J. K. Wing

Reasoning about Madness

The scientific method is a potentiation of common sense, exercised with the specially firm determination not to persist in error if any exertion of hand or mind can deliver us from it.

P. B. Medawar

*On the altars
They made him the red blood
Told what he wished to hear*

R. S. Thomas

1978

OXFORD UNIVERSITY PRESS

OXFORD LONDON NEW YORK

Oxford University Press, Walton Street, Oxford OX2 6DP

OXFORD LONDON GLASGOW
NEW YORK TORONTO MELBOURNE WELLINGTON
IBADAN NAIROBI DAR ES SALAAM LUSAKA CAPE TOWN
KUALA LUMPUR SINGAPORE JAKARTA HONG KONG TOKYO
DELHI BOMBAY CALCUTTA MADRAS KARACHI

© *J. K. Wing 1978*

British Library Cataloguing in Publication Data

Wing, John Kenneth
  Reasoning about madness.
  1. Mental illness
  I. Title
  616.8'9   RC454.4   77–30526

  ISBN 0–19–217662–5

*Printed in Great Britain by
Cox & Wyman Ltd
London, Fakenham and Reading*

Preface

The stimulus to write this book came from a suggestion by David Mechanic that I expand two papers, one on 'Schizophrenia: Medical and Social Models', the other on 'Psychiatry and Political Dissent', into a monograph on social psychiatry; one that would contain a discussion of its theoretical bases as well as its now very considerable empirical content. It soon became clear that such a book would take a very long time to write, but having worked up a few of the basic ideas, it seemed possible that a preliminary volume aimed at a wider readership might prove acceptable. The original papers, much altered, appear as chapters 4, 5, and 6. They formed the basis of lectures given at the Universities of London, New York, Salford, and Vienna. I am indebted to many people for reading and commenting on various drafts of the lectures or of these three chapters; in particular Julian Leff, Aubrey Lewis, David Mechanic, Zhores Medvedev, Jerry Morris, Richard Rodnight, Norman Sartorius, and Jerry Shields. Peter Reddaway and Ønulv Ødegård were particularly helpful with chapter 6 but the views expressed there, as elsewhere, are, of course, my own. Adam Hart-Davis, Adam Sisman, and Joe Weiner read through drafts of the whole book and their comments were invaluable in determining its final form. Christine Durston and Eve Gale undertook the typing.

J. K. WING

Contents

1. The meaning of madness

Historians would be well-advised to avoid the loaded phrase, 'lunatic fringe'. Lunacy, like beauty, may be in the eye of the beholder.

Christopher Hill

Madness as a social phenomenon

The first settlers in the New World carried with them ideas that still stir the blood on both sides of the Atlantic. One of those ideas, conceived in seventeenth-century England, was that neither democracy nor equality was possible without the free expression and debate of opinions. Before the time of the English Revolution, the uncensored exchange of divergent views was regarded with horror; it was heresy, treason, or madness.

But between 1640 and 1660, as Christopher Hill[68]* has pointed out, there was a glorious period of flux and intellectual excitement, when censorship was lifted and it was permissible to publish virtually anything. Indeed, so vast was the flow of tracts that it paid to be extreme, to set out deliberately to shock and provoke, in order to get a hearing. There is a close parallel with our own time, when the weekend colour supplements and the paperbacks, to say nothing of television, compete with each other to publish anything, from trash to high culture, that will catch public attention. The equivalents of the Ranters, Fifth Monarchy Men, Muggletonians and Millenarians of every description, rush into print. Now as then, literally any new idea concerning the way society ought to be reconstructed, no matter how far-fetched or controversial, seems to someone possible of achievement. In spite of the differences between the dissenting groups, they do have a single target, which is bourgeois society, whether liberal or conservative. But the passions that drive them are as likely to be turned against each other as on the common enemy, and the millennium seems as far away as ever.

To dismiss such ideas because they appear irrational may be an

* The references are to be found in alphabetical order at the end of the book.

appropriate reaction insofar as it protects us from descending into complete anarchy, but we should not deprive ourselves of the valuable insights they may allow into the nature of our own society and of society in general. 'There were lunatics in the seventeenth century, but modern psychiatry is helping us to understand that madness itself may be a form of protest against social norms, and that the "lunatic" may in some sense be saner than the society which rejects him.'[68] In seventeenth-century England, many political radicals claimed that madness was divine; that it was necessary to become a 'fool for Christ' in order to be able to prophesy and to reveal hidden truths. After all, God is by definition beyond human reason. Passages from the Bible could be interpreted to support violent departures from current social habits and orthodoxies. If all this was madness, there was method in it.

The parallels with today are close. Since the Bible is no longer fashionable, our own seers combine elements of psychoanalysis and of Marxism in unholy conjunction. A preoccupation with madness is evident. The form known as schizophrenia is particularly singled out as a sort of distorting mirror held up to society, in which, if we read the blurred images aright, we can discover the truth about ourselves and our future. Each prophet produces his solution—nihilist, anarchist, extreme left-wing and extreme right-wing—but all are agreed on the necessity for violent change.

So far, we have seen how the term 'madness' is used in a non-technical sense. It can stand for every variety of unreason from foolery to psychosis, and for any set of ideas or actions that is unacceptable or incomprehensible in terms of traditional social norms. Consequently, 'madness' has a shifting connotation. It carries different meanings according to the epoch, the society, and the social group involved, and according to the interests and preconceptions of the person who is using it. Shakespeare used his Fools, and characters such as Lear, to express truths that were all the more telling because of their paradoxical origin. This use of 'madness', as an indirect method of revealing truth, has been most effective artistically: the latest philosopher of 'madness', Michel Foucault,[46] is particularly concerned with its changing literary context.

But when we consider the tragic history of outstanding creative artists such as Nijinsky and Hölderlin, whose creativity was damaged beyond repair when they became schizophrenic, it is clear that creativity and illness of this severity are often thesis and anti-thesis, and that Foucault's conclusion is a just one: 'Madness is the absolute break with the work of art.' His mystical vision allows him to discern a synthesis but his primitive dialectic cannot separate the diversity of meanings embodied in his use of the term 'madness' (in spite of his claim to use it 'in the strict sense'); let alone bring them together again. At the same time it leads him to criticize Kraepelin, who tried to define different mental illnesses and so to differentiate them, not only from each other, but also from other varieties of social deviance, while praising Freud, who could see abnormality anywhere, particularly in social nonconformity. Kraepelin narrowed the range of social deviation that could be explained partly in medical terms; Freud greatly extended it (see p. 71).

This latter, more flexible, type of psychiatric interpretation, has been applied very widely, as in the psycho-biography of Woodrow Wilson by Freud and Bullitt, and in more recent attempts at psycho-history. Such academic exercises probably do little harm. Less professional attempts at instant psychiatric explanation have more serious implications. For example, there were several suggestions, in newspapers, just before Mr. Richard Nixon resigned from the American Presidency, that he was psychotic because he was out of touch with reality (the definition stems from psychoanalytic theory). The fact that everyone else expected him to resign was apparently taken as the criterion not just of his political judgement but also of his sanity. This tendency to equate social nonconformity with madness can be seen at the other end of the political spectrum as well. Leopold Labedz[90] quotes a remark said to have been made by the Editor-in-Chief of *Pravda* on 5 October 1967: 'At the moment, Solzhenitsyn occupies an important place in the propaganda of capitalist governments. He too is a psychologically unbalanced person, a schizophrenic.' R. D. Laing has argued that certain beliefs current in Western society (e.g. 'it is better to be dead than red') are so unthinkably horrible that anyone who accepts them must himself be 'stark raving mad'. We shall see in chapter 6 how dissenting political views can become 'reformist delusions'.

One of the most difficult and, one would have thought, most obvious problems about the use of the term 'madness' in this undiscriminating and pejorative fashion is that the procedure can be reversed by those at whom one is aiming. Dr. Robert Coles,[26] for example, has complained that some psychiatrists are willing to use their psychoanalytic apparatus on delinquents and other small-time dissidents but unwilling to do so when their targets are powerful politicians. The lesson is that if everyone we dislike can be called 'mad' then literally nobody (including ourselves) can be regarded as sane. The coin of protest is debased and we are left where we were. Whether we think that within madness lies truth, or that any personal characteristic or opinion we dislike strongly is a sign of madness, we lay ourselves open to reciprocal name-calling from those with whom we disagree. We cannot deal with the atomic bomb by calling its theoreticians, its technicians, and its sponsors 'mad'. They can pay us back in the same devalued currency. These are purely semantic jugglings and no substitute for rational argument.

Is the term madness then worth using at all, or is it always a manner of speaking, a cloak for somebody's prejudice? It would appear to be sensible to appeal to science at this point. Surely we have advanced somewhat since the seventeenth century? Is there no authoritative scientific view as to what constitutes madness, what its causes are, how it should be treated, and what lessons it has, if any, for practical people? What, for example, is the value of Kraepelin's theoretical ordering? The value would have to be demonstrated in a decrease in suffering and disability. If it was successful, any hankering such as Foucault's, after a return to the instinctive reaction of earlier times (to view anything that is incomprehensible in terms of the religious morality of the day, as part of the forces of evil), would have to be regarded, at best, as romantic and impractical but, at worst, as barbarous and inhumane.

I shall try to answer this question in later chapters of the book, but one further problem needs to be discussed first. There are several views as to what constitutes science. Some modern critics denounce the methods traditionally used in the scientific study of medicine as 'positivist' or 'scientistic', particularly when they are also applied to social problems, because they are thought to derive from the system of thought elaborated by Auguste Comte and known as 'positivism'. These criticisms are usually based more or less openly on a dialectical philosophy that can be traced back through Marx to Hegel. Therefore, before we consider whether medicine can be scientific, it is necessary to discuss briefly the systems of Hegel and Comte.

The scientific study of social problems

Hegel came to believe, after early mystical experiences, that what appear as facts to the empiricist are really trivial and irrational. The only way to approach Reality is by deduction; avoiding self-contradiction and using the method of dialectic, i.e. progressing from thesis to antithesis to synthesis. Thus, as Bertrand Russell explains it, Hegel's first thesis is that 'the Absolute is Pure Being'. But pure being can have no qualities and we can know nothing about it. Therefore the antithesis is derived: 'the Absolute is Nothing'. The synthesis is supposed to follow inexorably: from nothing comes being, i.e. 'the Absolute is Becoming'. This proposition in turn generates an antithesis, and so we make a sort of three-legged progression from Hegel's first thesis to the highest form of knowledge, each stage containing in embryo all those that have preceded it. The ultimate is Reality or the Absolute Idea. No statement can properly be true unless it is about Reality as a whole. Facts are therefore despised. For Hegel, the Absolute Idea was virtually embodied in the Prussian state. There was an inevitable progression through time; from the Eastern world, to the Greek and Roman world, to the German world. This historical development resulted in the perfection of national genius, finally realized in freedom for all; not, of course, in freedom of the press or democracy, but in acceptance of the law that value resides in the whole rather than in the parts, in the State rather than in its citizens. The State (particularly Prussia) is a super-being, as superior to any individual as the human body is to one of its limbs.

The debt owed to Hegel by Karl Marx, who substituted the idea of class for that of nation but otherwise kept intact the principle of inevitable historical development (or 'historicism' as Karl Popper[134] calls it), is fairly obvious. The method of dialectical materialism was for Marx the only true scientific method. Marx made substantial contributions to empirical sociology and his basic humanitarianism is unquestioned (this part of his work can be compared with that of Sidney and Beatrice Webb). But it was his very interest in science, which in common with other thinkers of his time he equated with determinism, that led to 'Marxism'. It seemed plausible to suppose that science could predict the future only if it were already somehow contained in the past. A social science must therefore also be based on discovering the inexorable laws determining the course of human history. 'Madness' and other deviance could then be explained in terms of a disjunction between the individual and the imperfect society in which he lives. The remedy is a radical change in society.

It was in protest against Hegel's philosophizing without regard to fact that Comte elaborated his six-volume *Course of Positive Philosophy*. He thought that a study of human history indicated that all sciences passed through three phases: theology—metaphysics—positivism. In the first phase, events were explained as the intended actions of supernatural forces. In the second, they were explained in terms of abstract principles, such as a vital force. In the third and final phase, events were observed and recorded and causally explained in terms of preceding events. Only this objective or 'positive' knowledge had any real scientific value. The physical sciences had already reached the third stage and the biological sciences were well on the way. But the crowning science was sociology, concerned with mankind itself, and this was still somewhere between the theological and the metaphysical stages. Comte's life-work was to establish the science of society.

Comte's psychology was basically instinctual, including egoistical instincts such as the sex drive and the desire for food, quasi-egoistical instincts such as a tendency to seek the approval of others, and non-egoistical instincts such as friendship. Without these, society could not arise. Between the more 'organic' phases of history—for example during the transition from the metaphysical to the positivist eras—there are periods of disorganization, during which the social solidarity that keeps the more egoistical drives in check breaks down, thus releasing 'madness' and other deviant behaviour (see p. 142). But, says Comte, if only the inevitable progression of history were better understood, how much suffering could be avoided! We could forecast the outcome of political struggles and thus make them unnecessary. Those who opposed progress would just give up and everyone's life would become more orderly. In order to make these ideas accessible to 'the man in the street', Comte developed a new religion, based upon positive science. His ideas of government were conservative, not to say fascist.

Once the science of sociology had been laid down in this way it was difficult to see how it could be extended further. As his successor, Emile Durkheim, remarked: 'the science was brought to an end with its foundations barely laid.'[110] Nevertheless, positivism has been modified or elaborated in various ways and has had a profound effect on current European and American thought. Critics have been particularly concerned with its assumption that statements of value cannot be derived from statements of fact. In the field of morals this means that the ultimate positivist state of society, being by definition good and in any case inevitable, is the only standard for morality, and can be derived 'scientifically'. The end justifies the means. History is the judge. Might is right.

Stated in this way, it is clear how much the philosophies of Comte, Hegel, and Marx had in common. Each adopted what Popper calls the 'historicist' doctrine of the social sciences; that we can predict the long-term social development of mankind in the same way that we can predict astronomical events, hundreds of years ahead of their occurrence. Each also adopted a special version of 'scientific' method—Comte, empiricist; Hegel & Marx, dialectical—the function of which was to demonstrate the truth of the theory. Each thought that this was the only way sociology could become scientific. They and their followers also believed that, once the predictions had been made, the task of using this knowledge belonged to the politician, whose job was to ensure a smooth transition towards the inevitable future. From this position, it was a simple step to the view that politicians should act not only as midwives but also as progenitors, sowing the seeds of the future in the present, and that all other considerations should be subordinated to this supreme aim.

Because of the subsequent divergent lines of development, through J. S. Mill and Marx respectively, Comte and Hegel are often seen as totally opposed to each other. Comte's historicism was essentially conservative, while Marx looked forward to a time when the State would wither away. Their methods, too, developed separately, although long-term social prediction remained the aim. In the hands of some of Comte's followers, positivism became an empty fact-grubbing without recourse to theory, and the term is often used nowadays as though it had no other meaning. The dialectic could be and was used to justify virtually any theory on the ground that it was a truth-finding instrument in its own right.

In spite of these brave beginnings to the social sciences the historicist approach is of very doubtful scientific value. As Popper[135] points out, long-term predictions are successful only when derived from the observation of recurrent events occurring in relatively isolated and stable systems. But these are rare. For example, the solar system is relatively stationary and isolated because of the immense regions of space surrounding it. Thus we can observe those regularities in the motion of the sun, moon, and planets that Ptolemy, Brahe, Copernicus, Kepler, Galileo, and Newton explained in terms of their physical laws; these in turn enabled predictions of further observable regularities to be made. Each modification of the laws allowed yet more precise prediction.

Similar regularities are to be observed in biological systems, although predictions cannot be made over such long time periods. There seem to be relatively stable repetitive cycles, amenable to observation and experiment in order to test hypotheses concerning the forces that keep them in a state of balance, or homeostasis. To a lesser extent, this is also true of ecological systems and even, to some degree, of behavioural systems such as habit formation, particularly when biological processes appear to be involved.

As soon, however, as we investigate psychological or social systems that can be affected by internal language (the most human characteristic), our ability to predict over a long time period falls sharply away. We can estimate the result of a referendum involving a simple Yes-No decision, but only by asking a sample of the individuals concerned how they propose to vote, and only over a very brief period of time. Most social behaviour depends upon countless such decisions. A social discipline like economics, which has been more intensively studied than most, can hardly yet be called scientific. (Perhaps meteorology is a useful analogy.) Society is changing and developing all the time: it never stops. The kinds of predictions that can be made about social systems are incomparably narrower and more limited than those possible in biology, let alone physics. This does not mean that social science is impossible, only that grand sociological theories are not in order.

Durkheim's work, *Suicide*,[38] illustrates the way in which social regularities can be used to test purely sociological hypotheses. In the preface he writes:

Sociological method as we practise it rests wholly on the basic principle that social facts must be studied as things, that is, as realities external to the individual. There is no principle for which we have received more criticism; but none is more fundamental.

Although, at first glance, suicide can only be fully understood in the light of an individual's subjective interpretation of his or her own personal situation, in fact all sorts of social factors that the individual might well fail to mention in a suicide note are associated with it. Rates of suicide vary in predictable ways with age, sex, religion, education, family position, marital status, and occupation. However convincing the evidence that an individual committed suicide in a state of depression or desperation, we can always imagine an individual equally depressed or desperate who would *not* have killed himself. The observation that Catholics are less likely to commit suicide than Protestants is a *social*, not a psychological datum. Durkheim, influenced by Comte, put forward theories of social cohesiveness that purported to explain much conforming and nonconforming social behaviour, and his theories of different types of suicide have stimulated a series of further investigations that has not yet ended (see p. 58). Although he did not entirely depart from the straitjacket of Comtean theory, and was not too assiduous in searching for material that might contradict his views, we can be grateful that, in moving away from Comte's cruder historicisms he began to lay the foundations of a scientific sociology.[110, 182]

Many of the present-day critics of Durkheim and other founders of scientific sociology do not recognize how much broader a vision they have gained by standing on the shoulders of their predecessors. Nor do they recognize that much of what was objectionable in positivism is also objectionable in Marxism: for example, the assumption that social changes can be recommended only if they conform to some process of revealed historical progression (known only to initiates), and that deficiencies in society can be made good only if a revolutionary advance is made towards the final state of perfection.

H. A. L. Fisher wrote in the preface to his history of Europe:

Men wiser and more learned than I have discerned in history a plot, a rhythm, a predetermined pattern. These harmonies are concealed from me. I can see only one emergency following upon another as wave follows upon wave, only one great fact with respect to which, since it is unique, there can be no generalizations, only one safe rule for the historian: that he should recognize in the development of human destinies the play of the contingent and the unforeseen. This is not a doctrine of cynicism and despair. The fact of progress is written plain and large on the page of history; but progress is not a law of Nature. The ground gained by one generation may be lost by the next. The thoughts of men may flow into the channels which lead to disaster and barbarism.

The historicist reaction to such a view, which deprives historicism of its only claim to scientific status, is characteristically to produce a conspiracy theory. The prophet knows how to make heaven on earth, and any falling short of the ideal—whether war, or unemployment, or 'madness'—is attributed to the manipulations of groups of people with malicious motives. Consider the reaction of a Marxist scientist to the passage from H. A. L. Fisher quoted above: 'The concealed reason underlying such an attitude was that any serious and rational attempt to interpret history would be bound to lead to criticism of the economic system or, even worse, to Marxism.' The only motive J. D. Bernal[12] could imagine for a liberal historical analysis was that it must be an attempt to distract attention from the obvious truths of Marxism.

Historicism and contemporary behavioural science

There are strong historicist currents in contemporary psychiatry and the relevant social sciences. The most radical schools suggest that 'madness' is a symptom of the degeneracy of modern society; a symbol of how far we have strayed from the correct path towards Utopia. The ultimate goal varies but, whatever it is, the appropriate conspiratorial ideas are brought forward to account for any deviation. For example, the right-wing psychoanalyst, Thomas Szasz,[176] has a vision of a free-enterprise capitalism in which mental illness will not occur, because the villains of present-day society, psychiatrists employed in public health services, will have been restrained from carrying out their criminal activities. The concept of mental illness is a 'viciously mendacious rhetoric' designed by psychiatrists so that they can 'torture rather than treat, murder the soul rather than minister to the body', because they are paid by socialist governments to do so. Szasz can see no difference between the 'medical criminals' of the United States and those of Nazi Germany. who were deservedly hanged. Soviet psychiatrists appear almost saintly by comparison. The virulence of this imagery (Szasz[175] also compares psychiatrists to the torturers of the Spanish Inquisition) matches that of the fierce denunciations of other prophets. Bruno Bettelheim[13] can hardly distinguish his particular demons, the parents of autistic children, from concentration camp guards.

Apart from their historicism, and a marked disinclination to produce any evidence for their views, a preoccupation with violence is almost all these theorists have in common. The nature of the ultimate vision, the diagnosis of the reasons for delay in realizing it, and the prescription of a remedy, show infinite variations. Another psychoanalyst, R. D. Laing, regards 'the family' as the villain of the piece, although he genuflects towards Marxism from time to time. We shall consider his prescription in chapter 5. Others are more deliberately neo-Marxist. The incoherent and chaotic nature of some of the more fragmented and transitory doctrines is sometimes mistaken for mysticism or rationalized as anarchism.

It is not necessary to begin the name-calling process in reverse. Because of the falsity of the underlying historicist philosophy, these movements have no more direct relevance to the urgent social issues of our time than the preachings of the more fanatical seventeenth-century divines. This does not mean that we cannot learn from them indirectly. As Christopher Hill suggests, we should use our lunatic fringe to tell us something about our society, although this does not mean that we have to adopt their sillier fantasies. Indeed, we could hardly do so, since they are so diffuse and contradictory. And even if all the *real* conspiracies came to an end, we should still be faced with the same sorts of social problem that we have today.

Residues of dialectical or positivist theories and methods also cloud much of what passes for conventional, and even academic, sociology and psychiatry. We can easily recognize the windy theorizing and preoccupation with pseudo-problems that represent the tail-end of the Hegelian tradition. On the other hand, a sterile operationalism and a preoccupation with vacuous methodological exercises identify the remnants of the positivist outlook.

Theorizing without respect for the test of facts, and data collection without any intention to test theory, are equally unscientific.

Neither positivism nor the dialectic can lead to a progressive acquisition of new knowledge. The view of science that I shall adopt in this book is Popper's[135] commonsense trial-and-error approach:

. . . a critical and adventurous rationalism. The creation of daring myths, conjectures, theories, which are in striking contrast to the everyday world of common experience but which nevertheless explain some of the regularities within that experience.

These theories are examined in order to eliminate those that do not stand up to the severest tests that can be contrived. Scientists cannot aim at ultimate explanation but they can aim to come closer and closer to truth, since each time they disprove an idea they can understand that there is a reality against which that idea has been judged. The most important function of theories is to create opportunities for new kinds of tests, in order that by eliminating what is false we may approach what is true. 'The direction of science is determined primarily by human creative imagination and not by the universe of facts which surrounds us.'[93]

One does not have to be an experimental physicist or biologist to work scientifically: the approach can be applied in the fields of psychology and sociology as well. But, as we have seen already, and will see again in this book, these fields attract prophets, most of whom are not concerned in any way with testing their predictions. They want only to be believed. Such people are not difficult to spot. However, there are also more subtle theoreticians, who appeal to facts and appear to have arrived at their conclusions by the use of scientific method, but who actually are presenting no more than their own individual vision, which has the validity of a work of art rather than a work of science. Edmund Leach's[94] criticism of Claude Lévi-Strauss summarizes the characteristics of these academic visionaries very well. He points out:

Lévi-Strauss on myth has much the same fascination as Freud on the interpretation of Dreams, and the same kind of weaknesses too . . . Supposing the whole Freudian argument about symbolic associations and layers of conscious, unconscious, and pre-conscious were entirely false, would it ever be possible to *prove* that it is false? And if the answer to that question is 'no', you then have to ask yourself whether psychoanalytic arguments about symbol formation and free association can ever be anything better than clever talk.

Leach's main criticism is that Lévi-Strauss is insufficiently aware of the need for testing his theories and is quite uncritical about his source material:

He always seems to be able to find just what he is looking for. Any evidence, however dubious, is acceptable so long as it fits with logically calculated expectations; but whenever the data run counter to the theory, Lévi-Strauss will either by-pass the evidence or marshal the full resources of his powerful invective to have the heresy thrown out of court . . . He consistently behaves like an advocate defending a cause rather than as a scientist searching for ultimate truth.

The criterion of testability—how can we tell whether our ideas are wrong?—distinguishes the scientific from the non-scientific theory. Evelyne Sullierot, who published an anthology of the amorous writings of French women, said that the phallus was never mentioned by any of them, thus disproving the Freudian theory of penis envy. Freudian theory can accommodate a small problem like that. Because of the concept of defence mechanisms, which can be used whenever convenient, there is no form of evidence that can possibly disprove the theory. However, this advantage also accrues to the alternative theory as well, which is no more meant to be tested than the one it is challenging. Peter Fuller,[49] reporting the 29th Congress organized by the Freudian International Psychoanalysis Association, was struck by the contribution of Janine Chasseguet-Smirgel.

Unlike Freud, she held that knowledge about sexual differences and about the existence of the vagina was innate, in both boys and girls, but that it later became subject to repression. In a convincing reinterpretation of the material in Freud's little Hans case, she demonstrated that Hans was aware, at some level, of his mother's vagina, and that only Freud's own 'sexual phallic monism' had prevented him from seeing this.

Which theory will prevail will not depend on which theory survives the more stringent tests.

There is of course no need for everyone to be consciously rational all the time, but we have a criterion by which to test any claim that a particular point of view is rational. Lévi-Strauss, Freud, and Marx have all made contributions to science, as well as setting up grand theories that explain nothing because they attempt to explain everything. But it is their grand theories that have inspired our lunatic fringe.

The emergence of a scientific medicine

When we examine the history of medicine, and even more the history of psychiatry, it is plain that science, in the sense of a systematic trial and error approach to problem-solving through the rational elimination of error, has only recently become influential. When members of the 'little savage tribes' described by Lévi-Strauss try to understand the various misfortunes that befall them, they do not require as many different types of explanation as people in western industrial societies. Crops may fail, babies may die, a man in the village may steal from his neighbours, another may run amok, a woman may develop hideous sores. Environmental disasters, physical handicaps, personal distress, socially undesirable behaviour, and madness can all be seen as the result of intervention in human affairs by supernatural forces. Such an infinitely flexible system of explanation requires interpreters. Morris Carstairs[22] found that villagers in Northern India lost belief in his powers as a healer when he asked them about their symptoms:

in their eyes, a healer who lacked the ability to *know* these things by virtue of his supernatural gifts, was scarcely likely to be able to contend with the spiritual cause of their complaint . . . It became plain that the great majority of remedies which I saw deployed were, physiologically speaking, quite irrelevant to the disease process itself. Instead, they were designed to bolster the morale of the patient and his family, and their effectiveness depended upon the authority and conviction which they imparted.

The western doctor is here distinguishing between two different types of theory, both of which, at the point of application, are psychosomatic. His own is based upon a knowledge of 'physiology' and the ways in which, when it goes wrong, various 'disease processes' may be produced. Each gives rise to recognizable patterns of complaint that can be matched against those of his patients, in order to suggest what remedies should be prescribed. That of the native healer is more diffuse but it too has developed by a slow and unsystematic process of trial and error and has, in practice, its own kind of successes. F. E. Clements described several types of theory used by primitive tribes, each of which gave rise to a type of treatment. The theory of spirit possession, for example, suggested treatment by exorcism, by mechanical extraction of the foreign spirit, or by transferring it to some other object or being. The theory of sorcery suggested treatment by counter-magic.

Some groups developed methods of treating or inducing various bodily and mental states that fit well into modern medical technology. Indian tribes in Mexico have since Aztec times used an extract from a local cactus, *peyotl*, in order to induce ecstatic states on special religious occasions. This is how mescaline was discovered. Others used an extract from a root which western pharmacologists subsequently purified as reserpine, one of the earliest tranquillizers. These were 'accidental' discoveries, incorporated into the general body of local myth, rather than systematically developed as part of a policy of rational inquiry. On the other hand, many such beliefs were not discarded in spite of the fact that they had harmful consequences, even to the point of threatening the very existence of the group. Dubos[36] described a South American tribe in which a disfiguring disease, dyschromic spirochaetosis, characterized by multicoloured spots on the skin, was so common that those who did *not* have it were regarded as abnormal and excluded from marriage. Dyschromic spirochaetosis is a serious disease, recognizable at once to any expert, but only those who had it were thought to be healthy.

All of us are exposed, from early childhood, to old wives' tales and folk-beliefs that are not dissimilar to the magical explanations commonly adopted by primitive peoples. The modern medical profession has inherited something of the mystery and charisma of the earlier religious healers and prophets, and naturally all doctors have acquired, during their early years, the assumptions about health that are current in their own society. The history of medicine is full of examples of ingenious but almost completely false theories about various ills and their treatments, put forward in pseudo-scientific guise by qualified medical practitioners. H. T. Pledge[132] suggests that this tendency reached its climax in eighteenth-century Europe, and that thereafter it was increasingly the province of quacks.

One of these ideas was the very simple one of John Brown of Edinburgh, that all ills are either depressions or excitements; to be treated, respectively, with alcohol or opium. His own ills were depressions and he died of the cure.

It is doubtful how far Pledge was right to suggest, as he went on to do, that professional doctors have been less likely to put forward and to act on such completely unauthenticated theories during the past couple of centuries. Certainly Bernard Shaw would not have agreed. There has been grand theorizing in the historicist manner, as well as a more positivist insistence on *ad hoc* treatments such as high colonic lavage, or surgical operations that for years were not recognized as harmful because no attempt was made to test their effectiveness. The paleolithic practice of trepanning, presumably to let evil spirits out of the skull, was not more unscientific.

The development of scientific medicine occurred against this background of folk-belief and ingrained social attitudes as to what constituted health and deviance from health. The formulation that certain patterns of mental and bodily change were explicable in terms of specific and testable disease theories depended a great deal on what was regarded as socially undesirable. It could be argued theoretically that great musical or mathematical ability is inherited, at least potentially, and that it will one day be possible to recognize which people have such abilities by measuring the activity of certain parts of the brain. There are the elements here of a disease theory, but because few societies are likely to regard musical or mathematical genius as undesirable it is most improbable (though not impossible) that either will ever be called a disease. As we shall see later, the term 'social deviation' has something of the same bias. The scientific approach does not vary whether we are investigating genius or jaundice; only the label changes. But whether we call the trait an 'ability' or a 'disability' depends mostly upon social norms. J. R. Baker[8] gives a splendid example of this process in his discussion of ethnic differences in endogenous body-odour. People with an acute sense of smell are aware of differences in the quality and intensity of axillary odour, which may vary between individuals and in the same individual at different times (for example, in relation to the menstrual cycle). In general, Europeans and Negroes are smelly, whereas most Japanese are not. The latter are therefore very sensitive to axillary odour and almost have a horror of it. However, some ten per cent of Japanese do have smelly armpits just like Europeans, possibly because they have Ainu ancestry. (The Ainu are of the same ethnic type as Europeans.) 'The existence of the odour is regarded among

Japanese as a disease, *osmidrosis axillae*, which used to warrant exemption from military service. Certain doctors specialize in its treatment, and sufferers are accustomed to enter hospital.'

As in other fields of human endeavour, medical theories and techniques gradually became refined; some were found more useful in explaining and relieving socially recognized disability than others. This progress was achieved at the expense of accepting that only certain problems were amenable to the new ideas, while the mass of amorphous complaints about deviance or ill-health had to be left to more traditional explanations or to agnosticism. Progress took two forms. One was concerned with bodily functions such as the circulation of the blood and mental functions such as the nature of genius. The other was concerned with the recognition of disease syndromes of increasing specificity: beginning with general concepts such as pallor or fever and progressing, by means of a growing understanding of the underlying biological mechanisms, to precisely delineated clusters of symptoms which allowed a specific diagnosis, such as iron-deficiency anaemia or meningococcal meningitis. The theories of medical scientists became more and more restricted and exact. The simplest way to test them was to apply them in practice. Thus John Snow[167] noted certain features of the cholera outbreaks in mid-nineteenth-century London: that the disease began with alimentary tract symptoms, that people who shared the same room with someone who had died of the condition did not necessarily contract it themselves, and that cases were dispersed widely over quite large areas rather than affecting everyone within a local district. In 1849, a severe outbreak of cholera occurred in central London. Most people who died had obtained their water from the pump in Broad Street and Snow tested his theory that cholera was somehow related to contaminated drinking water by removing the handle of the pump. The outbreak receded, but Snow knew that it had been on the wane already and looked for a more crucial test. He found it in an area of south London that obtained its water supplies from two different companies. These companies had both previously pumped water from the Thames at a point where it was heavily contaminated by sewage, but one of them had subsequently changed its source of supply to a cleaner stretch of river. Snow was able to calculate the mortality from cholera among people who drank water supplied by the two different companies and to show that contaminated water was associated with an enormously higher death-rate. Thus a means of preventing cholera was discovered thirty years before Koch isolated the water-borne organism responsible for the disease, the cholera *vibrio*. Koch's work in turn led to the discovery of additional means of prevention. In this way, step by step, a complete disease theory has been built up; the syndrome, the causative agent, predisposing factors (such as a state of poor nutrition), various means of prevention (including clean water supplies and vaccines for those particularly exposed), and methods of treatment.

This degree of completeness is unusual in disease theories, whose evolution takes a long time. Even in the case of so well known a condition as *diabetes mellitus* where knowledge has been accumulating for two thousand years, there are still considerable gaps. A condition such as Parkinson's disease, characterized by muscular tremors and stiffness, is even less understood than diabetes, although much useful knowledge has been acquired and much disability can be avoided in consequence. Theories about numerous other conditions are still only at the beginning of their scientific evolution, and in many cases doctors are not even certain whether a clinical syndrome can be described with the degree of accuracy necessary for experts to be able to diagnose it whenever it occurs.

Thomas McKeown[116] has pointed out that diseases began to be recognized with any degree of reliability only during the nineteenth century. Before that time, few conditions could be diagnosed with confidence; smallpox, plague, dysentery, tetanus, rabies, gonorrhoea, and syphilis. Some knowledge of the underlying anatomical and physiological processes had been very gradually built up but again understanding of the precise relationship between clinical syndromes and pathology or pathophysiology has been acquired only during the past hundred years. Apart from the successful use of mercury, iron, quinine, and digitalis, curative remedies were not discovered before 1900 and most medical and surgical therapies had poor results. Doctors could only hope to palliate. Nevertheless, there was a startling improvement in the expectation of life during the nineteenth century—the time of the industrial revolution. Our picture of the time is still largely Dickensian and it is difficult for us to grasp this point. The improvement cannot have been due to advances in medical treatment, since it largely antedated them. No doubt the recognition of the importance of clean water supplies had something to do with it, as had the technique of vaccination against smallpox. McKeown considers that a rising standard of living, particularly improved nutrition, was the most important factor.

The more dramatic advances in diagnosis and in the treatment of those diseases that affect individuals (as opposed to large groups) have probably contributed significantly only since the second quarter of the present century. Recognition of the limited impact of individual treatment on mortality does not, of course, denigrate the value of rational techniques of diagnosis and therapy in limiting morbidity, i.e. the disabilities caused by disease. It simply places recent advances into context.

We must also recognize that disease theories have made only small inroads into the much wider problems of ill-health and social deviance that less developed societies explain in terms of supernatural forces. Their healers treat loss of morale independently of cause, and are often quite successful, even though they miss most cases of curable disease and hence lose the opportunity to prevent much suffering and disability. Scientific medicine has achieved its success by concentrating on more and more specific problems. Although, within these restricted limits, doctors can be fairly confident that medical actions will be beneficial, they cannot afford to ignore the wider psychological and social context, not only because so many complaints are couched in these terms, but also because rational treatment cannot be prescribed in a social vacuum.

Thus two concepts of 'illness'—disease theory and social attribution—exist side by side. The South American tribe described by Dubos based their attribution of illness on a totally mistaken theory, derived from their experience of what was usual and their inability, understandable given the circumstances, to develop the habit of critical examination of hypotheses in order to eliminate those that are false. Recognition of the coloured spots as dangerous, in the absence of a tradition of scientific inquiry, could hardly be expected since cause and effect were not immediately obvious. E. H. Ackerknecht showed that malaria was so common in the Upper Mississippi Valley during the early nineteenth century that its manifestations were regarded as normal. Thus no one attempted to discover methods of prevention and treatment because no social attribution of illness was made and thus no disease theory was developed.

Neither of these two concepts of 'illness' is exclusively medical or non-medical. People who suffer from some chronic diseases, or their relatives, may acquire a more realistic and detailed knowledge of the nature of the disability and of what can be done than even many doctors. On the other hand, doctors need to use far more types of expertise than a narrow definition of the 'medical model' would lead one to expect. They have to act, on occasion, as teachers, psychologists, social workers, pastoral counsellors, and befrienders, as well as diagnosticians and therapists. Doctors are not necessarily well educated to adopt such roles: hence the temptation to apply their diagnostic skills to problems that require a different approach.

The ideal clinical synthesis is difficult to attain. Critics have tended to fasten on examples where the balance has clearly been wrong; either the medical approach has been too narrowly concerned with scientific disease theories while other personal and social problems are ignored, or disease labels have been used inappropriately to explain the whole range of human difficulties. Such criticisms are particularly relevant to psychiatric medicine, and the aim of this book is to consider how scientific advances can be fostered and applied without losing the art of healing.

2. Medical models

'This silly germ theory is something quite new,'
Muv said placidly. 'The truth is doctors don't
have any idea what really causes illnesses;
they're always inventing some new theory.'
Jessica Mitford

The scientific concept of disease

Putting forward a diagnosis is like putting forward a theory. It can be tested. Is it useful or not? The most obvious test is whether it is helpful to the individual concerned. For example, does it accurately predict a form of treatment that reduces disability without leading to harmful 'side-effects'? Does it give some idea of the future course and outcome? At the very least, can the sufferer or the relatives be given the consolation that there are other people with the same condition, that it has a name and that there are ways of coping with it? A further use of a disease theory is less obvious but in some ways just as important. It can lead to the acquisition of new information, for example concerning pathology, physiology, and aetiology. This may not be of immediate benefit to any one individual but it may lead to discoveries that will suggest future means of treatment or prevention.

There are two essential components to any disease theory. The first is the recognition of a symptom or syndrome; the second is the discovery of underlying biological abnormalities. Coronary heart disease is a good example. One characteristic symptom consists of pain felt in the central part of the chest and then radiating down the left arm. In spite of the fact that this symptom is entirely psychological—it depends upon an accurate description by the affected individual of his subjective experiences—it is sufficient for the doctor to hypothesize an abnormality in the blood vessels supplying the heart. The term 'biological' should therefore often read 'psychobiological', since we shall be concerned in this book mainly with processes that have both a psychological and a biological component.

Defining and naming the syndrome

The first requirement of a disease theory is the recognition of a cluster of undesirable traits or characteristics that tend to occur together; solidity is given to such a cluster if it can be shown to have a degree of stability over time as well. In that case we have a cluster that tends to suggest a particular course and outcome. None of this necessarily gives rise to a disease theory. One could say that shoplifting by *au pair* girls is such a cluster, in that there appears to be a statistical correlation between the various characteristics, and the outcome is, on the whole, favourable: shoplifting ceases when the girl returns home or grows up. Few, however, would put forward a disease theory on such a basis. The reason is that the third characteristic of clusters for which a disease theory might usefully be put forward—that the constituent characteristics can be defined without recourse to social phenomena—is absent. Shoplifting, vandalism, and divorce, for example, are defined purely in social terms. This does not mean that biological factors are of no value at all in explaining them, simply that the greater the social component in the definition, the less useful a disease theory is likely to be.

The second essential element in any disease theory is the hypothesis that the cluster of traits is 'symptomatic' of some underlying biological disturbance. The more the symptoms making up this syndrome are definable in non-social terms, the more likely are we to be able to suggest the nature of the underlying disorder. A telling instance, by way of introduction to psychiatric conditions, is the syndrome of early childhood autism. In 1799, soon after the French revolution, J. M. G. Itard[73] wrote a treatise which anticipated practically all the developments of recent years, describing the characteristics and the treatment of a boy discovered living wild in the woods of the Aveyron who would now be diagnosed as autistic. Itard was a forerunner of Montessori, and he had enormous influence on the way diagnosis, treatment, and services for the mentally retarded developed. His description of early childhood autism is easily recognizable today. But he did not realize that he was dealing with a distinct syndrome. The wild boy of Aveyron was, to Itard, either a unique example of lack of education (Locke's *tabula rasa*) or he was an ordinary idiot. It was not until Leo Kanner[81] recognized, isolated, and described the syndrome that any real advance could be made. Itard's insights could then be applied to other children with the same condition, but one hundred and fifty years had been wasted. No matter how the disease concept of autism changes in future (and it will change very markedly), Kanner's first step was of incalculable value, and humanity has reason to be grateful.[205]

No disease theory can be elaborated before the clinical syndrome has been recognized and labelled. The second step can then be taken, which is to test the validity of various explanatory theories.

Theories of normal functioning: dimensions and categories of disease

Most well-developed disease theories are based upon a knowledge of the homeostatic mechanisms that maintain some relevant bodily function, such as blood sugar, within known limits. When the normal cycle becomes unbalanced, the limits are exceeded, and a clinical syndrome such as *diabetes mellitus* becomes manifest. These linked theories of normal and abnormal biological functioning can lead to new knowledge; for example, about causes (and therefore prevention), about treatment, about resulting pathologies, and about prognosis. The theories can be developed in many ways, including backwards from the empirical discovery of successful treatments or forwards from a knowledge of the likely effects of a toxic agent; and the scientific study of a hypothetical disease syndrome can lead to an increased understanding of the normal. A large part of the value of the disease model lies in its flexibility. A single clinical observation may be sufficient to make possible a diagnosis, which can then be tested clinically or in the laboratory and can be used to suggest methods of treatment and to predict the likely outcome without treatment.

This formulation shows the complexity of the concept of disease. Very few diseases have a single cause. Tuberculosis, for example, has one necessary cause in the tubercle bacillus but this is by no means sufficient to give rise to the disease on its own. Other factors involve genetic constitution, previous contact with the bacillus, poor nutrition, and perhaps psychological precipitants. In poor countries, an improvement in nutrition would be a much better prophylactic than the issue of free streptomycin. The same is true of cholera; we have seen that an effective method of prevention was discovered before the cholera *vibrio* was isolated.

During the past fifty years a large system of disease theories has been built up which forms the basis of modern scientific medicine. To teachers, practitioners, and consumers, this system sometimes appears to be rigid and immutable, but in fact it is constantly changing. Standing as we do at the vantage point of half a century of achievement, it is easy now to see the relationships between groups of diseases that were once regarded as quite unconnected; and, conversely, we can see the necessity for breaking down other conditions, once thought to be unitary, into smaller sub-groups by means of newly discovered criteria. Furthermore, the processes underlying conditions such as diabetes and hypertension are now seen as complex and continuous rather than discrete, as they were in some of the simpler and more obvious disease models provided, for example, by acute bacterial and viral infections. Simple categorical disease theories—hypertension or diabetes being considered as present or absent—give way to a more flexible approach based on an increasing knowledge of biological control mechanisms. Underlying every disease syndrome there are quantitative theories of normal biological functions. The more complete and interlocking these are, the less relevant are the categories, except as keys to unlock dimensional secrets.

This does not mean that it would have been possible to reach our present position without having gone through a stage of categorization, or that we can afford to dismiss disease categories now. To argue this would be to misunderstand the nature and value of scientific classification.[64] Tycho Brahne and Linnaeus were part of a progressive scientific tradition, no less valuable because, with hindsight, we can see that their contributions, if regarded as the pinnacle of achievement, would have resulted in a static and sterile preoccupation with description and classification. In fact, astronomy and botany could not have developed without them. Kepler and Darwin built upon the foundations laid by their predecessors. The same is true of the early classifiers in medicine; where would Claude Bernard or Virchow have been without them? Classification and its concomitant, labelling, are not always empty and stultifying; they can be used creatively. They are, in fact, an essential step in the scientific process. Placing a label on a category, naming it, is one of the most fundamental characteristics of humanity and one of the most significant. Each disease label, apart from those most recently formulated, refers to a hypothetical dynamic system, normally kept in balance by known forces, but giving rise to a syndrome, and to other effects, when it goes out of control. The more we know about our normal systems of functioning, the more likely we are to see that the various disease syndromes are not discrete, but related.

Finally, there are practical reasons for retaining a categorical diagnostic system. Epidemiology depends upon counting heads. Decisions about treatment tend to be either-or, rather than continuous. It is unrealistic to suppose that, at the most basic level of medical, psychological, or social service, most practitioners are able to base their decisions on a complete grasp of all the relevant and most up-to-date dimensional theories: that would be impossible.

The terminology of handicap: another medical model

The fact that a disease theory is constructed on the basis of a syndrome of characteristics which are defined, as far as possible, in non-social terms and which are regarded as symptomatic of some underlying disturbance of biological functioning, does not mean that social factors can be ignored. One has only to consider the chronic infectious diseases, such as tuberculosis or leprosy, to see how enmeshed they are in a social matrix.

This dimension of chronicity is particularly important because of the gradual adaptation that takes place over a long period of time between the disease, the individual, and the environment. Many diseases result inevitably in chronic handicap, so much so that the diagnosis itself is not as important a part of the doctor's job as the assessment of the chronic impairments that result. For example, the diagnosis of Down's disease (mongolism) carries no implication for treatment. The only medical interest is in the particular pattern of impairments and their 'management'. Insofar as these impairments stem directly from the disease 'process', that is from the dysfunctions produced when the normal biological cycles are disturbed, they may be regarded as 'primary', or intrinsic. They may either be chronic symptoms as, for example, in *angina pectoris*, or direct impairments of function, as when a joint becomes stiff after trauma or inflammation. In other words, the term 'intrinsic' carries the same hypothetical implication as the term 'symptom'.

Such intrinsic impairments may be responsible for the affected individual adopting a 'sick role'; which may lead over a long period of time to extra personal and social handicaps that are not part of the disease process and that need not necessarily have accumulated at all if the context of treatment or rehabilitation had been different. These extra handicaps I shall call adverse 'secondary' reactions. (The formulation is close to that described by Edwin Lemert as primary and secondary deviation, which will be discussed in chapter 5.) It is worth considering them in some detail since they provide examples of the way in which disease and environment interact. Compare, for example, a violinist who injures the little finger of his left hand with a navvy who suffers the same injury. The implications and indeed the severity of the injury are quite different in the two cases. Compare also an individual who suffers a severe heart attack, recovers, and is back at work within three months as though nothing had happened, with someone who experiences a mild pain in his chest but thereafter is a 'cardiac invalid'. We are here dealing with apparent imponderables, with personal attitudes and habits. Rehabilitation must therefore be concerned, in part, with attitude change.

'Institutionalism' is another good example.[201] That there is a syndrome of institutionalism, in the narrow sense of personal changes induced by prolonged residence in relatively closed communities, is immediately apparent from numerous novels and memoirs. Thomas Mann, in a long and claustrophobic story about a tuberculosis sanatorium, describes in hypnotic detail the insidious encroachments of institutional life and the gradual disappearance of resistance to its procedures, until the hero (a passive young man who has lost his parents) no longer even considers returning to the world outside. A. E. Ellis, in *The Rack*, makes the same point:

. . . it ought to be the most terrible upheaval to come to live in the mountains, to leave everyone and everything one knows and loves, but instead one accepts it, one forgets that one ever lived in any other way and finally one doesn't even seriously think in terms of leaving—it is as though one's past life was something one had once read about in a half-forgotten novel.

In some cases, where the intrinsic impairments are very severe, a developing attitude of acceptance of a protected environment may be inevitable and even beneficial. However, if the degree of protection is greater than the intrinsic impairment warrants, the same dependence may come to restrict unnecessarily the individual's capacity to achieve his full potential. This has been very evident in the case of some mentally retarded individuals who have been taught to behave in a way which is more limited than their potential. This is adverse 'illness behaviour'. There are others, such as Trappist monks, who voluntarily submit themselves to situations in which institutionalism is inevitable. They welcome the restrictions imposed by the institutional environment and welcome also the peace that comes when they no longer have the faintest stirring of desire to leave the institution. In such cases it is doubtful how far institutionalism can be called a serious disadvantage; everything depends on the expectation of the individual and those whose judgement he respects.

To speak of intrinsic impairments and adverse secondary reactions is to imply a social goal which the handicapped individual is hindered from achieving. Just as in the case of acute disease, which is often recognized in the first place because it entails a loss of activity and ability, so chronic impairments are usually taken seriously only when they limit the individual's capacity to achieve what he or his immediate social group think is appropriate. The navvy with the crooked little finger does not worry too much about his intrinsic impairment, nor does the Trappist monk about his institutionalism. Nevertheless, each is impaired, though in different ways, and under other circumstances the disadvantages could be important even for them.

There is a third variety of disadvantage which may be called 'extrinsic', at least from the point of view of medical terminology, since it is not necessarily related in any way to disease or trauma. The individual who becomes ill or disabled may already be disadvantaged by poverty, a lack of vocational or social skills, or by colour prejudice. These disadvantages are bad enough without having illness as well; but of course, in spite of the term 'extrinsic', the least favoured groups of the community are the most likely to get ill and the least likely to receive fully adequate treatment. Children of lower working-class families, for example, tend to be of smaller stature and lower weight than other children, to speak later, to have a poorer vocabulary and a lower I.Q., to achieve less at school, to drop out of school earlier, to be more often brought before juvenile courts, to fail to take advantage of university education (which is less often obtained), and to have more teenage pregnancies and fewer stable marriages.[124] They come from larger families, with more overcrowding and greater unemployment, they are more likely to wander away from home in their teens in order to find unskilled work. Later in life they are more likely to be found working in casual jobs and living in common lodging-houses or reception centres, or sleeping rough. A great variety of medical statistics show them to have the highest rates of disease, disability, and mortality. Thus extrinsic factors are not necessarily independent of intrinsic ones; furthermore, secondary reactions such as institutionalism will be more likely to develop in people who have previously had few social ties and developed few social skills. When we come to consider the concept of 'personality disorder' we shall see how difficult it is to separate the innumerable strands which weave together to make each individual unique, though these may nevertheless carry their own implications for his future, depending on the circumstances he encounters as he moves through life.

The overall result of these various patterns of intrinsic impairment, adverse secondary reaction, and extrinsic disadvantage is that the individual is unable to achieve some personal goal; this condition we call 'social disablement'. It may be very minor and specific, or it may be very severe and general. In order to be able to help, it is necessary to try to judge what the handicapped individual's personal goals are. Even when the patient presents a highly specific and technical problem such as a minor sprain, the doctor must consider briefly, in his own mind, whether there is something more behind the symptom, something which is not being said in words. Obviously, each individual must make up his own mind about his aims and what help he wants in achieving them, but the doctor's responsibility is also clear; putting forward and applying disease theories is only a small part of it. Again we come back to social norms. The doctor is inevitably influenced, as are his patients, by the attitudes and expectations ordinarily held in the community. He would not be human, and he could not be a doctor, if he were not. There may be a danger that the doctor will impose his own social expectations on the patient, but there is also the opposite danger that the patient may not be expecting enough and that the doctor will not recognize this. It is against this background that we must now discuss the difficult concept of 'health'.

The concept of health

Health is a social concept. We cannot avoid the difficulty of definition by referring to the mere absence of disease or disability, because these concepts, too, evolve in a social context in which certain characteristics are regarded as less acceptable or less desirable than others. According to some radical ideologies, 'therapy means change not adjustment', the implication being that all impairments can be eliminated, either by changing the individual or by changing society. But these ideologies simply underline the element of value that is present in any definition of health. The World Health Organization puts forward an ideal of physical, psychological, and social well-being, thus shifting the onus of definition from one word to another. The point of view taken by the South American tribe described by Dubos cannot easily be fitted into an *ad hoc* definition made up by representatives of industrially developed societies, no matter how well-intentioned. They regard as health what scientists regard as disease. And who are we to say that the two are incompatible?

Physical fitness is, in some ways, easier to tackle. At least it is possible to make measurements of various factors in order to discover whether there is some underlying characteristic that sportsmen, for example, have in common, but that ordinary mortals lack. The nearest approach to such a characteristic is probably the efficiency with which oxygen is taken up and utilized. Even here, however, it is difficult to take seriously any standard that equates the long, thin, cross-country runner with the 25-stone weight-lifter. One is reminded of the retriever dogs who, when they inherited the earth, bred a special strain of human being with long, powerful, right arms capable of throwing balls repeatedly for hours at a stretch without tiring. The problem of defining health in terms of fitness is: fitness for what?

An answer which is not based simply on the ability to win contests is that fitness prevents or postpones the onset of disease or disability. Theories about the way biological functions are retained within normal limits provide guidance for the man who would be fit. He will not smoke; he will not take alcohol or dependency-producing drugs; he will take regular daily exercise according to a balanced plan; he will not overeat or neglect essential elements in his diet; he will avoid sexual intercourse with diseased persons; he will live in a non-polluted atmosphere and work at something congenial without being under any time-pressure; he will not, of course, commute or expose himself to situations that he thinks will lead to undesirable physiological consequences. Naturally, he will be very rich.

All this might promote fitness, but it gets us no nearer to health. Winston Churchill, for example, took a sardonic view of physical exercise and was certainly not fit, but he lived a long, productive, and useful life. Obviously fitness is important for some people and, statistically speaking, it is better to be fit than not. J. N. Morris has shown that regular physical exercise can help prevent heart disease, at least for a time, and there are many other useful rules which indicate how to reduce the chances of becoming ill. But we shall not solve the problem of health simply by considering the efficiency of the bodily machine.

The body-mind problem

One of the stumbling blocks to accepting a biological component in the explanation of any set of mental phenomena seems to stem from a crude version of the body-mind problem. How can ideas, images, or attitudes be 'symptoms' of an underlying bodily abnormality? There is no logical reason why physical and mental events should not interact; the problem is more one of degree and complexity.[135] If we take a subjective experience such as a pain in the chest and left arm, we have no difficulty nowadays in taking seriously the proposition that it may be caused, in part, by a narrowing of the coronary arteries. We do not even have much problem with the statement that taking too much alcohol or having a very high fever can cause an alteration in our psychological state, although the specific mental events experienced when drunk or in delirium will not necessarily be regarded as wholly due to the physical agent. We also know that very subtle psychological deficits, not at all apparent to the individual concerned, can accompany cerebral lesions such as division of the corpus callosum (the large bridge of nerve fibres connecting the two hemispheres of the brain). Moreover, it has been shown that by 'taking thought', a trained person can alter his blood pressure or pulse rate.

The more substantial difficulty is that some psychological phenomena that are regarded as symptoms are more complex than the experience of pain; so that they must have been affected by earlier learning processes and by inner languages, and thus are suspect according to our rule that symptoms should be defined as far as possible in non-social terms. Other experiences are regarded as symptomatic because of their abnormal form; this is true of delirium, for example. We shall see in chapter 4 that certain kinds of delusions and hallucinations may be hypothesized to be symptomatic because they are based on experiences which are rare, difficult to explain in social terms, and virtually invariant across a wide variety of social environments. In general, the form of a symptom is more important to diagnosis than its content. A patient may be afraid of cats, or deluded that there is a cat controlling him, or he may see a cat when no cat is physically present. He may fail to remember the name of his own pet cat. Four completely different diagnoses are suggested in spite of the fact that there is a common theme to all of these experiences.

A different kind of example of body-mind interaction occurs in anxiety. Everyone is familiar with the characteristic bodily accompaniments to the subjective experience of anxiety: a racing heart-beat, a dry mouth, a tremor of the hands and voice, a difficulty in breathing, 'butterflies' in the stomach, and so on. Furthermore, people who complain of severe anxiety states tend to have characteristic physiological responses to laboratory tests (see chapter 3). Thus the idea that certain psychological dysfunctions might be symptoms of disease states is therefore neither novel nor nonsensical. Everything depends on the evidence that can be brought together for or against any particular disease theory. Naturally, all reports of psychological experiences may be deliberately falsified, or unconsciously exaggerated, or even learned from others, but this is also true of the report of 'physical' symptoms. It is not particularly characteristic of psychiatric as against physical complaints.

One other problem may be mentioned here, although it is a difficulty only to those who think in primitive logical categories. Szasz suggests that mental illness cannot exist because we cannot see it. For example, Szasz says that we cannot demonstrate schizophrenia in the dead body of someone who is supposed to have had the condition during his lifetime, in the way that he thinks that pneumonia, say, can be demonstrated. But *no* disease can be 'seen' in this way. The pneumonic consolidation that is observable in the lung is not a disease. 'Pneumonia' is a theory put forward to explain a particular pattern of events, many of them psychological in nature and available only because the patient has described his subjective experiences. The pathology is part of this pattern, and in the case of pneumonia it may be possible to suggest a retrospective diagnosis purely on post-mortem findings, but it is not essential to see gross pathology in order to make a diagnosis. In a condition such as temporal lobe epilepsy, typically 'schizophrenic' symptoms may occur as an aura to an epileptic fit. At post-mortem, there is often some kind of gross or microscopic pathology in the brain. Does this invalidate the psychological symptoms, or must the fact that there is a pathology automatically rule out the classification of 'mental illness'? If no pathology is evident, does it mean that epilepsy does not 'exist'? This kind of semantic sleight of hand allows the polemicist to have it all ways at once. In fact, knowledge of a pathology is not necessary for a disease theory to be put forward. Modern medicine would never have developed at all if there had been such a rule.

Mental health and sanity

We have seen that health is a social concept that will not be pinned down within one comprehensive and universally applicable definition. The same is true of terms like 'mental health' and 'sanity'. All commentators who use them have their own personal or moral views, just as they have about 'madness' or 'insanity', but these terms do not form part of a physician's technical vocabulary. Certainly mental health cannot be defined as the absence of mental disease or disability. In fact, even the term 'mental disease' gives rise to false expectations. There are many theories related to mental diseases but none of them can claim to embrace all the phenomena of mental abnormality. To make such an assumption is to return to the vagueness, ambiguity, and misunderstanding induced by the term 'madness'. In psychiatry, as in the rest of medicine, there are only diseases, never simply disease. The persistence of unitary concepts of 'mental illness' is a grave handicap to the demythologizing and demystification of psychiatry. 'Schizophrenia' is not synonymous with 'madness'. 'Sanity' is not the opposite of 'schizophrenia'. It would be quite wrong to give physicians the responsibility of determining whether someone is 'sane', rather than asking whether a specific diagnosis can be made and, if so, what the implications are for treatment and prognosis.

There have been serious attempts to define mental health positively. Marie Jahoda[75] summarized the general characteristics regarded as important by various authors under the following headings: self-acceptance, integration of personality, ability to withstand stress, autonomy and independence of social influences, perception of reality free from 'need distortion', and environmental mastery. Each of these general characteristics contains terms that cannot be defined objectively except by making assumptions about social values. One can imagine a well-integrated burglar coming out quite high on all of them. Where the line can be drawn between health and not-health must obviously vary from country to country, class to class, and individual to individual; and it is questionable whether, from a scientific point of view, we need a concept of health at all. Virtually all that is scientifically useful seems to be better dealt with by discussing the prevention of disease, and here various concepts of fitness may be useful. The remaining component in the definition of mental health can then be seen for what it is – pertaining to art, myth, and social tradition, rather than to science.

It is possible to see how various types of political and moral philosophy have influenced views about mental health. In the United States and the Soviet Union, for example, the rival ideologies of psychoanalysis and Marxism have one thing in common —that they have been used to establish rather narrow standards of normality, definable in the last resort only by the experts. Departures from normal are regarded as pathological, i.e. medical terminology is taken over to describe what are mainly social deviations. On the other hand, the toleration of 'eccentricity' that used to be associated with the British allows a wide range of nonconforming behaviour to be included within normal limits. As soon as we start thinking of 'not-health', defined according to the standards of some particular society or social group, as 'disease', we find ourselves in the middle of the kind of problem that is discussed in chapters 5 and 6. The temptation to slide gradually and unwittingly into such situations is great, because concepts of health and ill-health affect 'illness behaviour', that is, the way people behave in relation to what they themselves formulate as problems connected with illness.

In chapter 1 we distinguished two meanings of the term 'illness'. People will come to doctors, or be brought to them, because of various characteristics of behaviour or experience that are defined by them, or by the social groups from which they take their standards (their 'reference groups'), as 'sick'. Part of the doctor's job is to put forward disease theories, to test them by applying the appropriate technology, and to reject them when they do not work. But illness behaviour does not mean that a disease theory must automatically be applied. In particular, it is not part of the doctor's job to validate automatically all illness labels applied by society. It is when doctors forget this vital distinction that a medical expansionism takes over, the results of which may be the opposite of those intended.

The assessment of treatment

A doctor is acting as an applied scientist only when deciding which of the various theories at his disposal is most relevant to the problem under consideration and what alternative courses of action they suggest. When he decides what advice he actually should give, he is no longer doing so. He has to take into account many different categories of information and sort them into some order of priority. Giving advice is an art, not a science. This is just as true of biological as of psychological or social treatments. The value of biological treatments for psychiatric disorders will be considered in more detail in the next two chapters. The social and psychological aspects of treatment are less familiar, although they have usually been pioneered by medical people. (This, in itself, exposes the extremely limited nature of the conventional definition of the 'medical model'.) The concept of treatment covers many different activities; prescription of welfare benefits, rehabilitation, advice on how to cope with handicap, prescription of sheltered environments, supervision, and control. In each case, other experts may be better qualified than the doctor, but at the very least he needs to have something of their skill in order to be able to make the appropriate referral. This conclusion may seem obvious enough, but there is little evidence that it has much influenced the curriculum of medical students.

Anyone who advocates a treatment is, in some sense, a salesman. No matter how fair-minded or qualified the claimant, the public needs always to be alert for the possibility of bias. So many people fall for the patter of the fairground hawker that it has to be assumed that a sizeable proportion of humanity are willing to be bamboozled. The claims made for social and psychological treatments are perhaps even greater than those for patent medicines or diets, or courses of body-building. Those who come across statements about the efficacy of this or that vitamin, or meditation routine, or course of relaxation, or exposure to undefined group pressures, or deep psychological analysis, would do well to ask whether a controlled trial has been carried out, and if not, why not. In such a trial, a group of people with the condition to be treated (clearly defined) are allocated at random to both a treatment and to a non-treatment group. Ideally, the trial should be double-blind,[24] i.e. neither therapists nor subjects know whether they are receiving the treatment or a non-active substitute, though in the case of psycho-social treatments this is difficult to achieve. Those who evaluate the outcome in the two groups should not know which is which and should be capable of independent judgement. The salesman should not be the judge of his own product. Under these circumstances, the treatment is given a rigorous but fair trial and its efficacy can be realistically assessed. One of the commonest treatments for schizophrenia 25 years ago was a course of deep comas induced by injections of insulin. A controlled trial showed that the outcome was no different when barbiturates were used to produce the comas. Since very few experts thought that barbiturate comas were useful in schizophrenia, deep insulin comas ceased to be used. Other physical treatments, such as electroconvulsive therapy, have not been fully assessed but have passed several quite severe tests. Many of the recently-introduced drugs have been shown, following controlled trials, to be very successful, both in treatment and in prevention of relapse.

In some cases it is impossible to carry out a fully controlled trial, because of the length of time needed for the treatment, the impossibility of keeping people ignorant as to who is receiving it, or the conviction of clinicians that to withhold what they regard as a useful therapy in order to provide a control group for the trial would be unethical. In such a case the potential consumer should be very much on his guard if he finds that claims are nevertheless put forward with confidence. There are other methods of discovering the strength of the case for treatment. What definitions have been given for the condition which is to be treated; is it clear who is supposed to benefit and who is not? Has any comparison group been used, and if so, how comparable were the people in it? For example, if the treatment is deep meditation under the guidance of a guru, has it been compared with a course of muscular relaxation under the instruction of someone who believes in it? Did the people taking the courses suffer from the same complaint, and were other relevant factors such as attitudes to treatment roughly comparable? Who decided whether the treatments worked or not, what were the criteria, and how much bias might have been involved? How many people are there with the condition for which the treatment is put forward and were they fully represented in the test groups? Was the test carried out with people who would probably have got better anyway, or who are likely to respond to a salesman's charm, or who do not like to admit that they have been cheated?

By obtaining answers to such questions it is possible to assess the strength of the case for the treatment and to judge the claims accordingly. The consumer with an inquiring mind will not be diverted from his critical study of the evidence by the therapist's use of modish terms such as 'search for dialogue', 'establishing a relationship', or 'initiating communication', which may sometimes be used simply because they tend to be accepted uncritically. The real high flyers in salesmanship, however, go directly for the big stuff; 'love', 'warmth', 'depth of insight'. Once such words are used, decent people tend to feel that they should suspend criticism. Who could criticize love? But at that point they have swallowed not only the bait but also the hook, line, and sinker. It is worth reflecting that those who have to tell other people how loving their therapy is might themselves have something to hide.

Social treatments

Strictly speaking, treatment (or therapy) should refer only to techniques of reducing the severity of symptoms or intrinsic impairments. A change in social circumstances brought about with the immediate aim of decreasing symptoms or intrinsic impairments can quite strictly be called a social treatment, and there is good evidence that such social change can be effective.[201,203] Social action is also necessary in order to counter adverse personal reactions to impairment, and to make up, as far as possible, any pre-existing disadvantages.[44,191] Rehabilitation consists of trying to identify these various elements in social disablement and creating the right conditions for minimizing them. It is basically a matter of increasing the number of options open to the handicapped person. This is true even when the intrinsic impairment is so severe that help has to be given within a protected environment.

Those who regularly 'fail' when they enter a series of environments created to help handicapped people tend to become labelled in some pejorative way. 'Psychopath' is one such label. Although it can have a quite specific connotation, it tends to take on overtones such as 'anti-social', 'lazy', and 'uncooperative'. The well-known 'therapeutic community' at the Henderson Hospital in London was set up by Maxwell Jones[79] in order to try to help people who had regularly failed in this way. The term 'therapeutic community' has been used in several senses. Tom Main[111] at the Cassell Hospital, for example, used a group technique with a predominantly psychoanalytic orientation to help much less damaged people. In that case, 'change not adjustment' was a legitimate goal. Other communities have been set up to help drug addicts, alcoholics, ex-prisoners, and many other groups. In spite of their differences, such communities do aspire to certain common characteristics. The first is a 'freeing of communications' between all individuals within the community, whatever their status, thus necessarily flattening the usual authority pyramid. The second is the analysis of all events in the community in terms of individual and interpersonal dynamics. The third is the provision of opportunities for new learning and for testing newly acquired skills. This allows the examination of social roles, that of doctor or nurse just as much as that of patient. All these experiences are shared in the daily community meeting, at which all members are expected to take part in the scrutiny of their own and other people's behaviour and motives. Robert Rapoport,[140] a social anthropologist, who studied Maxwell Jones's community, concluded that a useful attitude change did occur, but that a year later it had dissipated and could not be shown to have much affected the outcome.

The term 'therapeutic community' has been applied to many
very different social units since those days, whether the original
initiative came from doctors or from non-medical people. However,
there has been a dearth of scientific investigation, and it is still not
clear whether such a community can be identified in terms of
its social structure, and if so, what types of people it is most suited
to help. The global nature of the ideal, the ambiguity of the role
of leader (whom Maxwell Jones considers should have 'charisma'),
the tendency to assume that people with the most diverse social
problems can all benefit from the same regime, the lack of comparison with other techniques, and the notable failure to carry out
follow-up studies; all encourage large claims, often without proper
evidence. In such circumstances, the pressure to abandon science
and to rely on intuition is often overwhelming.

It is doubtful how far such medically inspired techniques can
progress until social scientists have separated some of the more
specific social processes involved. For example, Michael Argyle
and others[6,105] have begun to explore the effect of specific training
in social skills on people regarded as having 'personality disorders'.
The most serious difficulties treated were an inability to make
friends owing to a failure to take any interest in others, combined
with an inability to see their point of view or to behave in ways that
were rewarding to them; a failure in non-verbal expressiveness;
and a lack of ability in the verbal and non-verbal skills involved in
making conversation. These problems might reasonably be called
'social inadequacy', a cluster of traits that could interfere with
more conventional efforts at rehabilitation.

At this point we have come a very long way from the narrow
'medical model' put forward by some people, which would restrict
doctors to making diagnoses. Nevertheless, the progression
has been a logical one, and there has been no point at which it
would have been possible to stop and say: 'Here the responsibility of the medical practitioner ends and that of someone else
(the social practitioner?) begins.' Moreover, at no point could
we say: 'This is where ordinary medicine stops and psychiatry
takes over.' This is even more true of psychological than of social
treatments.

Psychological treatments

This impossibility of distinguishing between what should be regarded as specifically 'medical' and what should not extends to psychological as well as social theories of treatment. A specious distinction is made between dynamic and non-dynamic theories and these terms tend to be used pejoratively rather than descriptively. Both types of theory can be dynamic in the sense of providing an explanation for a sequence of events taking place over a period of time. The first type of treatment is based upon behaviour or attitude modification by means of empirical procedures such as reward and punishment, gradual habituation, suggestion, new role rehearsal, massive exposure to a feared stimulus, or deliberate acquisition of the ability to relax at times when a distressing reaction would be expected. These techniques are all familiar and commonsensical. They have been used by parents and teachers since humanity existed, but they have been extended and developed and systematized by psychologists and psychiatrists in various ingenious ways.

For example, let us consider one way of helping children with the condition known as early childhood autism.[205] A central characteristic of this condition is a severe impairment of the ability to develop an inner store of ideas in coded form. The normal human brain seems to have an inbuilt ability to abstract general rules from experiences. This ability is apparently present from birth, but is made immeasurably more speedy and efficient when the child begins to be able to use sounds as symbolic labels for these general rules. He can then build an inner store of abstractions from experiences, and further abstractions from abstractions, which are associated together in such a way that a new experience easily calls up appropriate memories from the store. The present can be judged in the light of the past; new ideas are formulated, and plans made for the future. The bank of ideas and associations grows and undergoes modification throughout life.

The autistic child may have no inner store of ideas at all or, if he is slightly less handicapped, he may have a few areas in which he can draw on simple associations, but with huge gaps between. His view of the world is therefore patchy and distorted. He has to be helped to build up a more coherent picture by people who understand his handicaps. Without this help he is likely to remain withdrawn, aggressive, and destructive, locked within a senseless confusion of impressions, which cannot be sorted into the system of categories and underlying postulated relationships that each normal child develops for himself out of his interaction with the environment.

Parents and teachers can be shown how to give this help.[205] For example, an autistic child may be able to understand the words 'large' and 'small' but not be able to identify colours from their names. If so, the former ability may be used to help acquire the latter. The first step is to make sure that the child can recognize and classify on colour differences, even though he cannot understand the verbal labels given to these categories of experience ('red', 'blue', 'green', and so on). This can be done by seeing if he can sort coloured counters into piles each of a single colour. Many autistic children will do this if shown what is wanted by visual demonstration, accompanied if necessary by suitable rewards for correct performance. If the child can accomplish this task, the next step is to select two colours, and then make a single large square of one colour (for example red) and a series of squares of the other colour (for example green), ranging from very small up to the size of one large red square. Then the child is shown the large red square and the smallest green square. He is told the names of the colours and taught (with rewards if necessary) to name, or point to, red or green when told. He will learn this because he can already name 'large' and 'small' and he will take his cue from the size of the squares, ignoring the colour. The series of green squares is then shown to the child, in ascending order of size, one after the other, and each is compared with the large red square. Each time he has to name or point to red and green. Somewhere along the line, as the squares become more and more alike in size, he will realize that it is the colour he is supposed to name and not the size. The penny may drop suddenly and the child will show a flash of understanding and intense pleasure. It is usually unnecessary to teach all colour names in this way once the first two are learnt. The rest come by pointing them out and naming them. This technique, well known to psychologists, can be adapted for learning other skills.

As in the case of Down's syndrome, it is possible to put forward theories about the origin and underlying nature of childhood autism, but the main techniques of helping the children, like the one described, are educational rather than medical. Precisely the same is true of congenital deafness; the child will be mute unless specific educational help is given.[138] The strictly medical role is limited to differential diagnosis and assessment, and help where necessary with, for example, sedatives for nocturnal restlessness. On the other hand, there is every reason why some doctors should become expert in all the techniques now available for helping mentally handicapped children. In fact, much of the progress in the field has been achieved by doctors who have ventured outside the limits of a restricted 'medical model'.

The other main type of psychological approach is quite different from this and, as a convenient shorthand, I will call it 'psychoanalytical', although a large variety of theories and applications, including some that stem largely from religious or political philosophies, are subsumed under this label. The therapist stands in the position of parent to the client, giving him a history by awakening and interpreting the echoes of long-forgotten reactions and emotions. Therapist and client strive towards an understanding of how things have come to be as they are. When client and therapist are satisfied, treatment is over. The client has his story. At worst, psychoanalytic theory is just another variant of historicism. At its best, the process is essentially creative. This is why it has so many literary and artistic admirers. Moreover, all the interesting facets of human life, such as gossip and dreams and jokes and coincidences, half-intended cruelties, passionate attachments to obvious nonsense, gross stupidities, and darting insights that have the force of visions, are included as important (indeed essential) elements of the plot, rather than being regarded as trivial or irrelevant.

The glue that holds the story together, in any particular case, is motivation. An account of an individual human life that does not include some indication of what made that person tick, what he was looking for, is bound to be wooden and dead. The general question, 'What is the meaning of life?', and the more specific one, 'What is the meaning of my life?', are as fundamental as any we can ask, and everyone has to find some kind of an answer. Many will work it out for themselves during the course of a lifetime. A few sceptics will make do without any story. The rest will adopt some ready-made ideology; whether its basis is religious or aesthetic or psychological or social is less important than the comfort it brings. All those who help others to find this meaning are healers, whether they are doctors, priests, novelists, or just individuals working on themselves or each other. The ideology used has no scientific significance. Rilke wrote in his Tuscan diary, 'Religion is the art of those who are uncreative.' Those who seek help in Freudian or Kleinian or Jungian theories may be illustrating his point. What is effective in psychotherapy is not the ideology of the psychotherapist, but something non-specific; the perception by the client that the therapist is unconditionally sympathetic, genuine, concrete, and non-arrogant. Whatever the theory, only therapists with these qualities seem to be successful.

Traditionally, the doctor has tried, with varying success, to span the two cultures of art and science. The danger is that theories and techniques appropriate to one type of approach will be substituted, without the fact being recognized, for those of the other. Thus psycho-analysis has continued to use the terminology of illness while rejecting the use of disease theories. Purely social problems and discontents become labelled with terms like 'neurotic' or 'psychotic' or 'schizophrenic', although the reference to disease is really no more than an analogy. The practical consequences, as we shall see in chapters 5 and 6, can be disastrous. But the process can act the other way about, and people who really are ill may not receive the treatment that would help them, because the whole process of diagnosis has been devalued.

Advantages and disadvantages of disease theories

It is always legitimate to put up a hypothesis so long as you do not harm anyone by acting as though it is true when it is not. To diagnose your neighbour, from his festinating gait, his bowed head, his weak voice, and his shaking hand, as a clear case of parkinsonism, is one thing. To tell him your diagnosis and give him some pills is another. The scientific value of disease theories is obvious, and further academic investigation is unlikely to cause harm. It is the application of disease theories in particular cases that can go wrong. Whether a diagnostic theory should be applied or not depends on the benefits and disadvantages of applying it, compared with the benefits and disadvantages of applying other theories. It is worth putting up with quite a lot of temporary discomfort in order to remain alive. There is no point at all in achieving relief from a minor symptom if the treatment carries a risk of major disaster. These are the two extremes.

In attaching value to what is or is not reasonable to recommend, doctors are making moral choices and must be influenced by social norms. But there are fairly obvious criteria to guide them: the severity of functional impairment, the degree of suffering, the complaint of the patient, the certainty of the diagnosis, the efficacy of treatment, the likelihood of undesirable side-effects, and the prognosis without treatment.

Critics of medicine suggest that doctors, particularly psychiatrists, get into the habit of making diagnoses when no disease theory is usefully applicable; even that no psychiatric diagnosis is ever applicable. There is a medical expansionism which capitalizes on the patient's willingness to feel better simply because a label has been applied or something has been done. Psychological and social theories of causation and treatment are also sometimes applied in this uncritical and unscientific way; they are not really meant to be tested. In such cases, making a 'diagnosis' is quite different from putting forward a set of differential disease theories, with the specific intention of trying to falsify those that are wrong and with a clear understanding of the benefits and disadvantages likely to accrue in each case. Any human complaint can be accommodated within certain psychological theories; contradictions are as welcome as consistencies. In such a case, the doctor may not act as an applied scientist but as a medicine-man, and there may be virtually no complaint that he may not be prepared to 'diagnose' and treat. Much of the criticism of psychiatry so evident during the past decade has been a reaction to a medical tendency, accurately recognized but over-generalized by the critics, to go too far. In the next two chapters, we shall see whether the principles of rational diagnosis, discussed here mainly in relation to general medicine, can be usefully applied within psychiatry.

3. The hierarchy of psychiatric disorders

> *It has been the fashion, where the dynamic forces in psychopathology were the centre of attention, to belittle description, calling it superficial, and to use 'descriptive psychiatry' as a term of disparagement. Such a view takes for granted our knowledge of the forces that lie behind symptoms and appearances. It ignores the corrective power of direct observation, which can save dynamic psychopathology from its ever-present danger of mistaking metaphor for explanation, and giving to airy nothing a local habitation and a name.*
>
> Aubrey Lewis

Psychosis and neurosis

The first two technical terms likely to be encountered in psychiatry are 'psychosis' and 'neurosis'. Like many psychiatric terms derived from Greek roots they promise a technical specificity that should help to clear up the confusion of terms like 'madness' and 'nerves'. In fact countless inconclusive battles have been fought over the implications of each one during the course of a century or more, and without further specification the meaning is still not clear.

The simplest use of these terms is classificatory, but even this use is by no means unambiguous. We talk of the organic, schizophrenic, paranoid, manic, and depressive 'psychoses' on the one hand and of the depressive, obsessional, hysterical, phobic, and anxiety 'neuroses' on the other. These terms are enshrined in the International Classification of Diseases (ICD).[210] Some psychiatrists use the terms as a crude indication of severity. A 'psychotic' state is one characterized by delusions or hallucinations, in which the individual is unable to differentiate his grossly abnormal thought processes from external reality and remains unaware of his deficiency. A 'neurotic' state is one in which the psychological abnormalities are much less severe, in the sense that they do not interfere with the discrimination between internal and external worlds and the individual is well aware that he has obsessions or phobias, though the knowledge may not help him to understand them. This can be a useful differentiation so long as it is recalled that states of partial and fluctuating insight occur. However, it cuts across the descriptive classification in the ICD. People given a diagnosis of schizophrenia (a 'psychosis') may have considerable insight and be well able to cope with their handicaps while someone with a severe anxiety state (a 'neurosis') may on occasion act in a blind panic and be totally out of control of his own behaviour.

These internal contradictions become even more confusing when a theoretical element is added to the definition. According to psychoanalytic theory, people in a state of psychosis regress towards an infantile mode of thought, in which no distinction is made between an internal and an external world. The American analyst, Theodore Lidz,[107] regards the essence of schizophrenia as an egocentric over-inclusiveness. 'The patient typically believes that what others do or say centers on him . . . that he is the focal point of events that, in actuality, are fortuitous or coincidental to his life.' Neurosis, in the psychoanalytic scheme of things, is due to a regression to a later stage of childhood. The neurotic individual can differentiate between fantasy and reality but has no control over the fantasy. Thus there is a continuum, with psychotic illness at one extreme, shading into neurosis and then into normality. The differences between abnormal mental states that, in the ICD, are recognized as denoting discrete illnesses, are explained in the unidimensional theory as resulting from the dynamic patterns of events occurring in infancy and early childhood. Only an expert psychoanalyst can construe them. Very little emphasis is therefore placed on descriptive diagnosis, which is regarded as a sterile exercise in classification, signifying nothing. The term 'psychosis', for practical purposes, becomes synonymous with schizophrenia, since manic and depressive psychoses are not regarded as essentially different.

Such a unidimensional approach can also have a completely different theoretical basis. For example, psychotic conditions are regarded by one school as the expression of a single underlying organic 'process'. The most important question in this case is how severe or intermittent or rapidly progressive the process is.

Variations of this kind are thought to explain the range of clinical pictures. Some unitary theories include the neuroses as milder manifestations of the process; others regard the neuroses as environmental rather than organic.

Whatever the theoretical basis for these unidimensional formulations they have one common disadvantage, which is that it is extremely difficult to be precise about the presence or absence of the abnormality. At what point, for example, does ordinary selfishness become 'egocentric over-inclusiveness'? Precisely how can someone with new and potentially constructive ideas concerning his country's economic or political structure be differentiated from someone with 'reformist delusions'? The criteria, by definition, cannot be laid down, partly because of the reaction against mere description, but mainly because of the dimensional nature of the theory. Each individual is unique and only long inquiry by an expert can gather together all the threads of information so that a decision can be made. There is an obvious danger that a condition regarded as 'psychotic', because of some very subtle and sophisticated interpretation of an individual's modes of thinking, might be thought to carry the same implications for action as a grossly abnormal delusional state. Great power is then placed into the hands of the expert interpreters, as we shall see in chapters 5 and 6. For the moment, we need only record a scientific objection to these grand theories on the basis of their vagueness and need for specialist interpretation, and the difficulty of discovering any means by which they can be tested.

A more complex but testable dimensional approach has been used by Eysenck who[42] postulates that psychiatric disorders can best be understood in terms of independent factors, each of which is normally distributed in the population. Three such dimensions, with a largely hereditary basis, are regarded as sufficient to explain most of the functional psychoses and neuroses: psychoticism, neuroticism and introversion-extraversion. Neuroticism is measured by a checklist of items representing, in the main, symptoms of anxiety, worry, and tension. The items composing the introversion-extraversion scale describe sociability and stability of mood. Someone who scores highly on both introversion and neuroticism would be likely to be diagnosed as having a neurotic depression or an anxiety or an obsessional neurosis. Someone who had high scores on neuroticism and extraversion would be more likely to be classified clinically as hysterical or 'psychopathic'. If it worked, the system would replace categorical diagnosis by assigning each individual to a unique point at the intersection of the relevant dimensions. Two practical considerations make this system difficult to use. The first is that it is too simple to cope with the great clinical diversity. Several conditions are characterized by a combination of high introversion and high neuroticism and there is no way of differentiating them. Similarly, as we shall see in subsequent sections, both 'hysteria' and 'psychopathy' are terms used for diverse collections of conditions; by no means all those given these labels are extraverted or neurotic. Adding the psychoticism dimension has not yet been demonstrated to differentiate between the functional psychoses.

The second difficulty arises from the first. It is not possible to derive, from a knowledge of the position of a point of multidimensional space, some useful statement such as a prescription for treatment or even a prognosis. For example, out of one series of patients with anxiety states, only half could be said to have had an introverted personality before the onset of symptoms. These are the two perennial problems of dimensional theories that are not firmly grounded in clinical facts and categories. Nevertheless, this type of dimensional approach is basically scientific and we shall see that some modification of it remains highly relevant for an understanding of most of the functional psychiatric disorders.

In this chapter and the next, we shall examine the evidence for supposing that a more orthodox medical approach can be practically useful. The most severe and chronic of the functional psychiatric disorders, schizophrenia, will be given a chapter to itself. First, however, we shall describe the principles underlying the conventional classification and consider the status of the common affective disorders (mania, depression, anxiety states) as illnesses. The second part of this chapter will then be devoted to conditions such as personality disorders, hysteria, and the lesser psychiatric syndromes which, for want of a better term, can be grouped together under the heading of 'mental ill-health'. This term avoids a pseudo-scientific medical terminology that could well be misleading. The terms 'psychosis' and 'neurosis' will be used only insofar as they are part of the conventional descriptive label of an illness—'paranoid psychosis' or 'obsessional neurosis', for example. No particular theory is implied by this usage and the terms are usually, in fact, redundant. The term 'psychotic state' will be used only to describe a grossly abnormal mental condition, in which the affected person's capacity for responsible judgement is obviously disturbed.

Principles of classification

As we have seen in chapter 2, diseases are usually recognized in the first instance by the delineation of clinical syndromes—clusters of traits (symptoms) that tend to occur together simultaneously or that follow a characteristic sequence over a number of months or years. As knowledge accumulates it becomes possible to classify according to the causes of the syndromes, or underlying physiological abnormalities, or even by response to treatment. Thus several varieties of anaemia can be recognized clinically, but precise diagnosis depends upon laboratory tests. In the last resort, the diagnosis of pernicious anaemia (as against, for example, anaemia due to iron deficiency) can be made by giving vitamin B12 and observing the therapeutic response. The same principles are used in psychiatric diagnosis, with the proviso that knowledge about aetiological (causative) factors, pathology, or underlying physiological abnormalities detectable on laboratory testing, is much more scanty.[198]

In crude terms, there are three types of psychiatric disorder: the organic conditions; the 'functional' psychoses and neuroses, for which no organic cause or pathology is known with any degree of certainty; and the disorders characterized either by a single specific symptom (such as depression) or by non-specific syndromes (such as worrying or muscular tension, concerning which no disease theory has been put forward with any degree of success). This last group we shall designate the 'lesser psychiatric disorders'.

The organic conditions include dementia, delirium, various types of severe mental retardation, and syndromes such as early childhood autism. All are characterized by cognitive impairments such as loss of memory, disorientation, or a grossly poor level of intellectual performance. Quite often there is a pathology or an obvious cause. For example, it may not be possible to differentiate clinically *delirium tremens* from other forms of delirium, such as that due to high fever, but the specific diagnosis can be made upon evidence of heavy alcohol intake before the onset of symptoms.

Dementia is commonest in old age, but it can result from head injury, from tumours of the brain or interruption of the cerebral blood flow, from encephalitis, and from chronic intoxication. Pick's disease is a form of pre-senile dementia that can most specifically be diagnosed from the nature of the lesions found in the cerebral cortex. Down's disease, or mongolism, can usually be diagnosed clinically without difficulty, but the common form is also characterized by a tripling of chromosome 21, easily recognizable under the microscope. These conditions do not present the same kind of diagnostic problems as the 'functional' disorders, and we need not therefore be concerned with them in detail. All the social issues that they raise, including problems of long-term management and the planning of services, are also raised by the second type of psychiatric disorder, the functional psychoses and neuroses.

The term 'functional' simply indicates that no structural abnormality or organic cause is definitely known; the syndromes can be formulated only descriptively, in terms of impairments of function. The schizophrenic and paranoid psychoses will not be further considered here except to say that their symptomatology takes precedence, in diagnosis, over that of the 'affective conditions', which include mania and various forms of depressive disorder. For example, if someone has symptoms of both schizophrenia and depression, as frequently happens, the diagnosis is likely to be schizophrenia or schizo-affective psychosis. In either case, the treatment will be aimed, in the first place, at the schizophrenic symptoms, since these are thought to carry the more serious implications. (The problems of drawing a dividing line between schizophrenia and non-schizophrenia will be discussed in chapter 4.)

Intermediate between the organic and the functional types of psychiatric disorder are those characterized by syndromes that would be diagnosed as functional except for the fact that there appears to be a clear organic cause. These are the 'symptomatic' psychoses. Thus experiences characteristic of the central schizophrenic syndrome (see chapter 4) may occur as a manifestation of disease of the temporal lobe of the brain and be followed by the familiar signs of an epileptic fit. The onset of the central schizophrenic syndrome may also be clearly related to excessive intake of alcohol or amphetamine, or to some clear-cut cerebral pathology such as a brain tumour. In the same way depression may occur following the ingestion of the drug 'reserpine' or occasionally as a side-effect of the contraceptive pill. In such cases the diagnosis is based upon the presumed aetiological factor rather than the syndrome. In due course, as knowledge accumulates, it can be assumed that the functional group will diminish as more and more precise diagnoses are made, utilizing aetiological and pathological as well as purely descriptive factors.

Beyond the syndromes of functional psychosis and neurosis, there are many other distressing experiences that may or may not form the basis for illness behaviour. These constitute the third large group of psychiatric disorders, including various syndromes such as worrying, irritability, poor concentration, lack of self-confidence, muscular tension accompanied by various aches and pains, and a subjective feeling of not being well in the absence of any demonstrable physical illness. None of these is specific enough to form a diagnostic entity in its own right. All of them quite often accompany the organic and the functional disorders, but they frequently occur in the absence of more specific syndromes and then need to be considered separately. Everyone experiences these non-specific syndromes at some time or other, often in association with stress, but fortunately the experience is usually transitory.

The threshold or cut-off point, beyond which it is difficult to classify syndromes because of their lack of specificity or because too few elements are present to make them recognizable with any degree of reliability, is of considerable theoretical interest.[52,197] Above the threshold point the individual symptoms can be reliably and accurately rated, the syndromes can be defined with a fair degree of accuracy, and rules for classification can be laid down explicitly enough for incorporation in a computer programme. Below the threshold point classification is much less accurate or reliable and is probably not worthwhile. This does not mean that these lesser psychiatric disorders are never severe or that they may not sometimes be related to psychosomatic disorders that are important in themselves.

The classification of the psychiatric disorders is hierarchical throughout; that is, the syndromes are ordered into a hierarchy according to their importance for diagnosis.[47,202] If an organic syndrome such as loss of memory or disorientation (inability to recognize places or people or to orient oneself in time) is present, this takes precedence in classification over any schizophrenic or depressive symptoms that occur at the same time. If there are no organic symptoms, the central schizophrenic syndrome is highest in the hierarchy—very often accompanied by many of the syndromes from lower levels.

The significance of this hierarchical element in classification is complex. It may be postulated, for example, that organic lesions can trigger schizophrenic symptoms because schizophrenia itself has an organic substratum. Among the functional conditions a reactive element may well be involved. Thus the experience of acute schizophrenia is found acutely distressing by most people. It is hardly surprising if they become depressed or anxious in consequence. There may, of course, be a more fundamental association as well, particularly in the case of anxiety, since the processes underlying attention and arousal are known to be disturbed in schizophrenia, as we shall see. The relation between mania and depression is also more than reactive. However, a reactive element can certainly be involved in affective conditions as well, since the experience of depression may secondarily induce anxiety just as chronic phobias may well be found depressing. In consequence the differentiation between depressive and anxiety states is often difficult. Every type of psychiatric condition is likely to be accompanied by the minor syndromes—worrying, tension, poor concentration, and so on—so that these come at the bottom of the hierarchy.

Hysteria[164] has not been mentioned in this classification. It comes under the broad heading of 'mental ill-health' and a separate section will be devoted to it in view of its importance in the history of psychiatry. The same is true of the personality disorders, about which so little is known at the moment that it is impossible to place them within a rational classification.

From this hierarchy of psychiatric conditions we shall pick schizophrenia (see chapters 4 and 5), the affective disorders, and the anxiety and obsessional neuroses, in order to examine how far disease theories of the functional disorders are useful, and how far other explanatory models need to be invoked. Personality disorders, hysteria, and the lesser psychiatric syndromes will also be considered, but without much expectation that disease models will be helpful in the foreseeable future.

The affective disorders

The affective disorders are so called because the primary clinical abnormality is an exaggeration of the normal moods of depression and elation. In some people there is a clear alternation between these affects—hence the terms manic-depressive and circular or bipolar disorder. Others swing only one way, either towards mania or towards depression, but not both.

The manic syndrome, when severe, is characterized by wild elation, gross over-activity and delusions of grandeur; the affected person believing that he has powers or talents or riches far beyond his actual means. There are lesser variants of the syndrome (hypomania) that shade into ordinary optimism and high spirits. The hypomanic mood is one of euphoria, readily changing to irritability if there is any frustration. One of the most recognizable clinical features is a rapid flow of talk easily diverted from its course by chance associations, and punctuated by puns, rhymes, snatches of song, and bursts of loud laughter. There is, however, a painful quality to the mood; it is not happiness. Hallucinations can occur, usually of voices speaking directly to the affected individual, saying things that are congruent with the mood such as, 'Go to the palace! You are the king!'

The depressive syndrome at its most severe presents in many ways the opposite of this picture. The patient may be so deeply depressed as to seem apathetic and so retarded as to be almost in a stupor. Occasionally these may be an extreme agitation rather than retardation. He may express delusions of guilt or inferiority, saying that he has committed appalling crimes and deserves severe punishment. He may hear a voice accusing him of unnameable sins and telling him he ought to commit suicide since he is not fit to live. This is the classical melancholia.

At their most severe, these two syndromes can reasonably be called 'psychotic', since judgement is seriously distorted and the individual is liable to act against his own interests and those of people round him. However, such severity is rare. Depressive disorders are much commoner than manic and most of them are unidirectional (not alternating with manic attacks). Depression of intermediate severity is characterized by retardation, particularly by a subjective feeling that thinking is difficult and inefficient and that bodily processes are slowed down, even when this is not apparent to the observer. Quite often retardation is complicated by motor restlessness. Guilt and self-depreciation are expressed, though not with delusional conviction. Appetite is poor and there may be loss of weight. Sleep is also affected, particularly early in the morning, which is the time at which the depression is worst and accompanied by a dread of getting out of bed to face the difficulties of the new day. The zest goes out of life, the edge is taken off all the appetites, the future appears bleak and hopeless and life seems hardly worth living. These symptoms often seem to be completely out of proportion to the problems the affected individual actually has to face. Some people experience such depressive swings quite frequently, so that they and those who know them well come to recognize the prodromal signs and have some idea of how long the phase will last.

There is yet another level at which depressive disorders may be manifested, on the whole milder though it can occasionally be quite severe. The mood is less consistently depressed, there is less retardation or agitation, less guilt or self-depreciation, and more anxiety. Sleep and appetite may still however be markedly affected. It is often assumed that this third syndrome is reactive to environmental pressures of various kinds while the other two are more 'endogenous'.

These three syndromes, named for convenience rather than theory 'psychotic', 'retarded', and 'neurotic' (or 'reactive') depression, seem to be on a continuum of severity. The first two are met most frequently in people who have had to be admitted to hospital because of difficulty in carrying on outside a protected environment. The third type is more often met in the out-patient department and in general practice. In all three types the lesser psychiatric syndromes such as worrying and muscular tension are very common. There is yet a further level below these three. In fact, it is in trying to define the threshold point below which depression can be said to be 'normal' that the dimension-category dispute can be assessed most clearly. All of us are unhappy from time to time. What makes us depressed may vary from one person to another, but someone who has never had the experience at all could hardly be regarded as normal. Some people, however, become more than ordinarily depressed, usually in response to real problems and pressures, although they do not experience the various extra symptoms making up the three depressive syndromes described earlier. They may well be worried and tense, sleep badly, and feel unusually irritable. Most psychiatrists would not feel that this was sufficient for a diagnosis of depressive disorder, in the sense that they would want to prescribe detailed investigations, admission to hospital, or pharmacological treatment. We can call such conditions 'minimal depressive disorders'.

It would seem fairly obvious from a clinical point of view that one dimension underlies these various disorders, from the most severe 'psychotic' variety to the minimal depressive disorders. If so, there are also qualitative change-points, equivalent to the boundaries between ice, water, and steam. The specialist sees mainly the more severe end of the spectrum, and most of the studies that have been carried out with a view to establishing an abnormality in some underlying physiological cycle, to discover possible causes, and to assess the value of various forms of medication, have been concerned with the more severe disorders, particularly the 'psychotic' and 'retarded' depressive syndromes. On the other hand, much of the sociological investigation of environmental precipitating factors and longer-term stresses has been undertaken on general population samples, and thus is, so far, more relevant to 'neurotic' (or 'reactive') depression and to the minimal depressive disorders.

Doctors have been impressed with somatic symptoms such as retardation, sleep disturbance, and weight loss; and they have put forward disease theories of various kinds. Identical twins are much more likely than fraternal twins to have a manic-depressive illness in common. Similarly, there is a tendency for either unipolar or bipolar types of affective illness to run in the family, though no simple genetic theories are applicable. Workers in New York recently studied people with affective illnesses, which were known to have occurred in at least two previous generations of their families. They found that a liability to affective illness (whether bipolar or unipolar) tended to be associated with the presence of a gene for colour-blindness of the type known to be carried as a recessive on the X-chromosome. Studies of this kind, which are still in their infancy, may suggest a whole series of sub-groups of the affective disorders, each of which may possibly have different clinical characteristics, course, and response to treatment.

The response to drugs with known pharmacological actions also gives rise to useful hypotheses. At the moment, one of the most promising lines of biochemical investigation concerns substances known as monoamines (e.g. noradrenaline and dopamine) that occur in certain neurones of the central nervous system. Since they are concentrated mainly in the fine nerve endings rather than in the cell body it is probable that they are transmitter substances. They are thought to play an important part in the control of functions such as sleep and appetitive behaviour in animals; for example, food-seeking and other 'goal-oriented' behaviour. These actions are not yet well understood. The monoamines are thought to have an important relationship with the affective disorders because of the fact that reserpine, a drug known to cause severe depression in some people, produces a marked depletion of the monoamines in the central nervous system. Certain drugs which are useful in the clinical treatment of depression (the anti-amine-oxidases) inhibit enzymes which destroy the monoamines. The other main group of anti-depressive drugs (the tricyclics) also seem to have an action that results in an increase in the amount of monoamines. Thus it is tempting to speculate that some depressive disorders at any rate are due to a deficiency of one or other of the biogenic amines at brain synapses; and there is a certain amount of direct evidence to this effect.[74]

It is not clear how mania fits into this picture. On the whole, the anti-depressive drugs do not help manic conditions. On the other hand, lithium salts, which are very helpful in the treatment and prevention of manic attacks, do seem to have some preventive effect in depression as well, though a less certain one. The mode of action of lithium is still unclear.

Thus studies of those severe affective disorders indicate that disease theories of various kind can be applied with benefit. Indeed the outcome of treatment is often excellent. Nevertheless, these severe conditions may arise out of a much wider matrix of depressive disorders of a less severe kind, that are quite common in the general population (the so-called 'iceberg'), and that seem often to be strongly dependent on environmental circumstances. They must eventually be related to the physiology of the emotions which underlies the ordinary reactivity of mood to everyday events. We can draw a parallel between moods such as depression and anxiety and biological functions such as blood pressure and pulse rate, which change from moment to moment as the environment alters. While this fluctuation remains 'within normal limits' there is no problem. But consider the reaction to a sudden and unexpected bereavement. Perhaps a young wife loses her husband in a car accident. She is liable to become depressed, to cry, to lose her interest in her usual occupations, to neglect her appearance, to find food tasteless, to lose weight. She may feel guilty about not having made enough of her husband while he was alive. She may even imagine, on occasion, in the middle of some activity which they used to share, that she hears his voice saying something very familiar, perhaps her name. She may find that she cannot cope with her work, that she is preoccupied, slow, and inefficient. None of this is unexpected, at least for a few weeks. In fact, it would be unusual if some elements of the syndrome did not occur. Nevertheless, this is a typical depressive reaction. From the medical point of view, it is reasonable to speculate whether the same biological factors are involved as in more severe depressions where no such precipitating stress is involved. However this is a purely scientific speculation. It does not mean that medical action need be taken as long as the course remains mild and self-limiting. Indeed, the reaction can be regarded as part of a positive reaction to loss; a period of adjustment to a new reality.

The factors to be considered in reaching a decision that a depressive disorder should be treated comprise intensity, frequency, and duration of symptoms; elaboration of a syndrome of depression beyond the simple mood-change (e.g. retardation, guilt, hopelessness, early waking, poor appetite, loss of weight, etc.); and inability to stop the syndrome by deliberately turning the attention to something else. All these criteria are clinical rather than social. Interference with social performance is a different kind of guide. Yet another is the degree of personal distress. In other words, the homeostatic process by which the emotions are usually kept within limits has gone out of control, just as in the models of physical illness we were considering in chapter 2. The analogy with physical illness is in fact quite close.

Work by George Brown and his colleagues[10] in London confirms that long-term problems—financial, housing, chronic illness in relatives, difficulties with small children, and so on—are often found in the background when depressed individuals are detected in surveys of the general population. Threatening events of more sudden onset are also important; for example, being evicted, losing a job or the illness of a close relative. More remote factors, such as the death of the mother during early life, may act to increase vulnerability. One of the most important protective features is the presence of a supportive relationship with someone else—a happy marriage best of all. A satisfactory job is another protective asset. Someone most at risk, therefore, would be a young mother with several small children, whose husband has left her and who has no close relationship with anyone else to help her take the strain, particularly if she is suddenly and unexpectedly faced by acute financial or other difficulties.[181]

What is not clear at the moment is whether these sociological facts can equally explain the more severe disorders and whether the disease theories that seem to have practical relevance to the retarded and psychotic depressions can also be usefully applied to the neurotic and minimal forms. Either way, it is still necessary to account for the variation in severity. It might be supposed that there is an interaction between biological and social factors; the more biologically vulnerable the more severe, and the less social precipitation is needed. This attractive theory has not yet been tested adequately.

There appears to be a relationship, as might be expected, between severity and outcome. Many of the mild depressive conditions noted in population surveys are short-lived and medical treatment is unnecessary. However, some manic and depressive conditions can be chronic or frequently recurrent and it is important to consider the secondary and extrinsic elements of disablement. Environmental manipulation is an important element of treatment, as well as acquisition by the individuals concerned of some understanding of the way they tend to react. It is clearly important that those who try to help people with affective disorders should become acquainted with all the common biological, psychological, and social mechanisms that can be involved in the genesis and treatment of the affective disorders. Any attempt to look only through the eyes of one group of professionals, whether doctors, psychologists, or sociologists, is bound to decrease the amount of help that can be given.[29] We shall consider in chapter 7 whether current knowledge is sufficient to suggest social changes that would prevent depressive disorders.

Suicide and attempted suicide

Throughout the world at least a thousand people kill themselves every day. The frequency varies in different parts of the world and in different social circumstances. Emile Durkheim,[38] one of the founders of sociology, published a book on suicide in 1897 in which he pointed out the relative stability of rates in different communities: consistently higher in urban than in rural areas, among the single or separated than among the married, and in Protestant rather than Catholic areas (see p. 8). Men commit suicide relatively more frequently than women. The peak rate occurs at about 50 years of age, and there is little drop thereafter. Physical illness is often associated, and alcoholism is an important contributory cause. Suicide, though rare in young people, is nevertheless one of the highest causes of mortality among them.

One of the best modern epidemiological studies of suicide was carried out in London by Peter Sainsbury,[153] who derived many of his ideas from Durkheim. He showed that the suicide rates of London boroughs had remained at approximately the same level for several decades. In accordance with Durkheim's hypothesis, the boroughs with high rates were socially isolated; they contained rooming houses and hotels, railway termini, and a large migrant population. Poverty was not associated with high rates if the area was socially stable. In part, this association might be explained, as in the case of schizophrenia, by the fact that isolated areas actually attract people who are liable to commit suicide.

Certainly, several clinical studies have suggested that a substantial proportion of the people who commit suicide have previously been depressed, and this suggestion is worth taking seriously since, as we have seen, depression is treatable. However, many doctors believe that suicide can be a rational act, undertaken by people whose mood, though obviously one of depression, is not 'out of control'. Many people who have killed themselves thought they had good reason to do so, at least at the time, and quite apart from the remote causes suggested by Durkheim, it is unwise to regard suicide as a symptom of disease. The numbers of suicides have been decreasing in Britain during the past few years (though not in the youngest age-group). This may be partly due to the fact that doctors have been changing to less dangerous sedatives and partly also due to the use of less dangerous forms of domestic gas, both of which were more common means of suicide in Britain than in the U.S. or other European countries. A voluntary agency, the Samaritans, supplying an emergency telephone and counselling service, may also have contributed to the improvement. Should such people, if their intention becomes known to others, be forcibly restrained from the act? This question will be considered in chapter 7 but the problem of 'intention' is also of interest in the present context, since there is a much larger group of people who seem to attempt suicide but do not carry the process through. Some have not intended to kill themselves; others have only failed to do so through accident or ignorance. Norman Kreitman[88] has suggested the term 'parasuicide' to avoid the implied assumption of intent in the term 'attempted suicide'. Parasuicides tend to be younger, more often women than men, less often physically ill or severely depressed and less likely to have used the most potentially lethal means, than those who have actually killed themselves. In addition, parasuicides are more likely to be members of a social group in which other people have engaged in similar behaviour in response to crisis situations. That is to say, there is a certain element of fashion in this behaviour. This makes prevention very difficult and there is no current decrease in rates of parasuicide as there is in completed suicide; quite the reverse—the rates are increasing in most West European countries. Norman Kreitman says that 'it is arguable that only a major change in the whole fabric of society, or at least in the relevant sub-cultures, is likely to make any appreciable difference to the currently very high rates of parasuicide'. It is also arguable that such a major change might make matters worse.

Anxiety and obsessional neuroses

According to Kierkegaard, the freedom of will that gives human beings the possibility of moral choice must inevitably be accompanied by a feeling of dread. Anxiety, like depression, is a virtually universal experience. Normal anxiety is even more obviously dependent on everyday environmental or internal stimuli than normal depression. Everyone gets anxious in some situations and if the reaction were completely absent, it would be regarded as abnormal. A degree of anxiety actually improves performance by providing a stimulus to attain a desired standard. Thus normal anxiety functions as a motivating force.

When there is some clear-cut object to be anxious about the emotion is usually called fear. Many people are afraid of dental treatment. Nearly everyone who experiences an air raid fears injury or death. Moreover, a substantial proportion of people will agree, when asked, that they avoid certain quite ordinary situations as far as they are able, because they know they will feel unpleasant anxiety if they enter them. The situation avoided might be a telephone booth, a car, an elevator, or a room with a spider in it. In the majority of cases this action is successful and the individual avoids the anxiety at small cost to himself.

The criteria for judging 'pathological' anxiety are similar to those used to judge the severity of depressive disorders. The main question is whether the condition has gone 'out of control', producing symptoms that cannot be dealt with by consciously turning the attention to other matters, or withdrawing from the anxiety-provoking situation in good order, or simply exercising the will. The symptoms that result can be very severe: palpitations, muscular tremors, 'butterflies' in the stomach, giddiness, sickness, breathlessness, muscular tension, and faintness. In a total panic, there may even be loss of control over bowels or bladder.

In 'free-floating' anxiety states, the sufferer experiences such symptoms continuously or in episodes of panic, even without specific precipitation. Such conditions usually improve a good deal over the course of time but sometimes they can persist with little change for as long as twenty years. There is no evidence that such people are more likely to develop the so-called 'psychosomatic' diseases—peptic ulcer, asthma, thyrotoxicosis, ulcerative colitis, hypertension, coronary heart disease, diabetes, etc. Nor are they more likely to develop other psychiatric disorders such as schizophrenia. The condition is, of course, in itself depressing. Men are as likely to suffer from anxiety states as women but the likelihood of occurrence decreases in both sexes with age.

Acute anxiety can occur in epidemic form. P. W. Ngui[130] reported an epidemic of the syndrome known in Malay as 'koro', which occurs particularly in male Chinese immigrants. The main symptoms are of anxiety, ascribed to a fear that the penis is retracting back into the body. The drama is played out in public, with relatives and well-wishers doing their best, by holding on to the penis or tying objects to it, to prevent it from disappearing. Ngui's epidemic took place in Singapore in 1967, following a rumour that 'koro' could be caused by eating meat from pigs dying of swine fever. For several days hundreds of people sought medical advice until strong reassurance was given through newspapers and broadcasts. The epidemic then quickly died away. Epidemics of anxiety symptoms have occurred all over the world, often precipitated by some fear-provoking report, which then spread by example through susceptible communities, such as schools.

Some fear responses seem to be innate. The classical example is that demonstrated by Konrad Lorenz. Newly hatched ducklings and goslings showed fear if a cross-shaped model was moved above them in such a way as to suggest the flight of a short-necked bird of prey. Moved in the opposite direction it suggested the flight of a long-necked waterfowl and provoked no alarm. Fear of heights may well be innate in human infants.

Probably the commonest form of pathological anxiety is that experienced in certain specific situations. Agoraphobia is a common example. (The Greek *agora* was a public meeting held in the open.) Other situations that give rise to such anxiety are enclosed or crowded places, heights, bridges, being alone, and being in the dark. Several such phobias can occur together. Quite often sufferers (young women are particularly vulnerable) have had a minor variant of the condition for a long time but there is a sudden onset of more acute anxiety following, for example, a change in routine which required the individual to stay at home. The symptoms can be extremely severe, chronic, and disabling. Social phobias overlap with these situational anxiety states. The individual is afraid of eating or speaking in public, of blushing when spoken to, or of doing something silly when entering a social situation.

There are more specific anxiety states caused by objects such as spiders, snakes, or fluttery things like birds or moths or bats. These usually begin during childhood, they are restricted to one or a few classes of object, and there are rarely anxiety symptoms except in the presence of anticipation of the object. Nevertheless the disablement can be severe if, for example, a sufferer insists on having any room explored by someone else to make sure there are no spiders before she will consent to enter. As many boys as girls seem to be affected by animal phobias, but adult sufferers are nearly always women.

In all these types of anxiety state, physiological tests demonstrate the abnormalities very clearly when the stimulus is present and often when it is not. There is a high pulse rate, increased palmar sweating, rapid respiration, impaired respiratory efficiency, increased blood flow, and muscular tension. In addition, unusual features in the autonomic response to stimuli can be demonstrated in the laboratory. More sedative is required in order to reach a given 'sedation threshold' than in non-anxious subjects; spontaneous fluctuations in the electrical conductance of the skin are more frequent, suggesting a higher level of spontaneous activity in the central nervous system; anxious patients do not adapt so quickly to a painful or anxiety-producing stimulus.

Sedative drugs are useful adjuncts in treatment, but tolerance tends to develop if they are taken habitually and it is usual to reserve them for special occasions. A psychological technique known as 'flooding' is often helpful. The individual is exposed for several hours to the situation he fears and finds that he can tolerate it. Such an experience may be more acceptable if finally shared in a self-help group. Specific phobias are often treated by desensitization—gradual habituation, beginning with the most minimal stimulus and working up to the most severe. Learning a technique of relaxation is very helpful as are methods involving 'meditation'.

Less is known about the social factors that precipitate anxiety states, perhaps because they are less common than depressive disorders. There is no doubt that social circumstances can act to maintain a severe disorder. If it is easy to avoid anxiety-provoking situations, the motivation for treatment may be low. The subject then prefers to put up with the impairment and may even deny that it exists.

Occasionally, anxiety states can be extremely severe and the subjective experiences may be described in very unusual terms: 'cold water trickling over my spine', 'the roof of my head lifted off', 'my stomach on fire'. There can even be hallucinations, as when a young woman who was terrified of the dark thought she heard the voices of two men in the shadows, plotting to attack her. Examples will be given in chapters 4 and 6 of cases of this kind that were treated as though they were schizophrenic, with serious consequences. Depersonalization and derealization also occur, sometimes as an alternative to severe and prolonged anxiety. The individual feels remote, detached from his body, floating above the surface of events, or seeing things as from a distance. Another symptom is fear of illness or hypochondriasis. Both depersonalization and hypochondriasis can occasionally occur, particularly in chronic states, as the most predominant feature; the anxiety symptoms having receded into the background.

Another group of neurotic conditions are termed obsessional and compulsive states. They are characterized by ideas, thoughts, or images forcing themselves into the consciousness against the sufferer's will, so that he finds himself preoccupied with some particular mental content (it might be germs, or knives, or the meaning of the universe) even though he tries to turn his attention elsewhere. These experiences, also, are often severely distressing and disabling. They can occur together with other phenomena in agoraphobic conditions or by themselves. The essence of the difference between an obsessive and a situational or specific phobia is that the former is 'not a direct fear of a given object or situation, but rather of imagined consequences arising therefrom'.[114] For example, one woman was more disturbed by the notion that she might injure herself on small splinters of glass (and driven to take useless preventive measures) than by larger fragments she could actually see and remove.

Because the objects of anxiety are less definite in the case of the obsessive phobias there is a greater likelihood of generalization, so that protective rituals spread to involve the whole of a person's life and the lives of other people round him (though this is always a risk in all anxiety states). One young man could never decide whether he had seen every possible source of danger when beginning to cross the road. He was afraid that a cyclist, for example, might have escaped his attention and that by stepping out incautiously he might cause an accident. Thus he stood hesitating on the kerb for hours at a time, unable to get across. Obviously his whole life became dominated by this obsession. He was unable to work, he had no social life and even his close relatives were finally unable to tolerate this bizarre behaviour, and he had to go into hospital.

Desensitization techniques are of less value than in the anxiety states but flooding offers more hope. As in all the functional psychoses and neuroses there is no evidence that psychoanalysis is better than other techniques of treatment, though supportive psychotherapy and specific counselling may enable the handicapped individual to cope better with his problems.

This completes our review of the functional psychoses and neuroses, with the exception of schizophrenia which will be dealt with in detail in the next chapter. It should be abundantly clear that dimensions do not contradict the categories as long as there are as many continua as there are discrete syndromes worth explaining. This is why unidimensional theories of 'psychosis' (let alone theories that also put 'neurosis' on the same dimension) are of little help in explanation. The complexity and richness of clinical phenomena cannot be restricted in this way. No doubt in time the various continua will be found to be interrelated; we can already make some guesses as to how. However, disease theories have usually been most successful when they have been applied, in the first place, to discrete syndromes. There seems no reason to suppose that this is not also true of the psychiatric disorders.

Personality disorders

The term 'personality' is commonly used to refer to that combination of enduring psychological characteristics by which we recognize other people as unique human beings. Even if the human race were to continue for ever, it is difficult to imagine that there could be another Winston Churchill or Franklin Roosevelt. The very idea of 'personality types' or 'personality disorders' therefore appears self-contradictory. Nevertheless, there is something useful in it. People do have traits in common. Approaches to classification have taken three main forms: *ad hoc* descriptive categories suggested by those, such as novelists, magistrates, soldiers, or doctors, who might be regarded as familiar with the way people react under a variety of circumstances and over a period of time; minor variants of disease theories, for example depressive or schizoid personality; and systems based on various psychological theories.

a.　The ad hoc *approach to personality disorders*
The first of these classifications is far and away the most interesting, but unfortunately each classifier suggests a different set of types. However, the gallery of personalities created by someone as familiar with human beings as, say, Anthony Trollope or Jane Austen, is not entirely to be despised by the would-be scientist.

Both knew that certain characteristics of an individual might remain with him for a lifetime and principally determine his interests, his occupation and the reactions of those around him. We need not consider all the *ad hoc* formulations of personality types that have been put forward, but one of them is worth considering in some detail; the concept of the 'psychopath' or 'sociopath'. This has its origin in early nineteenth-century descriptions of 'moral imbecility' or 'moral insanity'. J. C. Prichard, for example, observed that some criminals seemed to have no control over their behaviour and no ethical sense although they were intelligent and not suffering from delusions. Since then many psychiatrists have contributed to the description of a type of individual who characteristically behaves in an anti-social way without necessarily achieving much reward but also without being able to restrain himself even when it is perfectly clear that he will be caught and punished. For many years, this condition was regarded as a form of mental retardation. The British Mental Health Act of 1959 formally recognized a category of psychopathy which was regarded as separate from mental illness and mental retardation; 'a persistent disorder or disability of mind . . . which results in abnormally aggressive or seriously irresponsible conduct on the part of the patient, and requires or is susceptible to medical treatment.' Young people who have been found guilty of offences may be compulsorily detained for limited periods if this 'diagnosis' is made, but very little use has in fact been made of the provision.

Cases have been described in which crimes such as rape followed by murder appeared to be the culmination of a tendency that had been present since quite early childhood. Family members and teachers had been alarmed by the violent fantasies and the cruelties practised on animals and smaller children, by the lack of any remorse or sign of feeling for the victims, and by the complete lack of response to punishment. In such cases, the motivation appears to be internal and idiosyncratic. There is no parallel, for example, with the licensed killing of soldiers in wartime, which is clearly a social phenomenon, nor even with the murder of a bank guard during an organized robbery. The individual himself may be genuinely puzzled as to why he behaves as he does.

John Haslam,[63] that master of clinical description, published in 1809 the case of a boy of 10 who, since he was 2 years old had become 'so mischievous and uncontrollable, that he was sent from home to be nursed by an aunt.' He was treated with kindness, 'indulged in every wish, and never corrected for any perverseness or impropriety of conduct.' He nevertheless became the terror of the family. When he was 9, a keeper had to be appointed to supervise him and his regime became harsher. He did not respond to this regime either. He tore his clothes, broke everything that was presented to him, did the opposite of what he was asked and was completely indifferent to punishment. 'He was an unrelenting foe to all china, glass, and crockery ware, whenever they came within his reach he shivered them instantly.' He became attached to nobody and appeared incapable of forming a friendship. 'Of any kindness shewn him, he was equally insensible.' He was viciously cruel to small animals, 'oppressed the feeble, and avoided the society of those more powerful than himself. The keeper was already afraid of him.' Haslam notes that he was physically and intellectually normal and that he knew there was something the matter: 'for he said, "God had not made him like other children", and when provoked he would threaten to destroy himself.' Haslam showed him through Bethlem hospital. He was not alarmed by the patients chained in their cells but said, 'with great exultation, "this would be the right place for me". Considering the duration of his insanity, and being ignorant of any means by which he was likely to recover, he returned to his friends, after continuing a few weeks in London.'

When a long history of apparently motiveless crimes is present, a label such as 'violently aggressive psychopathy' is descriptively apt. There is very little evidence, so far, to link such a syndrome with any underlying biological abnormalities although there are a few hints, for example in the slow waves sometimes found in the electroencephalogram and in the fact that some people become much more aggressive following cerebral disease such as encephalitis. The correlations are low, however, and lead to no useful generalizations about treatment or management. Very few psychiatrists are willing to put forward a disease theory to explain the syndrome. John Bowlby put forward a famous hypothesis that early maternal deprivation was responsible for the development of a psychopathic personality but this theory has been considerably modified since.[151] No sociological theory has even this degree of plausibility.

It is understandable, therefore, that influential thinkers will suggest quite different methods of dealing with 'aggressive psycho-paths'. Some will say that prison is irrelevant, the only realistic alternative being a secure psychiatric unit. Others will argue that a medical solution is just as irrelevant and might carry its own social dangers. I would agree with the latter view until evidence becomes available that psychiatrists have something distinctive to offer. It is perfectly legitimate to postulate that a disease theory may eventually be found useful, because of the consistency of the behavioural pattern and its apparently non-social character. That is a scientific matter. But it is not legitimate to ask doctors to try to relieve society of the responsibility for recognizing and treating the condition, except in their capacity of experienced counsellors to a court.

This conclusion is just as appropriate when we consider individuals like Adolf Hitler, whose behaviour is so repulsive that we feel there must be some pathology to account for it. Hitler not only allowed himself to dwell upon and elaborate fantasies that most people hastily push out of their minds; he influenced others to put them into action. But a *post hoc* judgement of abnormality, made in the light of a full knowledge of how things turned out, is rather a different matter from reaching the same conclusion at a time when it would have been really useful, during the earlier days of his nefarious career when he was idolized by millions. Many leading statesmen then regarded him as a rational, self-interested, nationalistic politician like themselves. Certainly some people saw him as a danger to civilized life, but not because they made a diag-nosis of 'personality disorder'. The essence of the problem that Hitler presented—and it presents itself from time to time still, though fortunately not on such a scale—is whether preventive action should be taken when a man, without showing evidence of frank mental illness, claims that he is going to be cruel to other people. Is it necessary to wait until he actually is cruel? If so, the label of 'personality disorder' is entirely *post hoc* and tautological. If the recognition is to be made earlier, we need very good evidence as to the specific predictive features, otherwise we shall be locking up a lot of harmless people who have been unwise enough to air their private fantasies in public. It is very unlikely that any pre-dictive factors will be more than tentative and even less probable that they will be non-social in nature. These problems will be dis-cussed in more detail in later chapters.

b. Personality disorders as minor variants of disease

A quite different approach to personality disorders, deriving originally from Kraepelin, is to suppose that each of the main types of psychiatric illness has its own personality variant. Thus there are said to be schizoid, paranoid, cyclothymic, depressive, anxious, obsessional, and hysterical personalities. There is a good deal of clinical sense in this classification but it cannot yet be regarded as scientifically based since there is no means of reliably recognizing the personality types, no one has shown that there is a clear and strong relationship with overt psychiatric illness, and no practical conclusions have so far emerged that could be tested.

c. Theoretical systems of personality classification

The third approach is more theoretical and takes two forms. Psychodynamic theories are put forward in several different forms, but essentially they seek to understand the springs of all psychiatric disturbances (including schizophrenia, the affective disorders, the neuroses, and the personality disorders) in aberrations of psychological development during infancy and early childhood. Since it is very difficult to lay down with any precision which antecedents will result in which end-states, and since no predictive demonstration has been made by disinterested parties, it is necessary to depend on *post hoc* interpretations by experts. These often carry great conviction to disciples but cannot be seen as falling within a scientific tradition. The other sort of personality theory is based upon the idea of statistical deviation from a norm. A whole series of distinguished clinical psychiatrists and psychologists have put forward theories of this kind, including Pierre Janet, Karl Jung, Ernst Kretschmer, Kurt Schneider, Henrik Sjöbring, and Hans Eysenck. Most of these systems are related more or less explicitly to the clinical types described earlier, and the evidence regarding the special genetic, physiological, and psychological correlates of the dimensions has been put forward in each case with more or less success. It cannot be said that any of these systems has yet proved useful in practice, probably because they all oversimplify.

Of all the dimensions, intelligence probably has the best predictive validity, though there is a good deal of variation in detail. One person may be regarded as highly intelligent because of his excellent memory and verbal ability, while someone else without these advantages may do just as well because of his ability to reason logically. Each overcomes his deficits by using different assets but already we have said enough to show that their personalities must be different. Other dimensions, such as neuroticism or extraversion-introversion (see p. 46), have much less unity and predictive power. However, a substantial body of empirical data has been accumulated and gives reason to suppose that further scientific progress will be made, perhaps in association with population genetics.

Whichever classification of personality disorder is adopted—anecdotal, psychiatric, or theoretical—it is obvious that people with unusual personalities will tend to affect their environment as well as being affected by it. Someone whose personality does not 'fit' is bound to be more under stress and more likely to produce overt symptoms. Indeed, some people may even be instrumental in creating the very environmental stresses that they then break down under. Personality is therefore a variable that must be taken into account in assessing theories of the causation of mental illness and lesser psychiatric disorders.

Hysteria and socially shared psychopathology

Hysteria is one of the oldest concepts in medicine; one that has contributed more than any other to the powerful controversies that have always raged around the psychiatric disorders. Paradoxically so, because it is generally accepted today that disease theories of hysteria are only of very limited practical use, though they may yet turn out to be valuable pointers towards an understanding of the neurophysiology of mental processes. The term itself dates from the time of Hippocrates. The traditional theory was that hysteria was a disease of the uterus, which wandered about the body, thus causing a multiplicity of complaints, though physicians such as Aretaeus realized that it could occur in men as well as women.

Hysteria was probably used then, as now, as a sort of rag-bag for those complaints that no other diagnosis would fit. Greek medicine looked for natural causes even of 'emotional' disorders, but subsequent explanations reverted to the supernatural and treatments depended on whether the mentally ill were regarded as possessed by devils or were themselves stigmatized as witches. Either way the cure must often have been worse than the disease.

Thomas Sydenham, the great English clinician, wrote a treatise on hysteria in 1680 which returned to natural history. He described an enormous range of manifestations, so wide that hysteria was regarded as part of the differential diagnosis of practically every other condition. It could take the form of diarrhoea, muscular pain, cough, backache, or fits. It could affect men though it occurred most commonly in leisured women, and it could be precipitated by excitement, childbirth, or fasting. Sydenham was greatly puzzled by hysteria and was undecided between a somatic and a psychological explanation.

Towards the end of the eighteenth century, Franz Mesmer found that he could help some of his female patients by means of suggestion. His own explanation was in terms of a fluid in his body which he called 'animal magnetism'. He used both individual and group treatment and his methods and cures achieved great notoriety. Mesmerism was taken up in England by James Braid, a Manchester physician who popularized magnetism under the name of hypnosis. At the same time, John Elliotson published an account of surgical operations carried out under 'magnetic sleep'. By the middle of the nineteenth century the new ideas had reached the United States and were incorporated into some of the numerous religious movements of the time. The result was 'spiritism'. The spirits of dead people began to manifest themselves; they moved furniture, communicated by knocks and in other ways introduced an element of pleasing fantasy into small-town lives. Subsequently the spirits took to manifesting themselves visually and through intermediaries known as 'mediums'.

By this time hypnotism had rather fallen into disrepute but it was resuscitated by Liébault, Bernheim, and Charcot in France. Charcot was a great neurologist who first became interested in hypnosis when trying to distinguish between true and imitated epileptic fits. He described three stages in the development of hypnosis—lethargy, catalepsy, and somnambulism—and showed that hysterical conditions such as paralysis or mutism could be produced and made to disappear experimentally by hypnosis. Many of the characteristics of hysteria described by Charcot, and regarded by him as signs of disease, were in fact the result of suggestion. Bernheim argued that all human beings could in some degree be influenced by suggestion, and he made less and less use of formal hypnosis. Treatment by suggestion he called psychotherapeutics.

The fact that suggestions given during the hypnotic state could subsequently be acted upon without conscious memory of their origin, and that they could be recalled to consciousness by the hypnotist, together with other phenomena such as somnambulism and 'multiple personality', gave powerful reinforcement to ideas about a lower or hidden or unconscious mind which had long been invoked to explain dreams and the manifestations of the 'instincts'. Two of the people who were impressed by the work of Bernheim and Charcot were Pierre Janet and Sigmund Freud. Janet emphasized the relationship between hypnotist and subject. He thought that the subject's feelings contained definite filial and erotic elements as well as a desire for 'direction'. Henri Ellenberger[40] suggests that the differences between the explanatory systems developed by Janet and Freud can be understood if we remember that Janet's approach was characteristic of the French Enlightenment while Freud, and also Adler and Jung, were influenced by German romanticism. Janet developed a technique of rational psychological analysis based on uncovering the subconscious fixed ideas that he suggested had resulted from past traumatic events. A narrowing of consciousness obscures the connection between the symptoms and the trauma, but when the fixed ideas are revealed and discussed, improvement may occur. These processes are only subconscious in hysteria. In other neurotic conditions, particularly those that Janet called 'psychaesthenic', they are quite conscious. The rapport between therapist and patient is an important medium for therapy. Janet's ideas were systematically formulated over many years, but his system is virtually unknown outside France, and even in his homeland it has not been influential.

Freud, on the other hand, has been regarded as introducing a revolution in human thought equivalent to those of Darwin and Marx. Ellenberger quotes L. S. Granjel's comparison between Freud's thought and Schopenhauer's: both regarded man as fundamentally irrational, both thought that the springs of motivation were sexual in nature and both contemplated humanity with a thorough-going pessimism. Freud's ideas about hysteria were a more radical version of Janet's. (There was a good deal of acrimony at the time as to which had precedence.) Thomas Szasz, in *The Myth of Mental Illness*,[174] maintained that Freud's contribution was not to discover that hysteria was a mental illness but to advocate that so-called hysterics should be called 'ill'. Since the supposed central syndromes of hysteria were iatrogenic, that is, imitated from models supplied by doctors, what was really being explained by the new theories was no more specific than the wide range of ills described by Sydenham or the Greeks. Szasz points out that this tendency was in fact taken much further and that virtually any experience or behaviour that was thought to be socially undesirable, including delinquency, divorce, homicide, and drug dependence, 'and so on almost without limit', came to be regarded as a manifestation of illness, since it could always be understood in psychoanalytic terms. 'The prestige and power of psychiatrists has been augmented by defining increasingly large domains as falling within the purview of their special discipline.'

Although it is well-established that hysterical phenomena such as catalepsy, somnambulism and multiple personality were often induced by doctors rather than spontaneously produced by patients, during the era when magnetism and hypnotism were being investigated, similar phenomena often occurred in non-medical settings. States of 'dissociation' are regarded as desirable in certain societies, and are often connected with religious ceremonies. There are similarities in methods of inducing trances or states of possession, when individuals or groups may experience unity with supernatural forces and receive the gift of prophecy or of speaking in tongues. Virtually any psychiatric symptom may be mimicked.

In addition to phenomena that can be seen as analogous to those induced by suggestion, once the local supernatural and sub-cultural variations are allowed for, certain syndromes may develop that appear to be characteristic only of one particular locality. These are usually states of excitement or panic that can occur anywhere, but they are influenced by local tradition in such a way as to give the appearance of specifically identifiable psychoses. The Windigo psychosis of the Chippewa, Ojibwa, and Cree Indians illustrates how such states can develop. A. J. Lewis[102] writes:

These people suffer terrible hardships in the severe winters of north-east Canada. The scarcity of game obliges each family to live by itself, exposed to the risk of starvation; cannibalism sometimes occurs. They have myths about a monster, living as an ice skeleton during winter and dying in the spring, who devours human beings. They believe also that human beings may be led by witchcraft, to develop similar cannibal desires and to have their heart turn to ice. In fact some members of the tribe do become profoundly depressed and excessively anxious about starvation. Their perceptions then become disturbed and they see members of their family as plump, succulent, inviting beavers. Some of those affected have insight into their condition and beg that they should be killed before they give way to their cannibal urge; others actually kill and eat members of their family and eventually other people if they are not caught in time.

Psychiatrists in all countries have to become skilled in sorting out the various factors involved in any individual case. Although 'culture-bound reactive syndromes' are fairly common in some developing countries, comparable conditions occur everywhere.

The phenomena of 'possession' by evil spirits should also be mentioned. In mediaeval Europe these were well-recognized. Victims knew what was expected of them. The commonest symptoms were areas of anaesthesia or analgesia on the skin, convulsions, vomiting, blaspheming, and speaking in tongues with the voice of the devil. The churchmen of the time had an extensive repertoire of rituals, such as the benediction by salt and water, to drive out the devils.

It is in the nature of hysterical phenomena that they will occur from time to time as 'psychic' epidemics. One of the most famous of these took place in the village of Salem, part of the Massachusetts Bay Colony, in 1692. Its fame is no doubt partly due to the splendid account written by Marion Starkey,[171] who combines historical accuracy with the ability to tell a very good story. Only twenty witches were found guilty in Salem village, not a large number by the standards of Puritan and Catholic witchhunts in Europe; but the scale is small enough to make the whole affair seem comprehensible.

The tragedy began in the childish fantasy of a few small girls, inspired by a Negro slave woman's memories of her native Barbados. Even such an apparently innocent art as fortune-telling was, of course, strictly forbidden. 'God who reveals all things in His own good time does not permit His providence to be tempted. Only the devil will stoop to such devices.' The girls knew that well enough, since one was Betty, the daughter of the minister of the parish, Samuel Parris, and another was Abigail, her cousin. The Negro slave was Tituba, who relieved Mrs. Parris of all the heavier household chores. Soon Abigail, the older of the two girls and the bolder, had introduced several of their friends into the new mysteries. Twelve-year-old Ann Putnam was the youngest. (Her mother, also Ann, had recently been having vivid dreams, the meaning of which she urgently wished to unravel.) Several others were in their early twenties. All were unmarried. If Abigail was a pure mischief-maker, Ann the younger was the rapt initiate.

No contemporary account of the early stage of the affliction exists but by February 1692 several of the girls were 'possessed'. The outbreak probably began with Betty and Abigail and then spread to near neighbours, including young Ann Putnam. The manifestations or fits took numerous forms: fixed staring, hoarse choking noises like the barking of a dog, odd postures, uncontrolled leaping, incoherent babbling, writhing, and threshing movements. William Griggs, the local doctor, was utterly perplexed and finally handed the problem to the minister as the work of the evil hand.

Samuel Parris called in his colleagues, and between them they did their best to discover who was responsible for the witchcraft. Finally, Tituba and two village women—one, a female tramp, Sarah Good, the other, Sarah Osborne, moderately well-to-do but with a dubious past—were named. Tituba quickly picked up clues from her interrogators and confessed that she had been used as a witch. She claimed however that the other two women had been responsible. She also said, probably simply as an embellishment, that nine witches were involved in a pact with the devil. Thus, at a time when most people would probably have been glad to have settled the affair with only three rather unimportant witches accused, it began to take on a new dimension. Once more the afflicted girls were interrogated and young Ann Putnam named Martha Cory, a member of the congregation itself. Martha was not well liked in the village but she was respectable. She was brought before a preliminary hearing of the magistrates in the meeting house; the girls who accused her were seated on the front benches with a crowded congregation behind them. Martha denied all the charges and suggested that 'these distracted children' should not be believed. The girls shouted and shook and imitated Martha's every movement; they said they could hear a drum beating and see all the witches in Essex County assembling. 'You can't prove me a witch!' cried Martha before she was led away to prison to be held for trial. But such a statement was beside the point.

What she couldn't prove, what no one at all accused of such a thing could prove, was that she wasn't.

The girls had acquired breathtaking powers over life and death. Having breached the respectability barrier, new accusations followed each other in rapid succession. Both Ann Putnams together with Abigail, next named Rebecca Nurse, an old, deaf, ill lady of good family and supposedly unimpeachable reputation. Her preliminary hearing was a replica of Martha Cory's. Ann Putnam, senior, recounted how her small nieces, long dead, had appeared to her in their winding sheets, saying that Rebecca had killed them. Next to be accused were Rebecca's two sisters, then John Procter and his wife Elizabeth, and so it went on, including even a former minister in the village, George Burroughs. Some 22 were accused in April and 39 in May.

In all, 19 witches were hanged and more than a hundred suspects were in jail before ministers and public opinion alike became uneasy. When the wife of one of the leading ministers appeared in a young girl's dream everyone realized that things had gone too far. The girls became injudicious, even naming the wife of the Colonial Governor. That was the end. By mid-October the Governor had forbidden further imprisonments or trials for witchcraft.

Marion Starkey, who had taken courses in psychology with Dr. O. H. Mowrer, presents this story in more complete historical detail than previous authors. She was writing at the end of the Second World War, and several times mentions parallels with contemporary events. Her explanation is couched in terms of classical hysteria occurring in repressed teenagers brought up in a God-fearing Puritan community, whose ministers gave content to the epidemic and unconsciously guided it along its devastating course. Arthur Miller, in his play *The Crucible*, found parallels with the McCarthy era in the United States.

The episode does indeed raise echoes of Hitler and McCarthy. It also illustrates the case made by Szasz against regarding hysteria as a disease. Martha Cory and John Procter thought the girls were lying and that a good hiding would have put an end to their tricks. Probably most of the girls were as able to control their 'fits' as Samuel Parris was to control his religious fervour. They were acting rather than consciously lying, and they had an appreciative audience. A few others, notably Ann Putnam, senior, and

Abigail Williamson, cannot be explained quite so readily. They were more talented and perhaps better able to 'go out of control'. Such talents are represented in every community but they flourish in this shape only in special cultures.

Brilliant though it is, Marion Starkey's account of an epidemic of hysteria in seventeenth-century New England is somehow unsatisfying. It does not explain why it occurred at that time and place. Its emphasis on individuals and their motivations is curiously two-dimensional. The Sartre film version presents this quality even more intensely. An historical episode cannot be dealt with in purely psychological terms.

More recently, Paul Boyer and Stephen Nissenbaum[17] have published an analysis of the events in Salem village that is based on a detailed knowledge of parish and town records made during the previous twenty years. They know how the parish (an early democracy) voted, who paid how much in taxes, and which of the local inhabitants were elected to public office. They have read community petitions, family wills and deeds, estate inventories, lawsuit testimonies, and volumes of sermons. They begin by pointing out that the little sorceries practised by Betty and Abigail under the tutelage of Tituba must have been going on all over New England at that time. Outbreaks of witchcraft were no rarity. What was rare was the savage course run by the episode in Salem village. The expected outcome would have been for the whole thing to have blown over after the arrest of the first three women. Another example of witchcraft during 1692 was treated quite differently. The afflicted girl received a very great deal of public attention, but the minister used the opportunity to further the religious edification of his community.

Clearly the decisive factor was the interpretation which adults—adults who had the power to make the interpretation stick—chose to place on events whose intrinsic meaning was, to begin with, dangerously ambiguous.

The girls had not originally said anything about witchcraft at all. Some of them seemed to describe events with a divine, rather than a demonic, origin. Samuel Parris did not need to ask them leading questions about who was persecuting them. The village turned to him for help in understanding what was going on, but he was not entirely disinterested. Only ten or so girls in Salem village were actually afflicted and, after the first dozen local witches, most of those they named lived in communities scattered throughout the whole of Essex County. The girls would not have known these people personally, and their names must have been supplied. Boyer and Nissenbaum noticed that 12 of the 14 villagers who were accused lived in the eastern or outer half of the village, while 30 of the 32 people registered as accusers lived in the inner half. Following up this clue, they were able to trace a long history of local enmity between those living in the inner village and the more entrepreneurial, prosperous, and outward-looking inhabitants of the eastern portion, whose geographical and economic links were mainly with Salem town (the second town in the colony after Boston). It was the families of the inner heart of the village, led by the Putnams, who had been most eager to set up a new church, independent from that in Salem town. This would have been the first step towards complete civic separation of the village from the town. The first minister to the village, James Bayley, was appointed in 1672, but there was much wrangling between two local factions. One, led by Nathaniel Putnam, was opposed to Bayley because he did not sufficiently represent the inner core of villagers, the ones who most wanted their own independent church. James Bayley resigned in 1680, and George Burroughs was appointed in his stead. He fared no better; indeed John Putnam had him arrested for debt. (This was the minister later hanged as a wizard.) Burroughs left in 1682, and the quarrelsome reputation of the village was such that it was two years before another minister, Deodat Lawson, could be induced to take the vacancy. After a period of deceptive calm, a new controversy arose. This time, the Putnams supported the minister. Indeed, they probably arranged his election. Lawson set up a fully covenanted (independent) church in the village. The opposition was led by members of an influential family from the eastern section, the Porters. Salem town threw its weight on the side of Joseph Porter. Lawson left in 1688 at the end of his contract, and Samuel Parris was engaged by the group, led by the Putnams, that had the upper hand in the village at the time. The group pressed again for the full independence of the village church and this time they were successful.

Clearly there had been a running battle for years between the village factions, one having the best of it for a time and then fortune swinging to the other side. Samuel Parris knew his enemies in the village, many of whom retained their membership of other churches. Quite apart from the economic differences between the two sides, there were also bitter personal enmities. The Putnams, on the whole, were a declining family, while the Porters were on the way up. There had been a time, in the heyday of Thomas Putnam, senior, when the Putnams' wealth was concentrated and impressive, but, at the age of 54 and with eight children already (including Thomas, junior), he married a second time. Joseph Putnam was the only child of the second marriage, and he and his mother received the best part of the estate when Thomas Putnam, senior, died; a fact that Thomas Putnam, junior, and his wife Ann greatly resented. Joseph then married into the Porter family, taking much of the Putnam cash with him. The feelings of Thomas and Ann, and the rest of the Putnam family, can be imagined.

This is the background to the events of 1692, in which Samuel Parris and Ann Putnam, senior (the wife of Thomas, junior) played such a central role. It is very well to speculate about whether the afflicted girls knew they were lying; what is far more interesting is how much Parris himself, and leading members of the Putnam family, knew what was going on. It is impossible to tell from the contemporary records, which are couched in high-minded Biblical terms. It is true that the accused did not raise such matters, although many were sceptical about witchcraft. Rebecca Nurse and her sisters, and John and Elizabeth Procter, were friends of the Porters, and Isaac Porter attempted to rally opposition to the trials around the case of Rebecca Nurse. In the long run, the Porters won the battle, but only years later. Parris was evicted, and the fortunes of the Putnams continued to decline. The Porters, harbingers of the new capitalism, flourished.

We can see the connections between economics, politics, family interests and rivalry, and incidental personal motivations. As Boyer and Nissenbaum point out, this is the drama of history played out on a small stage. But does it throw new light on the role of the small group of hysterical girls who acted as accusers? They must have been given clues as to what was the purpose of the exercise. Ann Putnam, senior, herself belonged to the conservative faction, and she was mother of the younger Ann, who was one of the most influential among the afflicted girls. Precisely how consciously the manipulation occurred we cannot tell, but there can be no doubt of the fact.

Thomas Szasz would probably argue that the girls were consciously lying, their reward being the excitement and attention they got from the performance. This seems to be too simple an explanation. Other girls in the village were not affected in the same way. Among the group, Abigail stood out as bolder than the others, Ann Putnam, senior, as more odd. Betty Parris does not seem to have had a 'hysterical personality' at all. Several of the girls subsequently confessed that they knew what they were doing. They took their justification from the social situation, audience and all. We have to postulate mechanisms more developed in some people than in others but potentially available in any small community. Whether it comes to light in this tragic form or in some other depends solely upon the degree and type of stress experienced and on the nature of the social expectations. The epidemic of witchcraft in Salem village is unique, but it does illustrate, as Marion Starkey and Arthur Miller suggest, latent tendencies that can be brought out on a larger scale given the appropriate talent for exploitation. Hysteria is clearly social in nature; what comes of it depends entirely upon circumstances. It demands a basically non-medical paradigm, avoiding the mistakes of Charcot and Freud, but the more we know about 'personality' vulnerability (which might be biological in nature), the better.

Our ignorance of a hypothetical biological substrate does not mean that hysteria is not a matter for doctors. If Dr. William Griggs had been able to make the correct 'diagnosis' when the girls were first taken to him, and if he had been aware of the social forces operating in the village, he might well have been able to suggest a course of action that would have resulted in events taking a much more benign course. Naturally, he was himself deeply imbued with Puritan thinking, and his training in psychological and social matters was no doubt scanty. But there is no reason why doctors should not be as well acquainted with this sort of epidemic as they are with typhoid, also a very rare condition nowadays.

We are in danger of coming full circle, from saying that hysteria cannot usefully be explained as a disease to suggesting that it might be possible for some medical paragon to recognize hysteria, understand how the bitter personal feuds and social divisions in the village and the economic forces behind them might lead to exploitation of the afflicted girls, and work out a less damaging solution that would be acceptable to all parties in terms of Puritan

theology. No doctor, or for that matter any other kind of professional person, can be trained for such tasks. Still less could it be
done in complex industrial communities. But one central aspect of
knowledge that the doctor can be expected to acquire, by experience as much as by technical training, is the ability to recognize
people who are more likely to react hysterically than others.
Jaspers's description of the central trait of the predisposed personality is as follows:

Far from accepting their given dispositions and life opportunities,
hysterical personalities crave to appear, both to themselves and others,
as more than they are and to experience more than they are ever capable
of. The place of genuine experience and natural expression is usurped by
a contrived stage-act, a forced kind of experience. This is not contrived
'consciously' but reflects the ability of the true hysteric to live wholly in
his own drama, be caught up entirely for the moment and succeed in
seeming genuine. All the other traits can be understandably deduced
from this. In the end, the hysterical personality loses its central 'core' as
it were, and consists simply of a number of different exteriors.

It is worth reading the whole passage (in Jaspers's *General Psychopathology*).[76] Those who are not convinced that such a personality
can be reliably identified might do well to consider the description
of Trollope's Lady Eustace. Trollope was more forthright in showing his character to be a liar; he would have agreed with Szasz
on that point. But it is always difficult to see inside another person's mind, even when you know them well, in order to judge how
much is consciously motivated, and it is particularly difficult to
assess the level of consciousness in hysteria.

One further aspect of socially shared psychopathology needs discussion and that is *folie à deux*. Ernest Gruenberg[60] quotes an
occasion when a police van delivered four people to a Massachusetts mental hospital. One man, aged 60, was manic. Another was
mentally retarded. 'A woman was suffering from a psychosis which
the hospital was never quite able to classify. A 13-year-old boy in a
severely disturbed state was later called hysterical and required
unusual and ingenious methods for rehabilitation.'

Such a quartet would not necessarily be unusual in a mental
hospital but this one was peculiar in that it was a family group plus
lodger (the manic patient). At the time they were taken to hospital
they had been jointly engaged in discovering and destroying the
devils that were hiding inside the walls and furniture of their home.

Two other personalities (who were not brought to the hospital) were involved in the group project. One was the boy's dead sister, who was in a communicating relationship only with her brother, who in turn relayed messages to the remainder of the group. She, on the other hand, was in direct communication with God, whose messages she relayed to her brother. Through this two-stage communication system the physically present group had learned that the boarder was the second Messiah.

Gruenberg comments fairly enough that, although mental disorder can sometimes be related to social disintegration, in this and other instances it was clearly related to social integration. A better example of the uselessness of the term 'mental illness' to represent some hypothetical unitary condition cannot well be imagined. *Folie à quatre* (or even *à six*) might be a more appropriate term than *folie à deux* in this case. It is possible to work out in fair detail, simply from knowing the diagnoses and other information summarized above, what the relationships between the four people probably were. Any family or small cohesive group containing a mentally ill member is bound to be affected in some way. Similarly, society more generally is affected by mental illness, just as ill people are responsive to social pressures.

The importance of hysteria to doctors is that, by mimicking so many other conditions, including physical and mental illnesses, and by being so obviously amenable to social influences on role-playing, it poses several basic questions about the nature of illness. Norman Cohn[25] has shown that witches could not have been persecuted without a general acceptance by society of a stereotype of witchcraft. In fact there is no such thing as a witch; only the label, applied and accepted under duress, creates one. Once a few witches have confessed their status, a chain reaction starts, since the social attribution is confirmed. Szasz has used this analogy to argue that all functional 'mental illness' is a myth. He makes out a fair case while he sticks to hysteria, though even here we cannot be content solely with explanations in terms of social pressure and labelling. A truly satisfactory theory of suggestion has still to be put forward. When it is, Janet's ideas about dissociation may prove to have been farsighted. Szasz, however, takes his thesis very much further still, since he equates all psychiatric syndromes with hysteria. Thus the symptoms of schizophrenia are supposed to be always fabrications, adopted for various motives but basically created by doctors (i.e. iatrogenic). This argument will be considered in chapter 5. It is sufficient to state here that the evidence is against it. Szasz is certainly correct in his contention that the development of psychodynamic theories within medicine made it possible for some doctors to claim that virtually all human misfortunes should be regarded as illnesses. What he overlooks is that other doctors, at the same time, were putting forward more specific ideas that had completely the opposite effect. They separated the restricted areas in which practitioners could successfully use disease theories from the much wider areas where they could not. This did not mean that they refused to try to help people whose complaints did not fit into recognizable disease syndromes, simply that they realized that they would have to use non-specific techniques (among them psychotherapy, but including many others) or refer the patient elsewhere. The temptation to over-use medical labels must, however, remain high, and it is important that doctors should be educated to see the harm that can potentially follow.

Finally, it might be appropriate at this point to say a word about so-called 'psycho-history'. When Freud and Bullitt wrote their biography of Woodrow Wilson, Freud's contribution did not help to explain political events; nor, apart from disciples of psycho-analysis, would most people feel that they understood contemporary history any better for Freud's dynamic interpretations. Similarly, Norman Cohn's superb analysis of witchcraft in mediaeval Europe gains nothing from the appendix, in which psycho-analytic ideas float epiphenomenally on the tide of history like a sort of flotsam. Pathographies can be absorbing; for example Hunter and MacAlpine's diagnosis of George III's madness as due to porphyria or the controversies about Darwin's illness (was it Chagas's disease or hypochondriasis?). But they rarely help us to understand history.

The frequency of mental illnesses

If we ask how many people in the population suffer from a physical illness, there can only be one answer: it depends what kind of illness. If we count warts and athlete's foot, which are certainly illnesses, though usually very minor ones, the answer will be 100 per cent. If we count only serious illness, the onus of definition is shifted, and we have to specify the grade of severity we have in mind; the more severe, the less common. Precisely the same is true of psychiatric disorders. The psychiatric equivalents of warts are very common, but new cases of schizophrenia arise only rarely.

A sample survey in midtown Manhattan[170] may be used to illustrate the difficulties. Specially trained non-medical interviewers administered a questionnaire of mental health items to a sample of 1,660 adults aged 20–59. The information collected in this way was then rated by two psychiatrists, and each subject was classified in terms of severity of 'symptom formation' as: well (18·5 per cent), mild or moderate (58·1 per cent), marked or severe (20·7 per cent), incapacitated (2·7 per cent). Thus, nearly a quarter of the population were regarded as significantly impaired and more than 80 per cent as mentally unwell. This is the typical dimensional approach. The figures fill some theorists with foreboding and set off grand speculations about the decay of urban civilization, while the sceptics receive them with frank incredulity. Either way they give no information about the frequency of depressions of various kinds, of schizophrenia, or of anxiety states, and they tell us nothing about the need for medical help.

The British National Health Service (N.H.S.) provides a different kind of opportunity to study prevalence. Over two-thirds of the London population make contact with their family doctor during the course of a year. Michael Shepherd and his colleagues[161] have shown that some 10 per cent are given a diagnosis of 'neurotic' disorder. The psychiatric diagnoses of general practitioners are not always very sophisticated, but we can take the proportion seriously as an approximate estimate of those whose 'illness behaviour' is sufficiently motivated to take them to a doctor. Neil Kessel[82] has illustrated very graphically the problem of counting heads. He discussed with a general practitioner a sample of people belonging to the practice in order to discover how many had psychiatric conditions. Only 5 per cent could be given a diagnosis in the psychiatric sections of the International Classification of Diseases, but 52 per cent had psychological symptoms, complaints for which no physical cause could be found, or psychosomatic conditions. The margin of error is obviously so enormous that we cannot use such figures to give us useful information about the prevalence of psychiatric disorder even in the area in which the survey was carried out, let alone make comparisons between different parts of the world, or different types of society, or different historical periods.

Frequencies based on the numbers of people referred to psychiatrists are suspect for a different reason. They are much smaller (only about 5 per cent of cases regarded by a general practitioner as possibly psychiatric are sent on to a specialist) and are therefore subject to heavy selection. It seems unlikely that the same factors always play an equal part in selection, so that conclusions based solely on clinical observations of people admitted to hospital are probably unrepresentative and should not be generalized. There is, however, a remarkable similarity in the numbers. During the course of a year, somewhere between 1·5 and 2 per cent of the population of countries with well-developed medical services are likely to be in contact with a psychiatrist.[204] This is as true of Aberdeen (Scotland) and Hawaii as it is of urban areas like Baltimore, Rochester (New York), and London.[7, 207] All these places have developed psychiatric registers that record such contacts. There are differences of detail—in admission rates, in the extent to which in-patient care is used compared with day hospitals or out-patient clinics, etc.—but the overall frequency is very similar. Those referred to a psychiatrist, compared with those treated by general practitioners, tend to have diagnoses of schizophrenia, affective psychosis, and organic conditions, while the neuroses are relatively rarely referred (only about 1 per thousand of the general population during a given year, as opposed to the 10 per cent estimated to arise in general practice). This 100-fold selection suggests that only the most severe cases of neurosis are referred to the psychiatrist.

Surveys are now beginning to be made using standardized diagnostic techniques, including a standard cut-off point below which diagnosis is difficult, and above which standard classifying rules can be applied.[197] This makes it possible to compare randomly selected population samples more exactly with the samples referred to a psychiatrist. The work is still in its infancy, but the frequency of depressions of the severity commonly seen in in-patients is quite low in the general population, at any rate in London. Many of these people have been referred to psychiatrists, but there are some severe cases not receiving treatment. About 10 per cent of the population have milder conditions on the borderline. Below the cut-off point, there is another group of people with 'minimal depression' (7 per cent), and beyond this again, much larger numbers with only the minor psychiatric syndromes, such as worrying and muscular tension. Presumably this latter group makes up most of the very high morbidity reported by surveys of the midtown Manhattan type.

Anxiety and obsessional states of a degree of severity above the threshold point are less common than depressions. Single symptoms are, however, very common. Thus 28 per cent of women in an urban survey reported that they had avoided certain situations during the previous month because they thought they would experience unpleasant anxiety if they entered them. Very few were seriously incommoded by this, although it did place restrictions on their lives. One woman whose exacting job required her to visit old people on behalf of the local social services department could not go into a lift and therefore had to do a lot of stair-climbing. She was quite content with the situation. Others were restricted in the distance they could travel away from home unaccompanied, but very few expressed a wish to have treatment.

Thus the main problem raised by the high frequency of 'mental ill-health' is how much the people concerned need expensive and possibly irrelevant medical treatment (one in five of all N.H.S. prescriptions are for tranquillizers, anti-depressants, or sedatives) and how much a more supportive community might be able to help them cope better. This question will be considered in chapter 7.

As far as the really severe conditions are concerned, there is less doubt about frequency, since we can assume that most people will at some stage be referred to a psychiatrist; and we can therefore use official statistics, remembering always that the diagnoses written in hospital records tend to be rather unreliable. In England, some 15 new cases of schizophrenia arise per 100,000 population each year. The incidence rate (as this figure is called) tends to be higher in some parts of the world, for example in parts of the United States, but, as we shall see in chapter 4, this is largely due to the adoption of different diagnostic conventions. The prevalence rate (the number of cases present during a given period of time, say one year) tends to be higher in the case of schizophrenia, since there is an accumulation of chronic cases. An approximate estimate is 0·3 to 0·4 per cent of the general population. Estimates of the prevalence of other severe conditions are: mental retardation, 0·4 per cent of the population with intelligence quotients below 50; early childhood autism, 0·04 to 0·05 per cent of children; severe dementia, 6·2 per cent of those aged 65 and over.

All these figures can be summed to give an estimate of the prevalence of 'mental disorders', but such an overall figure has very little meaning. It is much more significant to compare specific rates in order to discover whether this or that condition is commoner at some particular time or place. Theories of causation can then be more precisely tested. Unfortunately, very little work of the necessary precision has been carried out, and we are restricted to a consideration of surveys that are methodologically inadequate. However, in view of the interest of the questions that have been asked (and often too confidently answered), such as whether the frequency of psychiatric disorders is increasing, whether the conditions of modern urban life foster them, and whether poverty, social class, or other social factors cause them, a section will be devoted to a consideration of the evidence available at present. All these questions can be discussed under the heading of 'the urban problem'.

The urban problem

Many of the great social theories of the day take on an extra depth and interest because they purport to explain mental illness as well as other social problems and prescribe a programme of community action that will make everyone healthier. We have already seen that questions of the kind, 'Does modern civilization cause mental illness?', have to be broken down into more manageable fragments, so that each of the elements can be more precisely defined. First, which features of our society are regarded as typical of 'modern civilization'? Second, which aspects of 'mental illness' are supposed to be affected? Can it be demonstrated, for example, that social conditions that increase the frequency of one type of illness do not lead to a diminution in some other kind? Most of the theories so far put forward have not been concerned with organic conditions but with a single dimension containing the functional psychoses and neuroses and the minor psychiatric disorders. Let us begin with the apparently simple problem of whether mental illnesses are increasing in frequency, since this underlies many of the more complex theories. The affirmative answer so frequently forthcoming derives its urgency from the fact that, at one end of the continuum, there are conditions that are severely disabling and distressing. If they are increasing, there is good reason for alarm. However, at the other end of the spectrum are minor disorders that are temporarily unpleasant but not severely or chronically handicapping. It is a matter of some importance where along the spectrum (or, better still, spectra—though most of the grand theories are not as sophisticated as that) the cut-off point is drawn, below which people can be regarded as not ill. Curiously enough, the theorists rarely specify.

No survey of technical expertise comparable even to those we shall be considering later in this section was carried out before the 1930s. Conclusions drawn about the distribution of mental illnesses in any historical period, from the Palaeolithic to the Victorian, are no more than guesswork. A study was carried out of the admissions to Worcester State Hospital, Massachusetts, over a period of nearly a century, during which it was the only public facility available and might therefore be expected to have dealt with most of the really severe cases of mental illness.[54] There was no change in the frequency of first admission for *dementia praecox* (schizophrenia).

Other studies bearing on the frequency of schizophrenia in various types of population will be reviewed in chapter 4. None of them provides unequivocal evidence that schizophrenia is commoner in urban than in rural areas or in industrialized compared with developing societies. Admissions to hospital are more frequent among single people, working in unskilled occupations, and living in isolated city areas; but the most likely explanation is selection rather than stress. There is a non-specific selective effect due to the fact that people without a home of their own or relatives to look after them are obviously more in need of admission if they become ill. There are also more specific effects. For example, individuals who later develop schizophrenia tend to be attracted by socially isolated city areas and move into them before the illness becomes overtly manifest.

There is an interactive effect as well. Social isolation, whether in the back wards of mental hospitals or in the rooming house districts of large cities, tends to increase the disabilities that commonly occur in schizophrenia. A substantial proportion of the people who make use of services for the destitute, who sleep rough, or who use the centres provided for homeless people, are suffering from schizophrenia. Most were not destitute when they were first admitted to psychiatric hospitals many years earlier. The decline occurred after they had left. In other words, once you are down, you tend to be ground down still further. There is a vicious spiral of interaction between chronically handicapping diseases and the environment. However, there is no good evidence that living in a socially isolated area causes schizophrenia. Studies of the other functional conditions, severe enough to merit admission to hospital or referral to a specialist, do not suggest that cultural factors are of paramount importance in affecting the rate of incidence. It is therefore worth considering the frequency of conditions of lesser severity.

A comparison of rural and urban areas gives an indirect method of assessing the changes that have occurred with urbanization in industrial countries. Nearly one-fifth of the world's population live in urban centres of more than 100,000 people. In the United Kingdom, the proportion is closer to one-half. The complexity of the problems caused by the growth of large cities hardly needs emphasizing to a nation of people who either live, work, or do their shopping in towns. Perhaps the most obvious features are the traffic, with its concomitant rush-hours, commuting, air pollution, and noise; the substitution of endless expanses of roads, houses, apartment blocks, and factories for woods and meadows; the existence of districts of substandard dwellings, overcrowding, and poor amenities; and a subjective impression that each individual in a village community possesses a unique identity which must inevitably become submerged and lost within the urban multitude. Thus David Riesman[145] writes:

The greatest danger . . . of modern city life is its disruption of human relations, resulting in an isolation, a loneliness of the individual which increases with the size of the city and its complexity . . . Human relations are only possible on a basis of communication. The complexity of modern city life demands an ever-increasing complexity of communication system, which however seems to have reached a point where communication is actually decreasing. The result of this process is the crowd . . . In the crowd, being part of the crowd, we are alone.

There seems to be a general feeling that cities are bad for the individual and that they must have adverse effects on mental health. As soon as one looks for a test of this general hypothesis it becomes apparent that both rural and urban areas vary greatly among themselves. Villages are not always havens of peace and prosperity, while some urban areas are just that. Moreover, in developed countries, even rural populations have some experience of life in towns. Most people, everywhere, experience several different environments—at home, at work and at play—during the course even of one day, let alone during a lifetime. Regional, social, and demographic trends will be likely to cut across and dominate urban-rural and inter-urban differences. Neither urban sociologists nor social anthropologists are much inclined to formulate general laws that will predict what sort of differences we should expect between people who live within the administrative boundaries of small country villages and those who live within a ten-minute walk of Piccadilly Circus or Times Square.

E. J. R. Primrose,[137] the general practitioner of a small Scottish village noted for its shotgun weddings and extraordinarily high prevalence of alcoholism, calculated that 9 per cent of the population, mainly women, were 'neurotic'.* Michael Shepherd and his colleagues[161] found about 10 per cent in London general practices, also with a much higher frequency in women. Alexander Leighton and his colleagues carried out studies in rural Canada and rural Nigeria.[98, 97] They found about one-fifth of the Nigerian village population to be definite 'cases', with the same frequency in men and women, but while the Canadian men showed a similar proportion, 40 per cent of the women were regarded as 'cases'. In terms of current symptom patterns, 76 per cent of Nigerian village men and 64 per cent of women were regarded as showing 'neurotic' symptoms, compared with 42 per cent of men and 60 per cent of women in the Canadian study. These proportions are very high, similar to those found in the midtown Manhattan survey referred to earlier. Olle Hagnell[61] carried out a thorough survey in rural Sweden. According to his own diagnosis, some 13 per cent of the population was 'neurotic'. When he tried to match Leighton's criteria the proportion became 35–40 per cent. The conclusion has to be that more secure and reliable case-finding criteria must be adopted before any generalizations can be drawn from comparing population surveys.

Other studies have concentrated on certain specific social factors thought to be causative of mental ill-health. When these are taken one at a time there does not seem to be a strong and consistent relationship. Aircraft noise may be taken as an example since many

---

* Quotation marks are included as a reminder that terms like 'neurotic' are not used in comparable fashion in these studies.

people are persuaded that it must be a factor in the production of 'neurotic' states. One study of admissions to the mental hospital serving an area which contained high and low 'noise zones' found that there were significantly higher rates from the high-noise area.[3] When a similar study was repeated at the same hospital, but with a number of minor changes in the criterion of residence within the high- and low-risk areas (for example, a hostel for elderly people in the high-noise area was excluded), the differences were much less impressive.[50] Clearly, more detailed studies are needed to evaluate the effect of noise and they are being carried out, but until the results are available it is not reasonable to make confident statements about the deleterious effects of aircraft noise on mental health.

Another factor often quoted is retirement but a recent longitudinal study[173] of the problems of people approaching retirement age suggested that similar proportions of people broke down whether they retired or not. What was important was the degree of preparation, the previous reaction to stress, and the extent to which people saw retirement (or remaining at work) as an externally imposed and unexpected directive, or something which fitted into their expectations for themselves.

Housing is another index which has been closely studied. Here there are certain specific factors. Marc Fried,[58] for example, showed that when people are compulsorily rehoused, they may grieve for a lost home as for a lost relative. The disadvantages of apartments in high-rise blocks, particularly for small children but also for phobic adults, have been clearly demonstrated, and planners have probably learned this lesson by now. Oscar Newman's[129] concept of 'defensible space' also has much to commend it. If only one single entrance serves many dwellings no one is sure who may legitimately enter and who may not. Some people (not all) will feel personally insecure as a result. Similarly, when people are not individually responsible for the boundaries of their property they will not feel it their concern to prevent it being vandalized.

Other studies have been focused on the new housing estates. Most people moving in tend to be young, with young children, and they are at a stage of family development when financial burdens are greatest. Taking factors such as these into account, the frequency of 'neurosis' on new housing estates does not seem to be much greater than on old ones.[62] (We shall see later that these factors are important in themselves.) A small proportion of people in each type of setting tend to be dissatisfied, though with different aspects of the environment in each case. There is a marked association between dissatisfaction and 'neurotic' symptoms. Stephen Taylor and Sidney Chave[178] sum up their results as follows:

Dissatisfaction with environment might be a cause of neurotic reaction. But it is much more likely to be a symptom, since a remarkably constant minority of people show both a measure of dissatisfaction and nervous symptoms, wherever they happen to live. Immediate environment may play a marginal part in causation; it may colour the clinical picture, and it may be blamed by the patient. But all our findings so far point to long-standing or constitutional factors.

These conclusions may be further illustrated by a small pilot study of housing environments carried out in south-east London.[192] Indices were used to describe three recently erected public housing developments—a thirteen-storey slab block of internal corridor apartments, a six-storey block of apartments with external access balconies, and a group of linked terrace houses around small enclosed courts or squares. According to these indices, the slab block appeared to be most isolating and the enclosed squares most conducive to social interaction, with the six-storey block in between. The neighbourhood of the slab block was bleak, lacking in amenities, and unwelcoming, compared with the neighbourhoods of the other two types of housing. On the other hand, the internal quality of the slab-block dwellings was much superior to that of houses in the squares.

Ten families were chosen in each of the three housing developments. None had been rehoused for medical reasons. Age and sex composition, length of residence, rent and income were not significantly different. In each case the mother was interviewed. The sense of belonging to the home was correlated with the quality and amenities of the dwelling; i.e. the slab-block dwellers were most satisfied and the square dwellers least. On the other hand, sense of belonging to the block or small group of dwellings was highest in the squares and lowest in the slab block. Social interaction was also reported to be highest in the squares and lowest in the slab block. There was no difference in the amount of mental ill-health reported in the adults or children of the three groups of families. These results tend to confirm those of the larger studies in that attitudinal factors were highly specific but did not, in sum, distinguish between the environments. The suggestion that architectural features may influence the degree of social interaction is, however, worth following up.

George Brown and his colleagues[18] have shown that poor housing is an important contributory factor producing mental ill-health among women. His work has thrown light on correlations found by the midtown Manhattan investigators between environmental stress, particularly in working-class people, and 'neurosis'. He considers that stressful factors can be subdivided into remote factors causing increased vulnerability to later breakdown, e.g. early loss of parents; long-term problems, particularly those associated with poverty, such as housing and financial difficulties and chronic physical illness, but also the presence of small children in the house; and recent precipitating events of a threatening nature, such as enforced rehousing, learning of a husband's infidelity, sudden illness in the family, and so on. These last seem to play the same role in causation as does acute bereavement, though most are less intense. As well as these adverse factors, the presence of various assets has also to be considered; a warm and supportive relationship with husband or boy-friend is particularly protective, so is a stable job. When all these factors are taken into account, it is found that mild psychological symptoms can often be understood in environmental terms, and the social class difference is seen to be largely a matter of differing frequencies of precipitating events, longer-term problems, and a lack of supportive relationships or work. For example, working-class women of this age are less likely to have satisfactory marriages and more likely to experience threatening events.

We must now begin to take into account the problems of another group of people, not so far considered, who do not so much complain of their own mental suffering (though they may do so incidentally, as a reaction to their other problems), but whose social deviance leads people around them to be concerned. We are dealing here with delinquency, crime, alcohol and drug dependence, attempted suicide, public and private violence and destructiveness, and the conduct disorders of childhood and adolescence. No one familiar with descriptions of the sinks and stews of Victorian London would be disposed to say that these were new phenomena, and it is a measure of progress that we can give so much time and thought to ways of preventing them.

Michael Rutter and his colleagues[152] found that schoolchildren in a predominantly working-class inner London suburb showed twice as much 'behaviour deviance', measured by a questionnaire completed by a teacher, as equivalent children living in the relatively middle-class Isle of Wight. Both minor psychiatric disorder and conduct disturbance showed this difference, as did educational attainment. The disturbed children in both areas tended to come from unhappy, disruptive, disadvantaged homes, but these were commoner in inner London. Thus Brown's conclusion that class differences within an inner London area could partly be explained in terms of poorer family relationships can be extended to explain class differences between areas, and there appears also to be an intergenerational effect. Some schools in Rutter's study were more associated with disturbance than others, as Michael Power[136] has also demonstrated. Donald West[187] found five background factors of particular importance for delinquency: low family income, large family size, parental criminality, low intelligence, and poor parental behaviour. Earlier ecological analyses, showing that delinquency occurred particularly in areas of high unemployment, overcrowding, poor housing, and few amenities (in a word, in poverty-stricken areas) were thus confirmed, but with the proviso that poverty affects the most vulnerable individuals. Lee Robins[146] pointed out that 'neurotic' symptoms in childhood and adolescence are usually of short duration and do not predict mental disturbance in later life. Deviant behaviour, however, has a more serious prognosis, since, 'in a large minority of cases it presages lifelong problems with the law, inability to earn a living, defective interpersonal relationships, and severe personal distress. In fact, if one could successfully treat the anti-social behaviour of childhood, the problems of adult crime, alcoholism, divorce and chronic unemployment might be vastly diminished.'

Accounts of the spread of drug use among young people suggest the importance of 'social networks', i.e. a set of personal linkages between members of a group which help to explain their social behaviour. Of course, the majority of people who have experimented with drugs have come to no harm, but the few individuals who define themselves and their circle in terms of drug use are at a high risk. It seems likely that a combination of family predisposition owing to the sort of factors described by West, Rutter, and Brown, together with reinforcing social networks or local reference groups, will go some way to explain the development of deviant behaviour. (Theories of primary and secondary deviance will be discussed in chapter 5.) A geographical area in which poverty and family instability were endemic would provide an environment in which a sub-culture could become established over a long period of time, so that its values came to be tolerated even by those who did not share them. At this point we have come close to describing a geographical phenomenon that is predominantly urban, although all these factors could occur together in a rural setting as well. Clearly there will also be selective in- and out-migration, with some people entering the area and some people leaving it because of its deviant characteristics, thus reinforcing its overall image.

This kind of sociological analysis should not lead us to forget that biological factors are also involved. An American study of two groups of teenage adoptees—one born of psychiatrically disturbed parents, the other not, both separated from their parents at birth—showed that the incidence of psychiatric problems requiring professional care was significantly higher in the former group. In this St. Louis study, 'psychiatric disturbance' included 'anti-social personality' as well as more orthodox diagnoses. The result might be due to stress effects *in utero* (most of the pregnancies were illegitimate) or to a genetic inheritance. Since there was evidence that a specific type of psychiatric disorder was transmitted, the latter explanation seems more likely. James Shields[162] has summarized other evidence that a genetic factor is involved, though not predominantly, even in the transmission of delinquency.

Although deviance defined purely in social terms should not be regarded, in itself, as evidence of psychological disturbance, many of the individuals concerned are not functioning at their psychological optimum and many do complain of mental ill-health. Many could be regarded as having 'personality disorders'. Social deviance is one cause of personal stress. Each of the other possible causes such as poor housing, retirement, noise, precipitating events of various kinds, lack of supporting relationships, and so on, contributes its own portion of pressure. It is the accumulation of social stresses, acting particularly on vulnerable people, that leads to mental ill-health.

It is useful to avoid over-generalization and to stick to what we know about each of these factors singly and in combination.[151]

Formulating our questions in terms of the urban problem may set us off along the wrong track. The acid denunciations of people like Lewis Mumford[125] ('A multitude of uniform, unidentifiable houses, lined up inflexibly at uniform distances, on uniform roads, in a treeless communal waste . . .') appeal to an aesthetic sense, but they are probably based more on a moral revulsion from the way the middle and lower-middle classes live than on any evidence that the inhabitants, at least of the outer suburbs, are more likely to be worried or depressed or sleepless than the inhabitants of supposedly idyllic rural areas. It is just conceivable, even, that our own time is not the most stressful there has ever been. A recent study by John Orley, of the population of two rural villages in Uganda, using standard techniques to ensure comparability, showed that the amount of depressive disorder was greater than in an inner London suburb.

It may be that the factor of sheer size, which we have not so far taken into account, makes social problems less manageable, rather than commoner. Theoretically, the stress of overcrowding, poor housing, and poverty is no greater in modern London or New York than it would have been in the Ziggurat of Ur. But cities are now the dominant environment for most people, particularly those who are most conscious of the need to improve the quality of life. It is the areas in which high multiple stress is experienced that matter, whether urban or rural, whether contemporary or historical. When such areas are both isolated and poor, there is likely to be a double load of morbidity. Moreover, the area takes on some of the characteristics of its disabled inhabitants, just like an institution. Members of the caring professions are constantly coming across psychiatric aspects of the 'urban problem' in their everyday clinical work. It may be the effect of a teenage sub-culture in a new housing estate on a vulnerable youngster, or the stress of noise from an urban motorway on someone already near breaking point for other reasons, or the fact that a handicapped schizophrenic patient has wandered away from home and been found sleeping rough in an isolated inner city area. These are urban problems, and the medical, nursing, and social work professions have important contributions to make towards helping to solve them. Psychiatrists might also help to develop interactionist theories that will predict how various aspects of the urban environment should be modified in order to reduce mental ill-health. However, these theories will probably not be concerned solely with urban problems but with much more fundamental social factors and their effects on human beings. In the meantime, it is so obvious on humanitarian grounds that the quality of life in some urban areas needs to be improved that town planners do not need to wait for psychiatric confirmation before they set to work.

'Madness' in the twentieth century

We have been concerned, in this chapter, with higher technical standards of description and classification. This concern will continue throughout the book. Only by improving our techniques can we hope to test our theories rigorously enough to decide which are inadequate. Copernicus cannot exist without Tycho Brahe, Darwin without Linnaeus. In view of this emphasis, it is hardly surprising that we are unable to reach unequivocal conclusions. Disease theories of the affective disorders, anxiety states, and obsessional conditions have a degree of practical usefulness and it would be silly indeed to deprive ourselves of them. On the other hand, it is clear that a large part of the iceberg of psychiatric disorder is submerged. The significance of the undoubted correlations between the lesser psychiatric disorders that float below the threshold at which diagnostic syndromes can be fairly clearly recognized, and various predisposing and precipitating social factors, is not yet clear. (Some conclusions about prevention will be discussed in chapter 7.)

We all know that mood fluctuates from day to day and even from hour to hour in response to changing circumstances. We know we are depressed by adverse fortune and made anxious by the anticipation of unpleasant situations to come. Phrases like 'living in poverty and misery' indicate an awareness of the interaction between environment and mood. We are less certain as to how far these rather commonplace observations can be extended so that, in the extreme case, the most severe mental illnesses are caused by equivalently serious environmental stresses. On the whole, the evidence is against a parallel equivalence between social causes and clinical consequences throughout the whole clinical spectrum. It seems more likely that biological vulnerabilities of various specific kinds play an important part in causation, particularly of the more severe disorders, and that the more strongly they are present the less important are social factors except as precipitants.

On the other hand, studies of the distribution of the lesser psychiatric disorders seem to bear out the popular belief that simple depression or anxiety, and the commoner non-specific syndromes such as worrying and muscular tension, are often immediately reactive to adverse pressures in the environment. These pressures are particularly common in inner city areas and areas of economic decline, where many different kinds of social disadvantage and deviant response may be mediated through family and other small group networks. General statements of the kind, 'mental illness is on the increase because of the harmful effects of modern civilization', have little substance when they are reduced to more specific components and subjected to empirical test. There may be a great deal wrong with modern civilization compared with our particular favourites from the past (or perhaps from the future) but our justification will have to be made in moral or aesthetic or spiritual, as well as in psychiatric, terms.

4. Schizophrenia

*I have often felt that the mad cannot explain
and the sane cannot comprehend.*

A doctor writing about his own
experience of schizophrenia

How not to use a diagnostic label

Rosenhan described how eight people gained admission to a
variety of psychiatric hospitals in the United States by complaining of disembodied voices saying the words 'empty', 'hollow', and
'thud'. In every case but one the diagnosis was schizophrenia, although the eight participants were lying about the hallucinatory
experience and complained of nothing else. Once admitted, the
conspirators noticed that all their behaviour was interpreted in
terms of their being 'abnormal'. For example, one of them who was
taking copious notes of everything that went on, found that this
had been reported by the nurse as: 'patient engages in writing behaviour'. Another participant in the project who obtained access
to his medical record found that his account of his relationships
with his parents during childhood and adolescence, which he
thought were in no way out of the ordinary, had been translated
into psychopathological terms. 'The facts of the case were un-
intentionally distorted by the staff to achieve consistency with a
popular theory of the dynamics of a schizophrenic reaction.' Most
of the conspirators found it was difficult to get the attention
of physicians or nurses in order to ask perfectly legitimate questions; in the majority of cases the staff member would simply
walk on with head averted. The pseudo-patients observed that
discourtesy and even ill-treatment was almost routine in some of
the hospitals.

The disturbing thing about this study is not that psychiatrists
can be fooled. Münchhausen's syndrome (addiction to medical
investigation and treatment) is well-known to experienced doctors,
but it continues to catch some of them out. Someone mimicking
the symptoms of disseminated sclerosis with skill and consistency
could well remain undetected. It would certainly be possible to

imitate schizophrenia, or any other condition whose diagnosis depends mainly on its clinical manifestations, if the faking were well done. In any case, it is essential, if physicians are to carry out their role effectively, that they should be able to expect people who come to them for help to be reasonably truthful. Many doctors have rejected Rosenhan's conclusions on these grounds.

However, the paper does raise three serious problems. In the first place, if the demonstrators really did restrict themselves to faking only the one abnormal experience (and it would have been understandable if they had embroidered their tale rather more than that), and if the diagnosis given really was unequivocally schizophrenia, based only on this one symptom, then the criteria for a diagnosis are so minimal as to call into question the value of making a diagnosis at all. The second problem is that there appears to be no obvious reason why anyone complaining of this 'symptom' (whether or not a diagnosis of schizophrenia could properly be made) should be admitted to hospital. Even if the diagnosis were correct, there is no treatment that could not equally well be given outside hospital. The third problem is that the participants say they were treated with discourtesy or indifference by the staff once they had been admitted to hospital.

Thomas Scheff[158] studied the processes of admission to mental hospitals in a mid-western state of the U.S.A., which involved a court appearance and a perfunctory diagnosis, and came to the conclusion that the psychiatrist was simply 'validating' the actions of those who wanted the individual out of the way, rather than using his own independent criteria to establish whether a mental illness was present. Erving Goffman,[51] in a more literary and polemical (but nevertheless highly informed) manner, has made a similar point. More recently, somewhat similar criticisms have been made of psychiatric practice in the Soviet Union, though comment has been focused more on the question of whether unconventional political points of view are being suppressed and discredited through the use of psychiatric diagnosis. Thus the opinion has developed 'that psychological categorization of mental illness is useless at best and downright harmful, misleading and pejorative at worst. Psychiatric diagnoses, in this view, are in the mind of the observers and are not valid summaries of characteristics displayed by the observed.' This quotation from Rosenhan's paper illustrates how criticism has become generalized from an attack upon the specifics of certain cases and certain service contexts to a complete rejection of the 'medical model' as used in psychiatry. The very concept of disease itself has come under attack.

An examination of the disease theory of schizophrenia may therefore be timely. It must be obvious from what has been said in chapter 2 that no sweeping claims will be made. All disease theories are, by their nature, limited and time-based. They are meant to be tested as rigorously as our wit can conceive and, to the extent that they fail the tests they are subjected to, they must be modified or rejected. If they pass the tests, we must assume that yet further tests lie ahead, and so *ad infinitum*. The scientist does not ask that his theories should receive preferential treatment. He knows that they must be criticized, and that well-informed colleagues are only too eager to point out any flaws. He asks only that all theories should receive the same treatment; those that are put forward as alternatives must stand up to the same examination as his own.

Development of the concept of schizophrenia

The basis of the original concept of schizophrenia was the observation that a severe and permanent deterioration in personality and intellect resembling dementia occasionally occurred in someone who had not had a feverish illness or head injury or other obvious episode to explain it. Morel, for example, reported in 1860 the case of an adolescent who had deteriorated in this way. He regarded it as an unusually early dementia. Hecker, in 1871, reported his observations about a number of cases in which similar deterioration had occurred at the time of puberty. Because of the fact that the young people concerned changed in personality, becoming markedly silly, giggling and affected in behaviour, Hecker called the condition 'hebephrenia'. Then Kahlbaum in 1874 described a condition which he called catatonia, because it was characterized by stupor and muscular rigidity. Kraepelin pointed out that these conditions were probably related, and eventually grouped them together as *'dementia praecox'*, the name being chosen because of the irreversible intellectual deterioration (dementia) and the early age of onset. Kraepelin did recognize that these features were not unique; that recovery was possible and that onset could occur later in life, but he thought that emotional deterioration, characterized by apathy and lack of drive, was the common pattern. Another group of cases, in which this feature was less marked, and in which more florid traits such as delusions and hallucinations were predominant, he called 'paraphrenias'. This separation was an uncomfortable one and when Eugen Bleuler suggested the term 'schizophrenia' to cover all these conditions, the idea immediately caught on. Moreover, Bleuler argued that all the characteristics could be interpreted in terms of the fundamental disorders of affect and thinking. Everyone with schizophrenia was regarded as having emotional flattening and a thought disorder based on 'loosening of the associations'. Other characteristics, such as delusions, were seen as secondary or accessory. Bleuler in this way broadened the boundaries of Kraepelin's concept, since minor degrees of emotional flattening and thought disorder, occurring without more obviously recognizable abnormalities, might be detected by eager clinicians in anyone whose behaviour was out of the ordinary, such as tramps, criminals, or eccentrics. Bleuler also introduced the term 'autism' to describe the emotional blunting, which resulted in the social isolation of people with schizophrenia within their own internal world. 'The reality of the autistic world may also seem more valid than that of reality itself; the patients then hold their fantasies for real; reality for an illusion.' This kind of 'autism' is similar to dreaming: although the individual is awake, as Jung remarked. It is certainly possible to see how delusions and hallucinations could be manifestations of such a state. However, Bleuler also used the term 'autism' in a much wider sense, to refer to mechanisms which might be present even in normal people. There is yet a further complexity, since there can be two varieties of severe autism, as Kretschmer pointed out. One he called the 'hyperaesthetic' or Hölderlin variety, in which the individual is oversensitive to his environment and therefore retreats into an inner fantasy life. The other is the 'anaesthetic' variety, in which there is a simple lack of affective response without any great inner experience. Both varieties could be present at the same time.

The term 'autism' was later adopted by Kanner to name the condition 'early infantile autism' which we have already met in the pages of J. P. M. Itard (see p. 22). This usage is doubly unfortunate, first because Kanner's syndrome has nothing to do with schizophrenia and second because the concept of 'autism' as a fundamental characteristic of schizophrenia was already impossibly complicated.[205]

However, the search for one single underlying trait which could explain all the others went on. Berze, for example, suggested that a general lowering of 'psychic activity' was the key factor, but was no more successful than others in providing criteria by which it could be reliably identified.

Gruhle, for example, pointed out that certain delusional experiences were 'primary' or 'autochthonous', in the sense that they could not be understood in terms of other psychological abnormalities; in fact, many other manifestations could be understood as attempts by the individual to explain his primary delusional experiences. Jaspers adopted this point of view when he defined 'true' delusions in terms of experiences that could not be understood by other people. It is possible, of course, to construct sophisticated theories, *post hoc*, which will make them 'understandable' in any particular case, but nothing follows from such explanations, which do not have the character of scientific theories. It is not possible to say, for example, that the explanation given by Freud of the famous Schreber case, will apply to all schizophrenia. On the contrary, it clearly does not. The function of this kind of explanation is to satisfy the person who makes it; no more. The ordinary individual does not have these experiences and cannot understand what they are. Other types of delusion, for example, ideas of persecution expressed by political refugees, Jaspers called 'apparent delusions'. Kurt Schneider[169] provided a list of 'symptoms of the first rank' which, in the absence of epilepsy, intoxication, or other evidence of gross cerebral damage, he regarded as likely to indicate a diagnosis of schizophrenia. Examples are the experience of hearing one's thoughts spoken aloud in one's head, so loud that it would seem that anyone standing near by must also be able to hear them; the experience that one's thoughts are repeated after one has thought them; the experience of alien thoughts being inserted into one's mind; the experience that one's own will is replaced by that of some other agency or force; the experience that several voices are commenting between themselves on one's thoughts or actions. Schneider did not suggest that these symptoms must be directly related to some underlying biological abnormality, nor did he think they carried a special prognosis compared with other characteristics of the schizophrenic syndrome. But he did provide the basis for defining a syndrome in a reliable way so that any expert could recognize it. In view of Rosenhan's experiment such reproducibility clearly has advantages, quite apart from the fact that it is impossible to test a disease theory until the syndrome has been clearly delineated.

The schizophrenic syndromes

It is commonplace for critics of psychological medicine to say that diagnostic techniques are unreliable; that no two psychiatrists can ever agree as to which category to use in any particular case. The problems of reliable description and classification of mental symptoms are indeed formidable. What is less generally known is that there has been a great deal of progress in this area during the past ten years, and that a series of technical advances has brought reliable diagnosis much closer. For convenience, the acute and the chronic characteristics will be discussed separately.

a. The acute condition

Two recent large-scale international studies may be cited by way of example. Both studies were based on a special technique of interviewing patients, known as the Present State Examination (PSE), which is simply a standardized form of the psychiatric diagnostic interview ordinarily used in Western Europe, based on a detailed glossary of differential definitions of symptoms. It is possible for psychiatrists trained in this technique to achieve a very considerable degree of agreement as to what symptoms are present. A set of rules, based on clinical experience but expressed precisely enough to be laid down in a computer program, is then applied in order to allocate each condition to a class, which is equivalent under certain circumstances to a diagnosis.[202] In both international studies, the agreement between the clinical diagnosis made by the participating research psychiatrists and the computer classification (known as CATEGO) based on PSE ratings was very satisfactory. The diagnostic rules have to be specified very precisely indeed, of course, in order to be able to incorporate them into a computer program.

The first of the studies, known as the U.S.–U.K. Diagnostic Project, was concerned with patients admitted to hospitals in New York and London.[28] It was set up because of the observation that schizophrenia was diagnosed more often in the U.S.A. than in the U.K. The results of the study indicated that much of this difference, if not all, was due to different diagnostic habits on the two sides of the Atlantic. The American psychiatrists had a broader concept of schizophrenia than their British colleagues.

The second study, the International Pilot Study of Schizophrenia (IPSS),[209] was carried out under the auspices of the World Health Organization and was in many ways complementary. Not only was the reliability of symptom-rating and the agreement between clinical and computer diagnosis confirmed, but it was confirmed under circumstances in which reliability would ordinarily have been expected to be low. Interviews with acutely ill patients were carried out in nine different parts of the world, by psychiatrists speaking languages as diverse as Chinese, Hindi, Russian, and Yoruba. Not only were diagnoses of schizophrenia, mania, and depression made in all these centres, but the computer reference classification, based on a standard process of classifying symptom ratings made during the standardized clinical examination, also produced the same result. The three broad clinical groupings could therefore be reliably differentiated from each other, and it is possible to state quite precisely what the descriptive criteria defining each type of syndrome were.

I will concentrate on the clinical picture in the group of schizophrenias defined in terms of the CATEGO criteria. The central group ('*Class S*' of the CATEGO classification) accounted for about two-thirds of all those who were given a clinical diagnosis of schizophrenia. This is defined in terms of symptoms such as thought insertion, thought broadcast and thought withdrawal, auditory hallucinations of a particular kind and delusions of concontrol. These are all very highly discriminating for a diagnosis of schizophrenia; that is, when present, there is a more than 90 per cent probability of this diagnosis being given.[156] Such discrimination makes for highly economical and efficient diagnosis in physical diseases, like the coronary pain described earlier. It does not, of course, mean that other symptoms are not present, and certainly not that other symptoms can be ignored when making the diagnosis. Often these other symptoms are themselves a reaction to the primary ones; an attempt on the patient's part to make sense of them. But the most highly discriminating symptoms are the most useful. Most of the symptoms in this central schizophrenic syndrome—*Class S*—were among those described by Kurt Schneider as 'symptoms of the first rank'. This phrase had no theoretical connotations; it simply emphasized their value for recognizing the syndrome.

In both international studies, about two-thirds of all the people given a clinical diagnosis of schizophrenia were recorded as experiencing the highly discriminating symptoms. In a few cases, people with these symptoms were *not* diagnosed as schizophrenic and it is instructive to consider the examples where the hypothesis fails. Let us examine one particular symptom, 'thought insertion'. The essence of the symptom is that the subject experiences thoughts *that are not his own* intruding into his mind. The symptom is not that he has been caused to have unusual thoughts (for example, if he thinks the Devil is making him think evil thoughts) but that the thoughts *themselves* are not his. In the most typical case, the alien thoughts are said to have been inserted into the mind from outside, by means of radar or telepathy or some other means. In such a case there is an explanatory delusion as well. Sometimes the patient may say that he does not know where the alien thoughts came from, although he is quite clear that they are not his own. In very rare instances, he may postulate that they come from his own unconscious mind—while still consciously experiencing them as alien.

There are several ways in which this symptom can be mistakenly regarded as present when it is not. The most obvious is when the individual fails to understand the question or, because of inadequate intellectual or verbal ability, is unable to reply clearly. Several other symptoms can be confused with it, notably those in which the individual believes that other people can 'read his thoughts'. This latter idea may well be based upon an exaggeration of the completely ordinary phenomenon of postulating someone's motives through observing his actions. The patient may come to feel, however, that such powers can only be due to a special ability on the part of others such as 'thought reading' or 'hypnotism'. In other cases there may be a strong religious element in such ideas, the patient believing, for example, that God knows what he is thinking. In yet others, a deep intensification of a normal mood such as depression or elation may affect an individual's experiences, including his thought processes, so that he says that his thoughts are as powerful as the sun's rays, or come from the Devil. Such ideas must *not* be taken to indicate that the symptom of 'thought insertion' is present. It should only be recognized when the individual describes an experience of *alien* thoughts —thoughts that he recognizes as not being his—being inserted into his mind.

This symptom is very rare. One can carry out a large-scale survey of people in a general population without coming across anyone who has ever experienced it. Moreover, it seems to be invariant with respect to age, sex, family circumstances, class, culture or nationality. In other words, it approximates as closely as we are likely to get, in a symptom of this kind, to a non-social phenomenon. This is what Jaspers called a 'true' delusion; one which could be traced back to an irreducible and non-understandable experience. Non-understandable, that is, except in terms of some *post hoc* theory, made up for the occasion. Of course, it can be faked or imitated on the basis of descriptions by other people who really have the experience, but no more than physical symptoms can. Rosenhan's experiment has demonstrated that it may also be necessary to consider deliberate faking.

Another example of a first-rank symptom may be given—delusions of control. Once again, this is based upon an experience which is described by the individual. He notices that his will is replaced by the will of some other agency or force, so that he is no longer in control of his actions or thoughts, or even of his gait or handwriting. Again, there are large possibilities for error unless the differential definitions are thoroughly known and the diagnostician has examined many people who have described the experience. For example, in the IPSS study, a Chinese priestess on the island of Formosa described how, when she went into a trance, she became 'possessed' by the God, who then directed what she should do and say. This *is* a social phenomenon. Being possessed in this way was part of her job. The experience did not occur against her will; on the contrary she sought and welcomed it and it is probable that, far from *replacing* her will, although this was the way she expressed the experience, it actually *enhanced* it. She became the God, rather than the God taking her over. Somewhat similar experiences are described by members of certain religious sects the world over. They are not part of the central schizophrenic syndrome.

These examples may serve to illustrate how a psychiatric

examination must be grounded in a thorough familiarity with the subjective experiences of human beings. This 'phenomenology' has a long and fruitful history in psychiatry. Obviously, the psychiatrist has to have this knowledge before he can hope to make a reliable diagnosis and it is all too apparent that some doctors are too preoccupied with their own theories to spend time listening to what the patient is telling them.

All of these 'first rank symptoms' can occur in organic states, for example, with a brain tumour, or temporal lobe epilepsy, or intoxication with various substances. Evelyn Waugh has given, in *The Ordeal of Gilbert Pinfold*, the most vivid account I know of a condition that could be classified as a schizophrenic syndrome if one did not know that it had followed a long period of self-dosing with a chloral and bromide prescription and with alcohol. Waugh also describes his poor memory and disorientation in time, which are both uncommon in schizophrenia. The diagnosis was probably bromide intoxication.

One of the first-rank symptoms experienced by Mr. Pinfold was hearing the voices of several people talking about him in the third person. Here is an example:

'We'll talk to Peinfeld when it suits us and not a moment before.'
'Who'll do the talking?'
'I will, of course . . .'
'All right, come on then. Let's see him now.'
'When it suits *me*, Fosker, not before.'
'What are we waiting for?'
'To let him get into a thorough funk. Remember at school one was always kept waiting for a beating? Just to make it taste sweeter? Well, Peinfeld can wait for *his* beating.'
'He's scared stiff.'
'He's practically blubbing now.'

Making due allowance for the orderly mind of Evelyn Waugh at work upon experiences that were actually more chaotic, this extract still gives a good idea of the story-like nature of some hallucinatory experiences and the way they necessarily make use of the individual's own memories and preoccupations. How an individual reacts to such experiences (indeed, much of the content of the experiences themselves) depends on what kind of a person he or she is. The explanations adopted, the secondary elaboration, the extent to which behaviour is affected, the reaction in terms of elation, depression, or fear all vary markedly, except that nearly everyone finds the experience intensely distressing and wants it to stop.

Psychiatrists do not restrict their diagnosis of schizophrenia only to cases characterized by first-rank symptoms. Many also include other types of delusional and hallucinatory syndrome. For example, the CATEGO *Class P* (accounting for 17 per cent of IPSS diagnoses of schizophrenic or paranoid psychoses) is characterized by delusions of persecution or grandeur or religion. The patient might feel that a gang of communists follows him about, that he has invented the atom bomb, or that he is a saint or a religious leader. Sometimes there might be only a single much overvalued idea, for example that a person's nose is too large, even though no one else can see anything the matter with it. This one preoccupation could ruin his life, drive him from one plastic surgeon to another, spoil his personal relations and deprive him of any peace or satisfaction, without there being any sign of the central schizophrenic syndrome at all. It is difficult to put up a disease theory in such cases, but whatever their origin, it is reasonable that the sufferer should be referred to a psychiatrist. Strictly speaking, all these conditions are best placed under the heading of paranoid reaction, or, sometimes, paranoid personality (see also p. 174). However, most psychiatrists tend not to make the distinction from schizophrenia; in most of the IPSS centres (there was one exception) *Class P* and *Class S* were not distinguished from each other. In only one centre were *Class P* cases regarded as suffering from paranoid and *not* schizophrenic psychoses, but it is clear that the distinction can be made.

Another small group constitutes CATEGO *Class O*, in which catatonic disturbances of behaviour or other abnormalities such as persistent talking to oneself, occur as the only 'psychotic' phenomena. This is a very doubtful category in the CATEGO classification and it accounted for only 6 per cent of those given a diagnosis of schizophrenic or paranoid psychosis.

This leaves a final 10 per cent of people given a clinical diagnosis of schizophrenic or paranoid psychosis who were placed by the computer classification into one of its classes representing manic-depressive or neurotic disorders. The proportion of discrepancies is thus very low and may come as a surprise to those who thought that a reasonable degree of concordance could not be obtained.

However, small though it is, this group of discrepancies is of great interest. It will be recalled that nine psychiatric centres were involved in the study, chosen because of their cultural diversity and large differences in language structure, and also because the psychiatrists taking part belonged to different schools of thought. In seven of these centres, the discrepancy between a diagnosis of schizophrenic or paranoid psychosis and CATEGO *Classes S, P, or O* was only 4·5 per cent. In the other two, it was 29·5 per cent. These two centres were in Moscow and Washington. Psychiatrists in both centres recognized cases in the central group (*Class S*) without difficulty. However, they also diagnosed others as schizophrenic who had no specific symptoms according to the reference classification. As far as the United States is concerned, this confirms the results of the U.S.–U.K. Diagnostic Project. That study suggested that the prevailing concept of schizophrenia was much broader in New York than in London, embracing substantial parts of what British psychiatrists would regard as depressive illness, neurotic illness, and personality disorder, and almost the whole of what they would regard as mania. (The discovery that lithium is a useful treatment for mania is likely to make the diagnosis of this condition more specific.) In the U.S.S.R., the Moscow school is also generally regarded as having a broader concept of schizophrenia than elsewhere, due to the use of special categories such as 'sluggish', 'periodic', and 'shift-like' schizophrenia. Categories in use elsewhere, such as 'latent', 'simple', 'borderline', 'pseudo-neurotic', and 'pseudo-psychopathic' schizophrenia also broaden the concept beyond the central and relatively easily definable groups.[59]

We shall return to the significance of these findings later. For the moment it is necessary only to point out that we have been considering, in this section, the recognizability and reproducibility of the descriptive syndromes of schizophrenia, not their validity. It is possible that the extra cases regarded as schizophrenic in Moscow, New York, and Washington could be shown, on some external criterion, to be related to the central groups. All we have been concerned with is whether it is possible to recognize the central groups, whatever the language of interview, whatever the culture of the patients, and whatever the clinical school of the psychiatrists. There appears to be evidence that this *is* possible.

Before we proceed to our next question, which concerns the

validity with which a disease theory can be put forward to explain this syndrome (and to justify the use of the term 'symptom' for characteristics such as thought insertion) we must turn our attention to the chronic condition.

b. *The chronic condition*

The clinical syndromes we have just been considering are often accompanied or followed by a condition of social disablement. Two main groups of chronic symptoms, which may be of various degrees of severity from mild to crippling, suggest the presence of intrinsic impairments. The first is a syndrome of 'negative' traits such as emotional apathy, slowness of thought and movement, underactivity, lack of drive, poverty of speech, and social withdrawal. These traits are highly intercorrelated. If one is present, the others are also likely to be, and they can be reliably measured by means of behaviour scales. Together they constitute a useful measure of the severity of one kind of intrinsic impairment. The intensity of the negative syndrome is highly correlated with measures of social performance at virtually any task, creative or routine, personal or social. For example, it predicts the individual's ability to communicate using verbal or non-verbal language. The most severely impaired person can convey little information through the use of language: the facial expression is wooden, the voice is monotonous, the bodily posture and gait are stiff, little use is made of gesture, and words are few and may convey little meaning. These limitations can be very handicapping indeed. This negative syndrome may be present before the first onset of more florid symptoms, it often accompanies an acute attack, and it is the most characteristic feature of the chronic state.

In addition to this variety of intrinsic impairment, there may be incoherence of speech, unpredictability of associations, long-standing delusions and hallucinations, and accompanying manifestations in behaviour. Even leaving out chronic symptoms such as delusions and hallucinations, since these are quite often forgotten between acute attacks, this second group of intrinsic impairments can be severely disabling. It seems to be based upon an impairment of inner language. The individual does not seem able to think to a purpose, but goes off at a tangent owing to some unusual association to a chance stimulus, and thus gives the impression of vagueness, confusion, and incoherence. Occasionally this may give the impression of creativity (no doubt the expression, 'the poetry of schizophrenia', is based on such a very rare occurrence), but usually the syndrome is constricting and handicapping. Most of the creative people who have been afflicted with schizophrenia have had their creativity abolished, not enhanced. (See p. 2.)

The two varieties of intrinsic impairment are not unrelated. Social withdrawal, for example, may be in part a reaction to the individual's experience that his attempts at communicating with other people are met with bafflement and a more or less polite brush-off. However, this is by no means the complete explanation of social withdrawal or of such characteristics as psychomotor slowness.

Apart from these two varieties of chronic intrinsic impairment, the liability to further relapse with acute symptoms of the kinds we have considered already may also be regarded as a kind of intrinsic disability. Following an acute attack, there remains a definite vulnerability to further breakdown of a similar kind. Nevertheless, about half of the people first admitted to hospital with a clear-cut acute schizophrenic syndrome suffer no further relapse over the following five years. In about one-quarter of the cases, there is a relapsing course, and in the remaining quarter a condition of chronic disablement is reached.[23]

In addition to the intrinsic impairments, there are often secondary and extrinsic impairments as well, and these will be considered later. Both the acute and the chronic syndromes are usually diagnosed as schizophrenic, but there are, of course, many other symptoms and signs as well. Any textbook will give a list of them. I have been concerned to pick out those that are the most characteristic. Perhaps more informative than a textbook is a collection of essays by the sufferers themselves.[196] We can now proceed to our next question: can a disease theory of schizophrenia be supported? What tests have been made, and what are the implications of the results?

Evidence for a disease theory

There are many ways of testing a disease theory once the syndromes have been identified. The evidence will be considered under the headings of epidemiology, causes (aetiology), pathology and biochemistry, psychophysiology, and treatment. Since it is clear that the syndromes described earlier are not all part of one unitary condition, we shall not expect any single disease theory to fit. Moreover, it is well recognized in medicine that one syndrome can have several causes. However, it is the highly discriminating symptoms that most obviously demand explanation. Ideally, one wants to elaborate a theory of normal biological and psychological functioning, explaining why such symptoms are not experienced by the vast majority of people. A knowledge of the factors maintaining this function within normal limits would in turn suggest possible causes of a disturbance in homeostasis, leading to the emergence of the symptoms. A further requirement would be to explain why the discriminating symptoms are so frequently accompanied by others, such as delusions of persecution, which are not in themselves discriminatory. Is this entirely a matter of the individual's reaction to or explanation for the more 'primary' experiences? If an explanation of the symptoms in *Class S* could be advanced along such lines, it would next be necessary to explain why people with *Class P* symptoms develop persecutory and other delusions without having had the 'primary' experiences. What is the mechanism in such cases? Are there other, hitherto unrecognized primary phenomena, or can the delusions be explained on a similar basis to the acquisition of other fixed but demonstrably untrue beliefs? In that case, a disease theory would be hard to sustain.

In what follows, it is assumed that investigators have used the term 'schizophrenia' mainly in connection with the central syndromes; i.e. they have used a fairly narrow concept. This assumption cannot always be sustained but it does seem likely that there was usually a predominance of *Class S* cases. It is to be hoped that, in future, more reliable criteria will be used for diagnosis, and that these will always be stated in scientific papers.

a. Epidemiology

The term epidemiology,[27] like the term schizophrenia, can be used in a broad and in a narrow sense. In both cases, the narrow sense is more scientific and more secure, while the broad sense is more interesting but more liable to be misleading. Strictly speaking, epidemiology is the study of the distribution of conditions, such as schizophrenia, in defined populations or sub-groups of populations.[124] In this sense, it is a method of investigation that involves the calculation of a ratio between the number of identified cases and the number of people in the given population who are at risk of contracting the disease. The rates in different groups can then be compared with each other in order to test or derive hypotheses concerning causes. The result is an estimate of relative risk, e.g. the overweight man has twice the risk of a coronary attack as a man of average weight or below. In its broader sense, epidemiology covers the whole complex of relationships between disease and environment; that is, it has roughly the same meaning as medical ecology. From either point of view, the problem of the definition of the disease in question is obviously crucial.

Much of our knowledge of the frequency of schizophrenia is based upon population surveys carried out by psychiatrists who interviewed respondents in an unstandardized way and then made a diagnosis using their own unspecified criteria. Case-finding methods varied in thoroughness; the populations studied were different in age and sex composition, in social and geographical stability, in birth- and death-rates, and in other relevant characteristics, and there were probably considerable differences in the reliability of the available census statistics. Nevertheless, a certain similarity was found in the estimated rate at which schizophrenia could be expected to appear in the adult population during the years of highest risk (ages 15–45). This was usually between 0·5 and 1·0 per cent.

In England, some 10 to 15 new cases of schizophrenia are reported each year for each 100,000 in the total population. The highest rate in men is in the age-group 15–24 years, after which the risk gradually decreases. In women the highest rate occurs a bit later, in the age-group 25–34 years, and does not decrease so sharply thereafter. There is little difference between the sexes in the overall figure.

Two early surveys appeared to differ very markedly from the others in their results. J. W. Eaton and R. J. Weil[39] studied an Anabaptist sect, the Hutterites, living in small, closely knit farming communities in North America. Their religious traditions dated from the sixteenth century and had been cemented by long periods of persecution and consequent migration. Property was owned in common, and everyday life was simple, austere, well regulated, and pious. Families were large since there was no birth control, but there was no poverty either, and practically no crime or violence.

It was thought by some that such rural peace, community support, hard work, freedom from urban stresses, and good order
would provide conditions in which mental illnesses would be
most unlikely to develop. Eaton and Weil surveyed the various
colonies—a few intensively, the others more briefly—and concluded that about 6 per 1,000 of the total population of 8,500 had at
some time suffered from a psychosis. This figure was not very
much lower than that arrived at in other surveys in Europe and
North America, except that it was mostly due to depressive psychosis, while schizophrenia was relatively rare.

Clearly the methods of case finding were subject to the clinical
idiosyncrasies mentioned earlier, and the screening of the population was not particularly thorough, so the results cannot be taken
at face value. In addition, the movement of individuals out of the
Hutterite colonies over the previous 20 years or so could not be
known with any accuracy. In fact H. B. M. Murphy[126] has 'calculated the 1961 schizophrenia admission rate for the Mennonites
and Hutterites combined, from Canada's prairie provinces, and
that rate is not significantly below average.'

The second example concerns a quite different area, the extreme
north of Sweden, where the climate is severe, summer is very short,
and for six weeks during the winter the sun does not rise at all. The
population live by small-scale farming and lumbering. Communications with the rest of Sweden are poor. Many families live under
very primitive conditions. Böök, who carried out this survey, used a
variety of sources to find cases, including mental hospital admissions, parish registers, the records of district physicians, and
information from key people in the settlements concerned, such as
parish clergymen and schoolteachers. Böök[16] made the diagnosis
in each case himself and gives a general account of the principles
he used.

According to his calculations, the prevalence of functional psychoses was some three times higher than among the Hutterites,
but, more striking still, schizophrenia accounted for 85 per cent of
the cases, while manic-depressive psychosis was almost non-existent. Böök's explanation is in terms of genetics and selective migration. He thinks that a schizoid personality is an advantage for
survival in those parts, while people with a high risk of developing
manic-depressive disorders are likely to emigrate.

These two surveys, with their completely opposite findings, are typical of the best of the early work, in which the case-finding instrument was ultimately a single clinician. Neither has been repeated as yet.

More recently, Dermot Walsh[184] has shown that schizophrenia rates are much higher in Eire than in England, and progressively higher from east to west. Morton Kramer was one of the first to draw attention to the fact that rates were much higher in the United States than in England, and indeed the U.S.–U.K. Diagnostic Project was mounted largely in order to investigate this fact. As we have seen, it was found that variations in diagnostic practice accounted for the difference. The Irish result is still being investigated.

Ødegård[131] found that schizophrenia occurred more commonly among Norwegians who emigrated to America than among those who remained behind and most American studies have confirmed this finding when comparing immigrant with native-born populations. A higher rate was also found among those who left Hungary during the uprising of 1956, but schizophrenia was commonest in those who did not give political reasons for leaving.[121] There is also a considerable consensus that schizophrenia is commoner in certain central districts of large towns. In their original and seminal study of Chicago, R. E. L. Faris and H. W. Dunham[43] thought that the poverty and social isolation of the central areas were in part responsible, but these characteristics do not inevitably go together in the centres of European towns. The poorer districts are not necessarily isolated, and the isolated districts are not necessarily poor. It is social isolation, not poverty, that is associated with high rates of schizophrenia. However, schizophrenic patients often move into these isolated areas shortly before they break down for the first time. Dunham,[37] in a study of Detroit, came to the conclusion that migration into the isolated areas was the main reason for the high concentration of schizophrenic patients there. Not all migration within a country carries this risk, however. It appears that, in Norway, for example, those who move to better themselves actually have a lower risk than those who drift to a big city such as Oslo.

A somewhat similar story emerges from the extensive studies of occupation and social mobility. A. B. Hollingshead and F. C. Redlich[71] found a higher incidence of schizophrenia among unskilled manual workers, and this observation has been repeated many times. However, patients tend to move down the occupational scale even before they are first admitted to hospital.[53] Similarly, people who are later going to develop schizophrenia are disadvantaged educationally, occupationally, and in their capacity to make social and sexual relationships, even before the onset of florid symptoms.

Thus most of the results of the earlier epidemiological work have tended to provide information about the course of schizophrenia rather than about its causes. The importance of this work is that it emphasizes the fact that the time when schizophrenia is first clinically recognized is not necessarily the time when abnormalities are first manifested. The patient may already have failed, even against expectation, to have advanced occupationally or to have made secure social relationships with family, spouse, or friends, and may already have been living an isolated and socially restricted life before florid symptoms first appeared.

b. Causes

Paul Meehl[120] makes an important series of disclaimers about his use of the term 'aetiology'. He explains that he does *not* mean any of the following: that the aetiological factor always produced the syndrome, that the form and content of the symptoms should be derivable only from the aetiology, that the course could not be substantially influenced by other factors, that the same aetiology would produce identical manifestations in different people, and that the largest single contribution to variation in the symptoms would always be that made by the aetiological agent. 'In medicine, not one of these is part of the concept of specific aetiology,' which means only 'the *sine qua non*, the causal condition which is necessary, but not sufficient for the disorder to occur.'

It is fairly clear that no one factor is sufficient to produce schizophrenia whenever it operates. There is, however, a good deal of evidence for genetic vulnerability in a substantial group of cases. The book by Irving Gottesman and James Shields[57] gives this evidence in detail, and another edited by David Rosenthal and Seymour Kety[149] summarizes the views of a large number of scientists working in the field, including many, such as Theodore Lidz and Lyman Wynne, who are basically environmentalist in their views. They too, however, accept that a genetic factor is important, and indeed, this can be regarded as common ground among those who have regard for facts. How crucial is this factor?

Very briefly, the evidence is as follows. The frequency of occurrence of schizophrenia in the first-degree relatives of index cases (parents, siblings, children) is approximately 10 per cent, compared with 3 per cent in second-degree relatives (uncles, aunts, nephews, nieces) and something under 1 per cent in the general population. When both parents are affected, some 40 per cent of the children have the condition.

It has been argued that figures of this kind can be explained on the basis that certain social factors may cause schizophrenia to develop and, at the same time, to run in families in somewhat the same way that wealth does. Thus my father and my son will tend to be approximately as wealthy or as poor as I am. My uncle or my nephew, while showing less similarity, will still tend to have an income which is closer to mine than to other people's.

This is where studies of twins are very useful, since they can be identical or non-identical (fraternal) in genetic make-up. Clearly, two identical twins should have the same genetic vulnerability to developing schizophrenia, whereas two fraternal twins need not. On the other hand, environmental factors should not be all that different between identical and fraternal pairs. In fact, in recent studies the rate of schizophrenia in the identical co-twins of pairs where one has already been diagnosed as schizophrenic, has been about 50 per cent, compared with about 12 per cent in fraternal twin pairs.

Perhaps it may be suggested that the relationship between identical twins is favourable for the development of schizophrenia on an environmental basis, because of the problems of weak ego formation and confusion of identity. In that case there should be a higher frequency of identical twins in populations of people with schizophrenia, but there is no such excess. Perhaps also, it may be thought that the environment of identical twins is often more similar in many ways than that of fraternal twins. This problem is overcome by studying pairs of identical twins who have been reared apart since infancy, so that their early environments have been even more different than those of fraternal twins living in the same family. In about two-thirds of pairs, both twins had schizophrenia or some similar illness. There have also been studies of the children of schizophrenic parents who were adopted at birth and brought up in families where no member was schizophrenic. The incidence of schizophrenia in these children is no different from what would be expected if they had been reared by their natural parents.

Thus one has to be strongly motivated if one wishes to avoid the conclusion that heredity is important in schizophrenia. As Seymour Kety[83] says, if schizophrenia is a myth, it is a myth with a strong genetic component. However, our problems are not over, since there is no question of any simple Mendelian model of inheritance such as that expected from a straightforward dominant or recessive gene. The first genetic theory of schizophrenia ever put forward, by Ernst Rüdin, involved two genes. Recent work has also supported multigene theories. However, the results are not so precise or specific as to suggest that a disease theory can be supported on this basis alone. This is true of many relatively common, partially genetic disorders, including maturity-onset diabetes, idiopathic parkinsonism, epilepsy, and senile dementia. The index cases in genetic studies are more likely to have clear-cut clinical abnormalities, since they are more highly selected, than their relatives, who tend to manifest what have been called 'spectrum disorders', including not only frank schizophrenia but also many other types of psychiatric disorder. In fact, Leonard Heston[65] found more able or creative relatives than he would have expected in a general population sample, though this finding was not a quantitative one.

The Danish studies, and the work of Gottesman and Shields, show that the broad definition of schizophrenia may be useful for scientific purposes. Further speculation and investigation along these lines will be useful. As we have seen, the chronic impairments most commonly associated with the central schizophrenic syndrome are those associated with social withdrawal, slowness, emotional blunting, and 'thought disorder'. In retrospect, it is clear that these negative characteristics are often present long before any manifestations of the central syndrome are recognizable. They are also found on their own in some of the relatives of some people with schizophrenia. Can we therefore suggest that, even when they occur by themselves without any previous florid attack, they can be diagnosed as a form of 'simple' or 'pseudoneurotic' or 'latent' or 'sluggish' schizophrenia? Those who use a broad concept of schizophrenia do, in fact, tend to regard these extra conditions as schizophrenic, not simply on genetic, but also on clinical, grounds. This is Eugen Bleuler's broad concept of schizophrenia, which was responsible for the differences between the IPSS centres in Washington and Moscow, on the one hand, and those in Aarhus, Agra, Cali, London, Prague, and Taipei, on the other. We shall discuss the social problems of using a broad definition in chapters 5 and 6, but these disadvantages do not invalidate its scientific (that is, its hypothetical) use. However, it cannot be assumed that any conclusions concerning therapy, responsibility, or prognosis that are shown to hold true for the narrowly defined condition are of any relevance for 'sluggish' or 'pseudo-neurotic' or 'borderline' schizophrenia. The ethical problems are even more serious than those involved in treating 'pre-symptomatic' diabetes, and the most important criterion is that no harm should be done.

More direct evidence concerning the somatic nature of schizophrenia is provided by the fact that an acute attack characterized by symptoms of the central schizophrenic syndrome can be precipitated by substances such as bromide or amphetamine or alcohol, and by cerebral abnormalities such as temporal lobe epilepsy or brain tumours.[34] These factors are obviously not sufficient causes of schizophrenia, but they might give some clue to the nature of the aetiology. Social precipitating factors are also now well attested, and the evidence will be considered in detail later in this chapter. These studies are concerned with the social and family environment of the individual at the time the symptoms of schizophrenia become floridly and acutely manifest. It is a hazardous matter to extrapolate from the present to the remote past in order to suggest that whatever precipitating factors are found now must have been operating during infancy, but some daring theoreticians have done so. So far, they have not been able to provide convincing evidence.[70, 211] The evidence for environmental theories of schizophrenia will be considered in chapter 5.

c. *Pathology and biochemistry*

There is no evidence for any visible structural abnormalities, microscopic or macroscopic, in the brains of people with schizophrenia, apart from those mentioned earlier where there appears to be a precipitating effect of a cerebral tumour and apart from the known association with temporal lobe epilepsy. New techniques have had to be developed in order to discover more subtle abnormalities and the most promising line of research at the moment is biochemical.

For many years, workers in the field have felt confident that there must be some specific abnormal constituent of blood or urine or sweat or tears, but in spite of a complex and formidable array of technical investigations it remained elusive. Substances such as amphetamine, mescaline, and lysergic acid diethylamide (LSD), provide an obvious starting point since they can cause a psychotic condition, even if it is often not very like schizophrenia. A good deal is now known about their interactions with brain chemistry, but none of the work is sufficiently well-established to support a disease theory. The same is true of claims from the U.S.A. and the U.S.S.R. that abnormal globulins exist in the blood. One of the best-known claims, probably because the name has a memorable quality, concerns the 'pink spot', so called because of a technique which indicates an abnormal substance excreted in the urine. Findings of this kind may be due to all sorts of extraneous factors, notably in the diet, and the pink spot story has been received with much reservation following similar claims that were shown to be mistaken.

There are good reasons for thoroughly examining certain chemical pathways that could produce a result of this kind. Any genetic predisposition to react adversely to stress would probably be reflected in specific biochemical abnormalities. Some of the phenothiazine drugs effective in the treatment and prevention of schizophrenic symptoms, for example one called fluphenazine, produce side-effects similar to the symptoms of a disease of the basal ganglia of the brain which is characterized by muscle tremors and stiffness and is called parkinsonism. Parkinson's disease is thought to be due to a deficiency of dopamine, one of the amine transmitters involved in transmitting impulses from one nerve cell in the brain to another. Cells containing dopamine in the lower part of the brain degenerate (particularly the *substantia nigra* in the brain stem). Fibres from these cells connect with the large system of basal ganglia in the mid-brain, which are involved with the integration of bodily movements. Giving L-dopa, which acts as a precursor of dopamine, to people with parkinsonism, helps to correct the muscle tremors and rigidity.

Since the phenothiazine drugs produce side-effects similar to the symptoms of parkinsonism,[163] it was hypothesized that they act as antagonists to dopamine at the nerve junctions. Schizophrenia may therefore be due to an over-activity or hypersensitivity of a biochemical system in which dopamine is important or to a deficiency in a dopamine antagonist. Such a hypothesis would also help to explain amphetamine psychosis, since amphetamine stimulates dopamine sensitive receptors.[74, 168]

One part of the upward projection of fibres from the *substantia nigra* goes as far forward as the limbic system of the brain which encircles the brain stem and hypothalamus just below the cortex and which is concerned with the emotions and memory. One of the most interesting of current speculations is that the dopamine pathways in the limbic forebrain are the key anatomical site for the abnormalities that underlie schizophrenia. This line of investigation is only one of several that promise advances in basic knowledge that may eventually lead to more rational therapy.

d. Psychophysiology

Some ten years ago, Peter Venables discovered that people with chronic schizophrenic impairments, particularly those who showed the syndrome associated with social withdrawal, far from being less alert and attentive, actually appeared to be 'over-aroused'. The physiological indices used measured both central and peripheral functions: the threshold at which two flashes or two clicks presented rapidly one after the other became fused and experienced as one event (an index involving cortical functions): and the level of skin conductance in the hand (this measures sweat gland activity). The more socially withdrawn the individual the more 'aroused' he appeared to be.[182] This paradoxical result started a long line of investigation which is by no means complete yet. The term 'arousal' has many connotations and should probably be avoided. For example, it can be said that severe anxiety or an acute manic attack is also accompanied by high 'arousal', but neither is at all like chronic schizophrenia. On the other hand, people with schizophrenic impairments do tend to have a higher heart rate and a wetter handshake than expected, i.e. they seem to be 'physiologically anxious', even though they may appear to be much less anxious than most people because of their unvarying facial expression and tone of voice, and because they tend not to use non-verbal means of indicating emotion. The disturbance of communication is quite unlike that found in aphasia or early childhood autism, but it is none the less profound for all that. Verbal and bodily communications may be distorted as well as narrowed, so that unexpected messages are received by people in the patient's social environment.

Karl Jung suggested that an impairment of attention with a consequent release of unconscious associations would explain many of the observed phenomena in schizophrenia. Very little of the subsequent work has extended this observation, but this is a key area in which progress needs to be made. There are also several promising lines of inquiry to be followed up in comparing acute and chronic states in schizophrenia. Much of the other research into psychological variables, such as psychomotor slowness, using such indices as reaction time, and into the characteristic disorder of associations, has simply illustrated the early clinical observations of Emil Kraepelin and Eugen Bleuler.

e. Treatment

There are now many forms of medication that will reduce the severity of the more florid schizophrenic symptoms and quite often suppress them completely. The drugs known as phenothiazines are the most widely used. Not only do they help during the acute attack but they act to prevent further relapse if taken regularly. The evidence for both therapeutic and preventive effects is derived from several well conducted controlled trials.[69, 95] The drugs do not cure schizophrenia any more than insulin cures diabetes. They do not always suppress all the unpleasant experiences, and they are quite unsuccessful in doing more than ameliorating chronic impairments such as slowness and apathy. However, the effect on the acute symptoms is often dramatic, and it is not due to a mere sedation (the so-called 'chemical straitjacket'); in fact sedative drugs are of very little use in schizophrenia. One common form of administration is by injection: a small dose of 25 mg. of fluphenazine is usually sufficient for preventive purposes and lasts about a month. At this dose level short-term side-effects are uncommon but they can sometimes be troublesome. Many people value the relief from distressing symptoms afforded by the phenothiazines, but some find that they dislike an effect which is described in very diverse terms but which amounts to a feeling of being 'damped down'. A few people find they are very depressed while taking them. A very few find that they can cope with the abnormal experiences by removing their attention from them, and they prefer not to rely on drugs.[195] In certain social surroundings the need for medication is much reduced, as we shall see in the next section. By no means everyone needs to continue taking the drugs indefinitely. Even before the new drugs were introduced, there used to be a proportion of cases in which the first attack would clear up and another never occurred. Manfred Bleuler[104] is of the opinion that 'the number of benign schizophrenic psychoses with complete and lifelong recovery after acute episodes has not been increased by modern therapy to any statistically significant degree.' We are still unsure about the frequency and severity of long-term side-effects. Nevertheless, psychiatrists in former times would have given a great deal for a treatment of such proven efficacy.

The phenothiazines have a beneficial effect on several other psychiatric conditions as well as schizophrenia: on mania, for example, and on the psychoses produced by alcohol or amphetamine or cerebral disease. Moreover, the liability to relapse often remains, so that when medication is withdrawn schizophrenic symptoms reappear. On the other hand, drugs such as lithium or amitriptyline, which are often effective in mania and depression, are much less useful in schizophrenia and may even make the condition worse. To be completely speculative, it can be suggested that there are lower brain centres, such as the limbic and reticular activating systems (which underlie the phenomenon of cortical arousal), whose functioning is essential for more highly integrated nervous functions. Phenothiazine drugs probably act at these lower levels through a biochemical effect, for example that which blocks the dopamine receptors, tending to restore the normal cycle of functioning. However, either a cycle at another brain level is also disordered, and not affected by phenothiazines, or the phenothiazines correct only part of the disturbance in the limbic system. We need not despair of further progress in unravelling these complex matters.

Conclusion

With one crucial exception, the evidence in favour of an explanation of the central syndromes of schizophrenia in terms of a disease theory or theories is very similar to that for *diabetes mellitus*. The most florid clinical forms can be reliably recognized by trained clinicians. The aetiology is unknown, but there is some evidence in favour of multigene inheritance, with all that implies by way of the likelihood of 'latent', 'sub-clinical', and 'asymptomatic' cases. A good deal is known about somatic and social precipitating factors. Methods of pharmacological treatment are highly effective in suppressing and preventing the acute manifestations, and techniques of long-term management have been worked out. Where a disease theory of schizophrenia is thoroughly incomplete is in the absence of a firm link between the clinical syndrome and an underlying homeostatic mechanism, equivalent to that which controls carbohydrate metabolism and which is known to be defective in diabetes. Of course, it is clear that the pathophysiology of diabetes itself is by no means understood, but if we could get so far with schizophrenia it would be a very long step.

All that can be claimed, therefore, is that a disease theory can be postulated, at least for the large central group of the schizophrenias, and that it seems to be useful in both of the ways mentioned earlier. It is helpful to be able to make the diagnosis, first of all, because this will lead in a large number of cases to the reduction of impairments. Secondly, making the diagnosis also allows us to further the scientific investigation of this condition. Progress to date is highly suggestive that further advances are likely to be made. Such advances, in turn, are likely to benefit our patients.

The main alternative to a disease theory, which attempts to take into account the same sort of evidence, states that the functional psychoses are not qualitatively distinct diseases but represent the end-points of personality characteristics running through the general population. The problem is to know what is meant by personality characteristics here. The first-rank symptoms discussed earlier are not obviously extreme examples of normally distributed traits. They are very rare and nothing like them appears to occur during the waking hours of most people. Indeed Karl Jaspers used this fact as a diagnostic criterion. This does not, of course, contradict a dimensional theory, since some hypothetical underlying function might be normally distributed in the general population, those with high values being specially at risk of developing symptoms when precipitating factors were present. The multigene hypothesis of Gottesman and Shields, together with the observation that precipitating factors precede the first typically schizophrenic attack as frequently as they precede relapse, would fit this formulation. It is, however, speculative.

People who develop the central schizophrenic syndrome tend to be characterized by certain pre-morbid traits. These traits, and those found among relatives, might be specifiable in terms either of unusual thought processes (perhaps shown as heightened creativity in some people) or of so-called negative characteristics: blunting of affect, poverty of speech, slowness, underactivity, social withdrawal, poor ability to make complex judgements, and decrease in the use of verbal and body languages in communication. It has not been shown that these characteristics can be measured reliably in samples of the general population, and no survey has been carried out, so that it would be premature to consider the nature of their distribution. However, it may be suggested that traits which occur quite commonly in the general population may be related to schizophrenia, even though the lifetime risk of this condition is less than 1 per cent.

Eventually, it will be necessary to formulate both psychological and biological theories concerning the underlying functions which, when they exceed known limits through the operation of aetiological factors, give rise to specific schizophrenic symptoms. The psychological theories would deal with the mechanisms preventing most people from experiencing their thoughts being repeated or spoken aloud or broadcast, and with how the breakdown of these mechanisms is related to predisposing traits. The biological theories would deal with the same questions at different levels: physiological, biochemical, and anatomical. As we suggested in chapter 2, there need be no contradiction between disease and dimensional theories. They will turn out to complement each other.

The social reactivity of schizophrenic syndromes and the efficacy of social treatments

a. Intrinsic impairments

In the formulations of earlier psychiatrists, it was sometimes considered that chronic schizophrenic impairments (or deterioration, as it was called) were ruthlessly progressive and that very little could be done to ameliorate them. We now know that this view was wrong. If the mechanisms underlying attention and arousal are, in truth, disordered in schizophrenia, it is clear that reactivity must be higher than in many other conditions where a cerebral disturbance is postulated. Some early clinicians did, indeed, point to the fact that even patients who were apparently insensible of their social surroundings, in a catatonic stupor, could nevertheless describe later many details of what had gone on around them. Some appeared to be in a state of 'vigilance'; they were *too* aware.

Recent experiments have demonstrated that even those who are most withdrawn and slow respond rapidly to changes in the social environment.[201, 203] Encouragement to take more interest in simple tasks and join in social activities is quickly effective if it comes from familiar and trusted individuals and is not accompanied by too much emotional involvement. It is also important that the patient retains control of the extent to which he participates, so that he does not expose himself to a level of social stimulation that he experiences as painful, or at least only in small and carefully graduated doses. Much of the harm that was done in institutions such as old-fashioned mental hospitals occurred because these basic facts were not appreciated. The appearance of the severely handicapped individual with schizophrenia tends to lead the observer to suppose that attempts at communication would be fruitless. Because of an inability to use ordinary verbal and non-verbal languages, perhaps particularly the latter, fewer and fewer attempts were made to 'reach' the patient. Indeed it could fairly be said that the social environment (or lack of it) was partly constructed by the patients themselves. In one hospital that was studied in detail it was found that patients spent the largest proportion of their waking hours doing absolutely nothing.[201] Thus the impairments were confirmed and deepened and became even more severe than they need have been.

The reform movement introduced into British mental hospitals, largely as a result of the changes following the introduction of the National Health Service, demonstrated that much of this harm could be undone. This was true even in the days before the introduction of the new drugs in 1954. Indeed, the pioneer hospitals were already by then declining in population and experimenting with new methods of community care. However, the phenothiazines demonstrated beyond argument that schizophrenia was not immutable; and this demonstration did much to ensure the acceptance of social methods of treatment. The best hospitals had the least need to use the new drugs; fewer patients took them and the doses were smaller.

However, just as, in many cases, preventive medication needs to be continued over a prolonged period of time (it is not yet certain if it ever needs to be permanent), so the extra social stimulation needed must also be kept up. This can be seen as the passive exercise of functions which the individual is unable, for the moment, to exercise actively for himself (a basic principle of rehabilitation). Even so, the negative impairments do not necessarily disappear completely. At an industrial rehabilitation unit[200] it was easy to pick out those with the schizophrenic handicaps by comparison with other attenders who were there because of physical handicaps of various kinds. Those with schizophrenia were plodding, lacking in initiative, and unsociable, although not unfriendly when approached. One of the most important lessons to be learned about this sort of disability is that, because impairments do not disappear entirely but seem to persist at a minimum level, it does not mean that no progress is being made. First, there is the vital point that any let-up in the provision of an adequate degree of social stimulation is likely to be followed at once by an increase in the degree of impairment. Secondly, there is always the hope that eventually the individual may be able to take over for himself. It is never safe, in schizophrenia, to talk of permanent disability.

We are now sure that these principles hold true for all social environments. They were discovered in the best mental hospitals but are equally applicable in protected environments of all kinds, including the home. A patient may be just as inactive in a poor day centre as in a poor hospital. The individual with schizophrenia is vulnerable to understimulating social environments, whatever the setting, and is likely in such conditions to suffer an increase in what might be termed the 'clinical poverty syndrome'.

Another type of chronic impairment, the liability to relapse with acute symptoms of schizophrenia, is also highly dependent on the social, environment but in a different way. Events which ordinary people take in their stride may prove highly threatening to someone with this vulnerability. George Brown and James Birley[19] have found that even promotion at work or getting engaged to be married, usually regarded as positive and rewarding events, may lead to relapse. Witnessing a street accident and having to appear in court is a more neutral example. Overtly threatening events, such as the death of a relative or a well-loved pet, have the same effect. Admission to hospital in an acute attack very frequently follows such events. Clearly, the effect is non-specific, a generally reduced resistance to excitement or 'stress' of any kind. Everyday life is found to be stressful at a lower threshold than is true for most people.

The work underlying these findings was undertaken within a Unit of the Medical Research Council that specializes in social psychiatry. Other projects have been concerned with relationships within the families of schizophrenic patients. Very little scientific work has been carried out in such a setting, in spite of the enormous claims that have been made, some of which have labelled the relatives in a particularly insulting way as incompetent and 'schizophrenogenic'. The facts are far more interesting. Brown, Birley, and Wing[20] found that schizophrenic patients who returned home after an acute attack to live with a critical, hostile, or domineering relative had a much higher risk of relapse during the ensuing nine months. The more the face-to-face contact with such a relative, the greater the chance of further breakdown. Christine Vaughn and Julian Leff[181] have recently repeated these findings. This suggests that techniques adopted by the patient to secure a certain social distance between himself and other people may in some cases be protective. For example, sleeping during the daytime and being active at night would have such an effect. Attending a day centre would also result in a reduction in the time spent face to face with an over-involved relative, quite apart from the benefit derived from any therapeutic social environment that was created there.

There can, of course, be similar effects in other types of social environment, not only at home. Again, it is the principles of vulnerability and reactivity that have to be understood. For example, it has several times been observed that people with chronic schizophrenic impairments should not be exposed too suddenly to increased therapeutic stimulation even in protected social environments, since this often leads to a relapse with a reappearance of symptoms of the acute state.[200]

On the basis of what we have said up to now, we can suppose

that socially overstimulating environments may be harmful in a different way from socially understimulating ones, since they produce an increase in different kinds of impairments. In other words, people who have experienced an acute attack of schizophrenia have to walk a tightrope with different kinds of danger on each side, and it is easy to become 'decompensated' either way. In psychological terms, it could be suggested that there is a cognitive defect which makes it difficult to communicate with other people. This is naturally most evident in interactions with close kin, and it is exacerbated in conditions of anxiety and high arousal. When this first occurs it tends to be normalized by relatives, who try to intrude further upon the patient. It is also explained by the patient in various ways which appear to him to be 'normal' (hypnotism, thought transfer, rays, witchcraft, etc., depending on the culture). At this stage, much of the high anxiety is self-generated, since the patient is preoccupied with new experiences. However, the more intrusive the social environment the less the patient is able to withdraw, and the more the symptoms are perpetuated and provoked. Going into hospital, wandering off alone, and other such solutions, may provide a relief by reducing the degree of environmental stimulus.

After several attacks, the patient may come to terms with his experiences and find (whether he consciously formulates this or not) that a degree of withdrawal is protective. Relatives, too, may learn for themselves just what degree of stimulation is permissible, so that a working solution is arrived at. Patients usually do not wish to be entirely alone, but they do like to remain in control of the intensity of contact. The role of relative, however, is a very difficult one, since it is unnatural to acquire the degree of detachment and neutrality required; it is much easier for professional people to adopt such a stance. The relatives of handicapped people may easily become over-protective and over-involved. In the case of schizophrenia, this over-involvement has specific effects in increasing the liability to further breakdown. When this shows itself in symptoms such as violence, noisiness at night, refusal to eat, or delusions involving the relative, a circular effect is set up. The relative expects such reactions on future occasions. This is a much more likely explanation of the findings than the assumption that the original cause of schizophrenia is somehow familial.

The alternative temptation for the patient is to withdraw altogether into contemplation of private experiences. When a patient is allowed to do so in the understimulating conditions of some large hospital wards, or in badly run hostels, or in reception centres, or even in an attic at home, the negative impairments become more and more obvious.

On the whole, treatment by neuroleptic drugs seems to be more beneficial in reducing and preventing the acute relapses than in minimizing the negative impairments. It may be suggested that removing the individual from a situation of 'stress'—whether caused by everyday events, or by the psycho-social intrusion of an over-involved relative, or by over-enthusiastic rehabilitation and resocialization experts—will in itself be beneficial, although the neuroleptic drug administered at the same time will get most of the credit.

The relation of these clinical handicaps to physiological arousal remains speculative, but it is possible to suggest a link. When the arousal level is optimal for a given patient, which is usually when he is living in a structured and stimulating, but emotionally neutral, social environment, rather little in the way of neuroleptics may be needed. When socially disturbing events occur or when the pressures of the social environment are too intrusive, maintenance phenothiazine medication reduces the likelihood of relapse. Phenothiazines are the quickest and most certain way of restoring equilibrium once a relapse has occurred. Paradoxically, however, phenothiazines may also be useful in reducing over-arousal due to socially understimulating conditions. Here the patient may become completely preoccupied with internal stimuli and cease to be in touch with the outside world altogether. The social measures we have discussed are the most effective way of avoiding this dangerous condition; hence the lesser need for drugs when the patient is living in a good hospital or with a protective family. If this formulation has any validity, social treatments and pharmacological treatments must always be prescribed together.[196,199]

b. Secondary impairments

Secondary impairments are personal and social reactions to the fact and circumstances of illness, both by the patient and by other important persons, such as relatives, employers, workmates, and professional people, who reflect back to the handicapped person an indication of his social status and worth. If they think he is less of a man because of his illness, he will tend to think so, too. If he is helpless, he may have no choice but to depend upon his environment to help him. A congenitally deaf child must rely on others to teach him to talk and help him to communicate. The more severe the intrinsic impairment, the more inevitable is the development of secondary impairment as well.

Handicapped people have to (or wish to) opt out of certain social responsibilities. Therefore others must take them on. If the others are professionally trained for the job, there tends to develop what Goffman called a staff-patient split, each side taking up rather stereotyped attitudes towards the other. The longer the patient experiences dependence, the more he will tend to prefer it. Staff, in turn, may exaggerate the severity of intrinsic handicaps, and thus a vicious circle is set up, with unnecessary dependence developing as well as that which is unavoidable. The acceptance by the handicapped person of limitations which are not actually necessary is the essence of secondary impairment.

The most obvious example of secondary impairment in schizophrenia is institutionalism, at the heart of which is a gradually acquired contentment with life in the institution that culminates in the individual no longer wishing to live any other.[201] Institutionalism is thus caused partly by a reflection back to the handicapped person of his own altered status as a human being. He is seen as a patient, rather than as an employee, a father, a customer, or a companion. The patient role is a restricted one, replacing many others which he might have been able to undertake. Partly, however, institutionalism is caused by forces within the patient—his own previous experience of illness, his self-confidence, his potential for developing alternative skills, and his determination to achieve independence.

These factors have been illustrated in several studies of schizophrenic patients in mental hospitals. The core of 'institutionalism' is that the longer the patient has been in hospital, the less likely he is to want to leave. Other attitudes and personal habits are affected in the same way. The patient loses any ability he might originally have retained to play a wide range of social roles, he does not replenish his stock of useful current information (such as how much a postage stamp costs), he does not practise travelling on public transport or shopping, and he gradually ceases to make plans for the future or simply repeats some vague formula if he is asked about them. Fewer visitors come and even if the patient is allowed to go outside hospital, he will tend to do so less and less.

Hospitals differ markedly in the social conditions they provide. Although exposure to a socially impoverished environment is not necessarily associated with increased negative impairments, with the major exception of an imposed idleness, it is fairly obvious that social poverty is likely to encourage the development of secondary impairments. Thus institutionalism, pauperism, and neglect contribute to the disablement of hospital patients as well as to their discomfort. This is not the place to speak of ill-treatment, which in British hospitals is rare but which has been documented in some recent cases. One does not need the apparatus of scientific research to demonstrate that cruelty is unacceptable.[142] However, if the hospital management is aware of the social techniques that can limit intrinsic and secondary impairments and maximize the assets of individual patients it is very unlikely that such abuses can occur.[144]

Once attitude change has taken place, as in institutionalism, it is very difficult to remedy. Probably attitudes to discharge or to work outside hospital can be changed in schizophrenic patients only by methods aimed specifically at this end. Thus in one of our studies, we successfully changed the attitude to work by getting moderately handicapped, long-stay schizophrenic patients to go to an Industrial Rehabilitation Unit outside hospital (after adequate preparation), and found that those who improved did in fact find jobs. What we did not anticipate was that there was no change in the attitude to discharge. Even those who began working out still wanted to live in. These attitudes are very specific.

Although this analysis of secondary impairments has been based mainly on the problem of institutionalism, it is, of course, true to say that nowadays far fewer long-stay patients are accumulating in hospitals. Nevertheless, there are 'new' long-stay patients in hostels, day centres, and sheltered communities, and it is important to remember that the principles of the development of institutionalism are most unlikely to be different in kind for these people than for the 'old' long-stay patients in mental hospitals.[66] Indeed, in some respects the problems are more difficult. Sheila Mann and Wendy Cree,[112] for example, found that after only two or three years in hospital the 'new' long-stay patients already wanted to stay where they were. This is what one would expect as the process of selection focuses to a greater extent on those with more severe intrinsic and extrinsic handicaps, and the 'hospital' becomes more and more a sheltered community. Even those who spend most of their time at home and do not have to remain in sheltered environments of various kinds nevertheless risk developing secondary handicaps, other than institutionalism. Brown and his colleagues[21] found that 20 per cent of their schizophrenic patients, admitted to hospital in 1956, left home during the subsequent five years and did not return. Divorce is much commoner among schizophrenic patients than in the general population. The secondary problems arising from unemployment, solitary living, poverty, and even destitution, are important causes of an attitude of indifference or despair. Once you are down, you tend to be ground further down; people handicapped by schizophrenia are no exception to that rule.

Among those who stay at home, there are some who have outstayed their welcome. There tends to be a discrepancy between the attitudes of relative and patient: the relative sees the patient as disabled and often a bit of a trial to live with, the patient himself regards his circumstances with a touch of complacency. We have heard a good deal about the effect of relatives upon patients, but much less about the effects the other way round.

As time goes on, there is no doubt that patient and relative, if they stay together, come to acquire a tolerance which neither might have had before. The relative, however, does so at the expense of restricting his or her life. Often the parent of an unmarried schizophrenic is an elderly widow who is grateful for some companionship and for someone to do a bit of shopping if she is physically disabled, and is not too worried by not being able to live a life of her own. Under such circumstances, even a patient with a turbulent history of frequent breakdowns eventually settles into a routine. It is another kind of institutionalism—less expensive, of course, and less demanding on the patient than a good hospital with its workshop, leisure activities, and socialization programmes would be, and sometimes a good deal more restricting on the activities and interests of relatives. Few, however, complain. The major problem raised by those relatives articulate enough to be able to make a point is worry over the patient's future. One father called it the WIAG syndrome ('when I am gone').[31]

However, this contented, if restricted, outcome for family life, at least for the unmarried patient, is sometimes reached only after a lengthy and profoundly distressing time, during which the patient's condition is constantly unstable and the relatives do not know what will happen next. It is not surprising that many patients find themselves homeless and drift to common lodging-houses, reception centres, or sleeping rough.[179, 208] It does not need very many patients from each area each year to account for the large numbers found in Salvation Army hostels and shelters for the destitute. Nor is it surprising that the rate of suicide is so high among people with schizophrenia.

c. Extrinsic impairments
The concept of extrinsic handicap is far from self-explanatory when we are discussing schizophrenia, since the epidemiological evidence makes it clear that impairments are frequently present long before an acute and florid episode brings the condition to the attention of other people.[160] Already there may be deficits in vocational, intellectual, and social functioning which can be ascribed only to an early manifestation of the disease. The evidence on this last point is overwhelming.[185] Some of the factors that might otherwise have been called extrinsic are better called intrinsic. The tendency to slowness and social withdrawal, on the one hand, and the liability to breakdown with florid symptoms, on the other, are already present and possibly recognizable in some cases, simply waiting for the appropriate conglomeration of environmental forces to reach threshold level and precipitate the first 'attack'. Of course, this is by no means always the case. Sometimes schizophrenia seems to fall from a cloudless sky, and the tragedy then seems all the greater.

It should also be recognized that many of the factors which have been demonstrated to be associated with a poor prognosis in schizophrenia, such as prolonged unemployment, lack of social and vocational skills, being single as opposed to married, and being socially isolated, are also predictive of a poor social outcome in other conditions or in people who have no psychiatric condition at all. Moreover, there are often pre-existing independent or accidental factors which make the course of a subsequently occurring schizophrenia more severe and prolonged than it need otherwise have been. It is important to recognize these and to try to correct them during the course of rehabilitation, because the more developed a person's psychological and social skills, the better equipped he is to compensate for a handicapping condition.

d. Adjustment, as well as change

We have been concentrating on the problems of the severely handicapped but it should be remembered that milder degrees of disability often occur and that many people recover completely after one or two attacks. One such individual, who still experiences occasional symptoms but nevertheless enjoys a happy family life with his wife and four children and who carries out a satisfying and responsible job, has laid down a number of rules, based on simple conditioning theory, for helping to avoid a relapse. Whenever he experiences a primordial symptom—for example, that other people's eyes seem to be observing him and that they seem to be 'radiating'—he consciously relaxes and reminds himself of how such experiences used to lead, after an initial panic, to fully fledged delusions and hallucinations. He finds that he needs no medication; in fact he will not allow himself to use it, since he wants no crutch to help him deal with his disability.

Another individual found that he often experienced a recurrence of delusional thoughts when he got emotionally worked up:[195]

I begin to notice coincidences which otherwise I might not have noticed. Then I might start testing some delusional theory. Let me see whether that car turns the corner behind me. If so, is it still there several turnings later? Then it must be following me! I now feel that I have sufficient knowledge of myself to know that this kind of thinking is dangerous. I can control my mind sufficiently to prevent such thoughts getting out of control and destroying my inner self.

Whether many people can achieve the degree of control attained by these two is unknown, but it is highly encouraging that it can occur even in a few cases. This is true self-rehabilitation. Rehabilitation often has to mean adjustment, not change, particularly when social disablement is severe. To argue the contrary is often denying that handicap exists, at the same time as asking handicapped people to carry the burden of social reform. Occasionally, the principle of using one's own weaknesses as a stepping-stone to changing society can work. Bernard Shaw became a skilled public speaker by means of forcing himself to overcome his shyness. Such tactics are rarely indicated in schizophrenia. If we regard all psychological problems as identical in nature, we shall quite often do harm.

Finally, a word about course and outcome. It should be clear that there is no such thing as a 'natural history' in a disorder as reactive as schizophrenia. If everyone lived a non-demanding life, there might be less, and less severe, schizophrenia. There is a suggestion that the prognosis is more benign in certain areas, such as Nigeria or Mauritius, because of a complex of reasons including greater tolerance and less social pressure.[127,155] If so, the social and familial factors that were discussed earlier are likely to be involved. But many human beings would be frustrated if all challenge were eliminated. Those who attempt to reach rather further than others have done before do tend to be admired by society, at least if the circumstances are right. They represent something in human nature. But obviously they run more risk than if they had ventured nothing.

If schizophrenia is inherited, some of the genes, in some contexts, may well be valuable. Perhaps in paleolithic hunting societies the suspicious man, or the man who had an inner light, might have had survival value for the group. Similarly, the genes for diabetes might, in epochs when near-starvation was the rule, have been more useful than they are today. Speculations of this kind do not help handicapped people, but they may provide a corrective to our habitual modes of thinking about disease, which naturally concentrate on its harmful aspects.

Through the eyes of relatives

It is only after one has had an opportunity to digest all the evidence reviewed in this chapter that one can reasonably approach the problem of how far relationships between family members, particularly between adults and small children, are likely to be a primary cause of the schizophrenic syndrome. We shall look in greater detail in chapter 5 at what evidence can be mustered for this theory. The relatives themselves have views on this and other matters and have now formed an association, the National Schizophrenia Fellowship, to promote the welfare of sufferers and their families:

Part of the peculiar difficulty for relatives is that schizophrenia lies somewhere between those conditions like blindness which, though severely handicapping, do not interfere with an individual's ability to make independent judgements about his own future, and those, like severe mental retardation, in which it is clear that the individual will never be able to make such independent judgements.[31]

In addition, relatives are only too well aware of the fact that they are living through a transitional stage in the organization of social and medical services. From a predominantly hospital-based system which is gradually running down, except for the treatment of acute illnesses, the intention is to create a system in which protective environments and supporting social and welfare services are provided by the Social Service Departments of local authorities. The run-down of hospitals in England and Wales is a fact; the number of beds occupied has decreased from over 150,000 in 1954 (354 per 100,000 population) to 110,000 in 1971 (225 per 100,000). The build-up of new facilities has lagged far behind, and the current financial crisis has not improved matters (see chapter 7).

Relatives find themselves being asked to undertake the main responsibility for the care of people handicapped by schizophrenia, without being given sensible advice about the nature of the disorder, about the importance of environmental conditions, about the indications and contraindications for medication and its detailed management, or about the best way to respond to disturbed and disturbing behaviour. Paradoxically, they are often regarded, in spite of this, as being responsible for the patient's condition in the first place. The small hostels, and groups of bed-sitters, conveniently placed near home, from which handicapped people could attend day centres or sheltered workplaces, and which would ensure an emotionally neutral and socially rich environment to which relatives could contribute, barely exist anywhere. As the *Lancet* commented in an editorial: 'A society which has, for its own reasons, decided that the long-stay hospital is not the place in which schizophrenics should be treated owes all possible skilled advice and support to those who have taken over the responsibility.'

Schizophrenia and madness

We have to defer an examination of the advantages and disadvantages of disease theories of schizophrenia until we have considered the alternatives in chapter 5. However, it will be useful to sum up what we have discussed. Most of what we have considered can be related to the common central syndromes of schizophrenia and the chronic impairments that accompany them. How they relate to the various syndromes represented in *Class P* and *Class O* is not so clear, and there is a good deal of uncertainty outside the limits of the central concept. The experiences complained of by Rosenhan and his colleagues (see p. 98) would not come within even the widest boundaries of the CATEGO classification of schizophrenia and the fact that this diagnosis was made in nearly all cases reflects the very broad concept used in much of the United States. A tenuous theoretical justification of the broad concept can be put forward in terms of the multigene hypothesis, suggesting that any oddity which is remotely reminiscent of the central syndromes or the chronic impairments must also be schizophrenic; but none of the evidence, for example on the efficacy of phenothiazine drugs or the dangers of over- or understimulating environments, is relevant to these peripheral groups. Speculation is admirable. Acting on the speculation as though there were some evidence for it is likely to be damaging. Odd experiences of the kind Rosenhan complained of (let us forget for the moment that the conspirators were lying) might be included under the catch-all term 'madness' which, as we have seen, has no technical referents and can cover almost any strange or unusual condition that cannot be explained in any other way. Schizophrenia, in the technical sense used here, is a restricted concept, useful only within the limits specified, and without reference to purely social deviations. It is completely irrelevant to violence at football matches, or the behaviour of politicians under pressure, or drug addiction or shoplifting. It cannot be used to derive theories concerning the creativity of artists or the activities of men of big business or generals. It is not even correct to say that all those with a diagnosis of schizophrenia are 'mad'; they may, in any lay sense, be completely 'sane'.

Finally, when applied to a particular human being, the term schizophrenia, used scientifically, is an abstraction based on a few specially selected experiences and aspects of behaviour. Although these are bound to affect an individual's personality when the impairments are severe, each person remains unique. The physician does not think he has said all that has to be said about an individual when he has made a diagnosis of schizophrenia. He has put forward a theory that he can test in various ways, but he would be a poor doctor (in fact, not a doctor at all but a technician) if he did not use a wide variety of other skills, including those social skills he has developed in common with other mature human beings. This is what is meant when it is said that medicine is both a science and an art. If the doctor is not something of a creative artist—as well as something of a social worker, priest, psychotherapist, teacher, and friend—he may well do harm, no matter how technically competent he is at diagnosis. Criticism of doctors suggests that this is precisely what does happen, and even worse, that they apply diagnostic techniques when none are applicable, and that harm does indeed result. On the other hand, if doctors do not apply disease theories when they are applicable, the consequences will also be serious. The evidence either way will be reviewed in chapter 5.

5. Alternatives and complements to medical models

There are certainly some cases where the psychiatrist might more profitably spend his time discouraging illness behaviour and teaching the patient to focus less, rather than more, on his psychological state; and other cases where the social contingencies of the disorder are far more important than the symptomatology.

David Mechanic

Terminology

We have seen that the term 'illness' can have two quite distinct connotations. In one usage, someone is regarded as sick (or regards himself or herself as sick), because of some experience or behaviour that departs from a standard of health generally accepted in that community. Such standards vary widely. In one society, multi-coloured spots on the skin indicate health, in another they indicate illness. Moreover, the norms of health are vague and shifting so that there can be a good deal of latitude as to what is regarded as unhealthy. Even the most specific terms are still very general: 'fatigue', 'pallor', 'backache', 'pain'. In the second usage, for which we are reserving the term 'disease', a limited and relatively specific theory about some aspect of mental or bodily functioning is put forward because it is thought to be relevant to the reduction of some recognizable impairment. A term like 'pallor' is no longer acceptable except as an indication to look for more specific characteristics, which may suggest one of the anaemias or some other condition, of which pallor is one indicator.

In fact, of course, these two usages represent two different types of theory. Over the centuries, the second type of usage has become more and more precise and differentiated from the first, as scientific knowledge has accumulated. In many fields of medicine, experts have no difficulty in applying common standards of definition, whatever country they come from. Measuring the level of glucose or haemoglobin in the blood does not depend on shifting social definitions, although a judgement as to what level requires medical intervention may vary according to local circumstances.

The term 'madness' should be used only in the first of these two ways. It is a lay term, covering a wide range of experiences or behaviours; from wit to delusion, mild foolishness to total senility. A degree of differentiation is introduced by terms such as 'nervous' or 'tense' compared with terms such as 'crazy' or 'daft', but all of these social attributions can have many different meanings depending on the context, and sometimes they can overlap each other to the point of identity. Used in this way the term 'madness' is of no scientific value. Restricted disease theories have been put forward, ranging from highly specific and well developed concepts such as phenylketonuria to much less complete theories of schizophrenia or depressive disorder. As in the rest of scientific medicine, experts from all over the world are now beginning to be able to agree upon standards of definition that are not dependent on local social values. There is, however, a special terminological problem, in that a substantial number of psychiatrists, for example in countries that have long based their psychiatric education mainly on the tenets of psychoanalysis, tend to use words that appear to have a highly specific technical connotation but that in fact cannot be defined with any degree of precision. Familiar terms like 'schizophrenia' may well be used in idiosyncratic ways or even as a synonym for 'madness'.

New advances in medicine filter very slowly through the profession and take at least ten years to get into the medical textbooks. It is not surprising, therefore, that they diffuse even more slowly into the sociological literature. In nearly all the work with which we shall be concerned in this chapter (that by David Mechanic[117] is an exception), terms like 'mental disorder' are used, not as collective names for a wide range of more or less specifiable and separable conditions, but as synonyms for 'madness' or 'nerves' in the lay or non-technical sense. This has certain advantages since the sociologist is interested in social norms and 'illness behaviour' rather than in disease theories. However, a circularity is introduced if it is not recognized that the same words can be used in a quite different, technical, sense. We shall have to clear away a good deal of such semantic undergrowth.

Social normality and social deviance

The early sociologists, as Edwin Lemert has pointed out, placed their own ethical tags upon aspects of society they wished to condemn or advocate. If they decided that some social characteristic such as poverty was evil, their tactics, like General Custer's, were simple; they 'rode to the sound of the guns'. For many of them, social problems included deviations from an ideal of 'residential stability, property ownership, sobriety, thrift, habituation to work, small business enterprise, sexual discretion, family solidarity, neighbourliness, and discipline of the will'. These were the ideals of small-town America. They have changed since, but a list of some sort could be drawn up for any group of human beings with a fair degree of organization, whether on a large scale such as the U.S.S.R. or on a relatively small one, such as the Quakers. All such lists incorporate assumptions of value.

Lemert himself was of a different generation. In the first edition of his book, *Social Pathology*, published in 1951, he said that he defined social problems purely as situations 'about which a large number of people feel disturbed and unhappy—this and nothing more'. Presumably he wanted, like a physician does, to study problems that were defined socially as distressing and about which people complained, but again like a physician, he wanted to get away from value-laden definitions of abnormality (he did not regard prostitution as either right or wrong) and to set up criteria that could be agreed by all scientists who worked in the field, whatever society they belonged to. To this end, his main focus of interest lay in the processes whereby 'problems' were socially defined and recognized and in the effects of these processes on the individuals concerned.

Many social scientists who begin with some form of historical theory reject this common-sense approach. They explain present-day social problems either in terms of a deviation from a past ideal condition of society or in terms of 'historical forces' that drive inexorably towards a future millennium. According to both types of theory, social problems arise because of the tensions set up between those forces moving towards and those moving against the ultimate goal. The job of the 'scientist' is to spot which is which.

Lemert himself was quite explicit about these types of theory, both of which were manifested at that time as variants of the concept of social disorganization (see p. 6). Either there was a nostalgic regard for a past society less 'disorganized' than ours, or a hypothetical 'cultural lag' between present-day communities and the longed-for ones of the future. The ideal steady-state society has been described most nostalgically by Lévi-Strauss:[100]

> Although they exist in history, these societies seem to have elaborated or retained a particular wisdom which incites them to resist desperately any structural modification which would afford history a point of entry into their lives. Those which have best protected their distinctive character appear to be societies predominantly concerned with persevering in their existence. The way in which they exploit the environment guarantees both a modest standard of living and the conservation of natural resources. Their marriage rules, though varied, reveal to the eye of the demographer a common function, namely to set the fertility rate very low and to keep it constant. Finally, a political life based on consent, and admitting of no decisions other than those unanimously arrived at, seems conceived to preclude the possibility of calling on that driving force of collective life which takes advantage of the contrast between favour and opposition, majority and minority, exploiter and exploited.

Lemert reserved his most stringent criticisms for Charles H. Cooley's social disorganization theory, in which social life was regarded as an organic process involving the mutual interaction of society and the individual. The difficulty with Cooley's theory of interaction was that so many factors, both personal and social, were postulated as being in continuous flux that it 'amounts to a confession of open-minded ignorance about how factors work together'. Above all, it gave no clue as to how personal disorganization and social disorganization interact to produce a 'sociopathic' person; in fact the two concepts were so vaguely defined that it was not even clear how they were differentiated at all. Cooley and his followers could readily inject their own value-judgements. The theory of social disorganization 'draws heavily upon analogies and literary allusions for its effectiveness and . . . at times grows mystical. [Cooley's] literary and philosophical predilections present salient difficulties when it comes to finding empirical referents for his ideas, a fact which probably accounts for the failure of his writings to inspire any considerable body of research.' Theories of social disorganization have not advanced much since that time.

Lemert equally dismissed psychological and psychiatric

explanations for deviant behaviour because, although they can help us to understand some of the subjective aspects of deviance, they shed no light on its collective aspects. Crime, prostitution, and drug addiction cannot be explained as the summated expression of individual motives or 'pathological' personality traits.

Lemert's own formulation of the way in which 'sociopathic' behaviour can be scientifically investigated has been very influential and is worth considering attentively. He begins with the fact of a diversity of social behaviour (when sufficiently unusual, this is named 'primary' deviation), some types of which result in 'social penalties, rejection, and segregation. These penalties and segregative reactions of society or the community are dynamic factors which increase, decrease, and condition the form which the initial differentiation or deviation takes.' An intensification of the initial or primary deviation, because of the societal reaction, so that it becomes a way of life, is named 'secondary' deviation. The theory is amoral, in the sense that deviations are not regarded in themselves as better or worse than 'normal' behaviour. It should be as interesting to study the behaviour of an exceptional athlete or an outstandingly beautiful woman or a precocious musical genius (all of whom pursue 'careers' formed in part by the public reaction to their deviation) as it is to study that of a criminal, a pauper, or a sexual delinquent. Nevertheless, like the doctor, Lemert is concerned mainly with deviations defined by society as undesirable.

Primary deviations may be biological in nature. Examples are deafness, blindness, paraplegia, cleft-palate, aphasia, spasticity, or fits. Such handicaps tend to become 'overlaid with culturally conceived ideas as to how far the handicaps can go', and it is these cultural stereotypes that give social meaning to the physical disability. The degree to which the primary deviation is socially visible (i.e. its severity and duration) is an important determinant of the societal reaction. Thus occasional drunkenness will not be noticed in most societies, whereas constant, severe inebriety will be noticed in nearly all. But no matter what the original reasons for the deviations, they are not significant until they are organized subjectively and transformed into active roles and become the social criteria for assigning status. The deviant individuals must react symbolically to their own behaviour aberrations and fix them in their sociopsychological patterns. The deviations remain primary or symptomatic and situational as long as they are

rationalized or otherwise dealt with as functions of a socially acceptable role. When a person begins to employ his deviant behaviour or a role based upon it as a means of defence, attack, or
adjustment to the overt and covert problems created by the
consequent societal reaction to him, his deviation is secondary.
This is the origin of the idea of a deviant 'career', which follows
when a critical point in development has been reached.

The examples that Lemert uses are instructive. Some, like blindness and speech defects, are biological in nature. Secondary deviation
follows when the individual begins to define himself as handicapped in the terms used by society in general, and to adopt an
appropriate way of life. Lemert's analysis covers much of the same
ground as the analysis of handicaps in chapter 2. The intrinsic
impairment leads to secondary abnormalities such as the so-called
blindisms, and to attitudinal and behavioural adaptations of
various kinds. The blind person inevitably has to come to terms
with his social environment and to take account of social expectations of how he should behave. For someone who is congenitally
blind the adaptation comes very early.

At the opposite extreme, Lemert uses political radicalism as an
example of a career that has not developed on the basis of a primarily biological defect. He says that there has always been in
every society a group of persistent critics who have come to be
defined as dissenters, agitators, free thinkers, infidels, heretics,
rebels, reformers, renegades, Bohemians, or radicals. The punitive
reaction of society to such groups has been responsible for some of
the cruellest pages of history. Primary radicalism may occur
through 'absorbing cultural traditions emphasizing social justice,
as with many Jews, or because of identification with a critical,
rebellious parent, or because of special social trauma breeding a
deep and painful disillusionment'. Such people may 'develop compulsive habits of thought and rigid symbolic reactions. They
become less responsive to suggestion and to group opinions, more
unyielding and uncompromising.' The secondary elements are
here very obvious: the need for support from specially constructed
philosophies, from friends, and from institutional groups that will
help the dissenting individuals to bear the adverse weight of societal opinion, and to draw strength from (and even to become more
radical because of) society's reaction. Crime and prostitution are
further examples of careers based mainly on social factors.

Somewhere between these two extremes come Lemert's other examples; alcoholism and mental illness. He considers that all mental disorders, whether neurotic or psychotic, can be regarded as abnormal variations in the amount and form of self-expression. Schizophrenia, for example, may be the result of an intolerable loss of self-respect, coped with by drifting (simple schizophrenia), fighting back (delusional misinterpretation), or panic (hebephrenia). These simple notions need not detain us except to illustrate the way in which the concept of primary deviation is applied to the mental disorders. The secondary adaptation then follows, in principle, in the same way as it does for other forms of social deviance. Clearly, the more severe and 'intrinsic' the primary deviation (or impairment: see p. 25) the more inevitable the secondary adaptation.

The theory of secondary deviation may be stated in two forms, one moderate and one radical. The moderate form of the theory is similar to the theory of intrinsic and secondary disabilities put forward in chapter 2. It states that certain primordial forms of behaviour, due to demonstrable biological, psychological, or social causes, bring people to public attention and that the ensuing societal reaction has the effect of stereotyping and defining the individual who, at the point at which he accepts and incorporates the societal definition into his own image, becomes a secondary or 'career' deviant. Institutionalism in schizophrenic patients is a case in point.[201] A person is admitted to hospital as part of the societal reaction to his primary deviation, and gradually over the years, he comes to accept the social environment of the institution as his proper world. The appropriate behaviour and attitudes develop, and eventually he ceases altogether to wish to leave or even to take any interest in the world outside. Institutionalism does not cause schizophrenia; on the contrary, it is a secondary response to societal pressures that are themselves reactive. (Institutionalism may, of course, be more likely to occur in people with certain types of primary deviation, such as severe physical handicaps, schizophrenia, severe mental retardation, very passive personalities, etc.) This is an interactional type of theory, but the components can be specified quite precisely.

The radical form of the theory states that there is no primary deviation, or that the secondary component is so overwhelming that for all practical purposes, the primary element is trivial and can be ignored. This is labelling theory. The label is the deviation. For example, 'mental disorder' is thought not to be recognizable in any specific form before somebody influential applies the label.

The more radical formulations of Lemert's theories have been developed by his followers, and two examples will be considered in some detail by way of illustration. One is delinquency, for which a medical model is not usually put forward; the other is 'mental disorder', which is disputed territory.

The new criminology

The critics suggest that defining 'delinquency' in terms of an appearance before a juvenile court (legal positivism) involves an assumption that the processes of criminal law have a validity of their own; that crime must be caused by qualities within the individual offender who is unwilling to adjust to society. But, the argument runs, the 'primary deviation' might have been a perfectly rational action, or set of actions, given the circumstances in which the individual found himself, or simply some activity in which almost everyone engages but for which only a few people, stigmatized for other reasons, are prosecuted. What needs to be changed is society, not the individual. Defining him as delinquent and forcing him to see himself in this light will merely make a career criminal of him while leaving the deeper social causes unexamined.

Putting the theory in these uncompromising terms has the signal merit that we can test it. D. J. West[187] studied a group of boys living in a poor area of south London where the frequency of prosecution for delinquency was high. Some 20 per cent of all the boys in the area were actually prosecuted. West also used indices of behaviour not recognized and prosecuted as, but equivalent to, delinquency. He found that his conclusions were much the same whether he used these extended indices, or simply the rate of prosecution, as the basis for analysis. This in itself suggests that the first appearance in court is not the first step in a process of stigmatization of boys who are otherwise indistinguishable from their peers. On the contrary, it appears that a vulnerable group of children could be identified, even at an early age, who were likely to become publicly recognized as delinquent later on. The main adverse factors were five in number: low family income, large family size, parental criminality, low intelligence, and poor parental behaviour. The more marked these factors, the more likely the occurrence of delinquency and the greater the chance that a first episode of delinquency would initiate a career.

The fact that these indices were predictive from pre-school age suggested to West that what we have called the radical form of labelling theory could not be supported. Since the main factors needed to produce a delinquent career were present before the force of societal reaction had been felt (i.e. before the first publicly recognized act of delinquency), the hypothesis of primary deviation has not been disproved, although its nature is not clear.

However, there is in addition reasonable evidence that a career of delinquency and crime may become consolidated first of all by social networks in schools, neighbourhoods, and gangs, and later by a sort of apprenticeship, served in detention centres, reform schools, and prisons, in which the skills, attitudes, and personal habits of criminals are learned, both from others more advanced in expertise and from the reaction of society. These factors probably act more strongly as the child gets older. They form a truly vicious spiral. West himself has produced evidence for deviance amplification of these kinds. The moderate form of labelling theory (Lemert's original formulation) is therefore applicable. What is difficult to explain, in terms purely or even largely of career indoctrination or societal reaction, is the fact that the most socially disadvantaged 20 per cent of West's group of children, according to the five factors mentioned earlier, not only became delinquent but also could be identified as vulnerable long before any official societal labelling had occurred. The other less vulnerable four-fifths—all from the same area and attending the same schools—did not show the primordial deviant behaviour nor did they become delinquent. This does not, of course, mean that they were paragons of virtue. Few children are.

The reviewer of West and Farrington's book in the *Times Literary Supplement* of 1 March 1974 tried hard to salvage something for the 'new criminology'. He did not attempt to discuss the results but selected for comment sentences from here and there in the book that showed, as he thought, the authors' conservative and middle-class prejudices. This is the characteristic historicist reaction described by Popper: to look for a conspiracy and to search out hidden motives in order to excuse a failure to deal with inconvenient facts. What the reviewer found particularly hard to swallow was that the authors did not clearly recognize that the quality of 'criminality' or 'delinquency' resides 'not within the "offender" but within the processes of social definition'. But this extreme version of labelling theory was precisely what they had disproved, and only further work, of an even higher quality, can re-introduce the idea.

West's five causal factors have been demonstrated in several other investigations. Shields[162] has summarized the evidence for a genetic influence, not of course predominant but worth taking into account. It is also necessary to consider the influence of physical impairments and malnutrition. These scientific studies begin to indicate the nature of the multiple underlying social and biological processes.

Mental disorder as social deviation

The radical or labelling theory of mental disorder is stated most clearly by Thomas Scheff,[157, 158] who has also provided the best empirical evidence in its favour. He argues, following Lemert, that society has a set of stereotyped responses to violations of social norms, i.e. to deviant behaviour. Labels such as 'ill-mannered', 'ignorant', 'sinful' or 'criminal' are stock responses. Someone who frequently violates social norms tends to be categorized in some such way, but there remains a group of assorted deviations that are regarded as inexplicable. These tend to be put down to witchcraft or spirit possession or mental illness, or just as eccentricity, depending on the society concerned. In the early stages, abnormality tends to be ignored or denied. Thus children sometimes show traits such as temper tantrums, head banging, fantasy playmates, or strange fears, but this behaviour is usually transitory and does not become labelled as evidence of mental illness. The small proportion of residual deviants who go on to deviant careers do so, according to Scheff, *because* of the societal reaction. 'Residual deviance may be stabilized if it is defined to be evidence of mental illness, and/or the deviant is placed in a deviant status, and begins to play the role of the mentally ill.' Scheff thinks, unlike Thomas Szasz, that the role-playing is not mainly voluntary, but that it is mainly involuntary. The stereotypes of mental disorder and insanity are learned during childhood, much of the imagery involved being fallacious. These stereotypes are, however, constantly re-affirmed in everyday conversation ('You must be crazy'), in the mass-media, and in popular fiction.

Once a person is labelled as mentally ill, these social expectations as to how he or she should behave become concentrated because of the reward and punishment system of psychiatric institutions and, once the deviant role has been adopted, all mentally ill people behave in the uniform way which confirms their status. Thus 'most mental disorder can be considered to be a social role'; career or secondary deviance has set in.

The role of the psychiatrist in this process is that of a professional licenser of the new role. Scheff investigated the process of admission to state mental hospitals in Wisconsin, at a time when all in-patients had to be admitted compulsorily through the courts. (The law has since been changed.) He came to the conclusion that the psychiatrist often acted as a legal, rather than as a medical, agent, confirming the label placed upon the patient (usually 'schizophrenia') without even spending the time necessary to make a proper 'diagnosis'. In a subsequent study of a Wisconsin county mental hospital in 1964, I interviewed all the patients who had been diagnosed as schizophrenic and had been resident for more than two years.[201] All were committed; there was no form of voluntary or non-statutory status in those days. None was allowed to go into the local town alone and only 5 per cent of the women could go into the grounds unescorted. (The British hospitals studied in the same project were completely different. Nearly all patients in the survey were under no form of legal order. Almost all could go into the grounds as they pleased, and were then virtually outside the hospital.) All but one of the 45 American patients who fitted the selection criteria were interviewed, using a standard procedure. It was possible to make a definite diagnosis of schizophrenia in only 29 of these 44 cases. In a further 9 cases, the evidence was non-existent or weak, but no alternative diagnosis could positively be made. In the remaining 6 cases a diagnosis other than schizophrenia could fairly confidently be made, according to the British system of diagnosis: 2 had been admitted with delirium tremens and 4 with depressive disorders.

The findings of the U.S.–U.K. Diagnostic Project and the WHO International Pilot Study of Schizophrenia, described in chapter

4, also showed that some people were admitted to hospital with a diagnosis of schizophrenia who would not have been given that diagnosis elsewhere. The paper by Rosenhan (see p. 98) demonstrates, if the evidence of people who are prepared to tell lies to further their reformist cause can be accepted, that a label of schizophrenia is all too easy to affix in an American state hospital. The story of Leonid Plyushch, which will be found in chapter 6, shows that a similar process can occur in the U.S.S.R. It can also happen in the United Kingdom, although the grounds for diagnosing schizophrenia are usually more limited there, and the resulting incarceration less damaging.

The importance of these studies for Scheff's case is that, once an individual had been admitted to a mental hospital with a diagnosis of schizophrenia, his chance of discharge was low and sank lower with every year he stayed.

Erving Goffman,[51] whose formulation of 'the moral career of the mental patient' is roughly equivalent to Scheff's, is particularly associated with the attack on the old-fashioned mental hospital as a 'total institution'. Given the twin facts of a large patient population (many under compulsory orders at that time) and a small, inadequately trained staff, it was inevitable that procedures that were adopted for the control of a few potentially dangerous or disturbing patients should be generalized to the relatively amenable majority. The major function was to prevent a mentally ill individual from harming himself or others, and to ensure that he could not escape. Routines of supervision and control were developed which would leave nothing to chance; hence the railed airing-courts, the windows that would open only two inches, and the warning whistle that every nurse or attendant carried. This rule applied throughout the whole range of activity of the hospital. As Goffman points out, much time and trouble can be saved 'if everyone's soiled clothing can be indiscriminately placed in one bundle, and laundered clothing can be redistributed, not according to ownership, but according to rough size'. Goffman argued that mental hospitals, in these respects, were fairly characteristic of the class of organization he called 'total institutions', which included prisons, orphanages, and concentration camps—any place which threw up impermeable barriers between the inmates and the outside world. Staff and inmates came to have stereotyped views about each other, all sorts of institutional rituals developed out of the reward and punishment systems, and a special jargon became the symbol of an isolated and secret society.

Goffman's style is literary rather than scientific. He is a master of polemic and of the telling anecdote. He is compulsively readable and his papers have persuaded many people that mental hospitals are evil places. He is also worth reading for his lighter touches—the hospital entertainments given by visiting groups of artists in search of a captive audience; the annual 'open' day; the attitudes of other inmates to the 'trusties'; and the ways in which members of the management committee carried out their duties, pompous or pathetic, but always helpless in the face of institutional routines. No one who has taken part in the 'underlife' of a large institution (Goffman includes convents, battleships at sea, and residential schools under this heading) can fail to recognize the brilliance of his journalistic insight. Science is a different matter.

King, Raynes, and Tizard[85] used Goffman's ideas to quantify a number of factors (rigidity, block treatment, depersonalization, and social distance) in order to compare several residential units caring for severely mentally retarded children. They found that hospital units tended to be institutionally oriented compared with homes run by local authorities, which were more child oriented. This was not a matter of size, nor was it a matter of official bureaucracies. One of the important factors was the presence of nurses in the hospitals, who were less likely to spend their time with the children, caring and playing and supervising, because of their official duties. The child-care staff in the local authority hostels were more autonomous and less hierarchical in organization. Senior nurses, for example, might spend much of their time in the office or the kitchen attending to official duties, while house-mothers were able to organize their time more flexibly to suit the needs of the children. Albert Kushlick[89] has argued that these professional limitations are not essential and that nurses can take a house-mother role if trained appropriately, but the fact remains that a nurse's basic training will not fit her for some types of work, just as a house-mother would not be much use in an operating theatre.

Another British study[201] (referred to earlier in the description of the Wisconsin county hospital) attempted to test the hypothesis that if the social environments of mental hospitals were different the clinical condition of the long-stay patients should also be measurably different. During the early 1960s, a test of this hypothesis was possible in England because of the varied rates of improvement from the old-fashioned type of 'total' institution towards more therapeutic communities. (It is worth noting that this improvement had begun long before Goffman wrote his seminal article on total institutions. It was due to the pioneering efforts of a number of social psychiatrists who exploited the new opportunities provided by the introduction of a National Health Service, which integrated the mental hospitals into the general hospital system: see chapter 7.) This reform had taken two main lines; one the introduction of new ideas concerning rehabilitation and social treatment; the other concerned with early discharge and the prevention of admission. Some hospitals made more rapid progress than others, and thus it was possible to find three that were markedly different from each other.

Standard measurements confirmed that one, in particular, was outstanding in the poverty of the social environment provided for patients with schizophrenia (diagnosed according to a fairly strict concept). This hospital contained patients with the highest degree of negative impairments. Moreover, during the course of an eight-year project it was found that, as new measures of social stimulation were introduced, the negative impairments decreased. Thus intrinsic handicaps seemed to respond to changes in the social environment, at least to a certain extent.

In addition to this evidence of the effect of environment on intrinsic disabilities, attitudes towards discharge were found to change with length of stay: the longer a schizophrenic patient had been in hospital, the more likely he was to say that he wished to remain. This relationship did not change much during the eight years of the study. Only very specific re-education seemed to have much effect on it. This gradual acquiescence in the way of life of the hospital and gradual loosening of ties with the outside world, so that the inmate finally loses any desire to leave, lies at the heart of institutionalism.

Thus it has probably occurred in the past, and the opportunity may yet exist today, that someone who is not severely disturbed in behaviour, or whose disturbance might otherwise have been transitory, has been committed to a mental hospital, given a diagnosis of schizophrenia, and then kept in for years while secondary disadvantages accumulated, so that finally he was no longer fit to leave and did not wish to do so. The evidence for the early part of this chain of events is descriptive and to some extent subjective. No study of alternative disposals, e.g. to prison as compared with hospital, as a result of equivalent behaviour leading to a court appearance, has been made; nor of what would have happened if no action had been taken at all. However, if we suppose that the account given above is correct, it would seem to confirm Scheff's thesis.

We must, however, distinguish between two concepts of 'illness'. Which one does the theory explain, the social attribution or the restricted disease theory? Clearly it is the former. Scheff emphasizes that he is concerned only with a 'uniform' lay concept of 'madness'; and points out that when the psychiatrist formally adds a label such as 'schizophrenia', he does no more than legitimize the societal definition. No technical expertise need be involved at all. If we further agree that the end-state of institutionalism is sometimes itself regarded as evidence of schizophrenia, all the links in Scheff's chain of reasoning are complete. 'Society' has created 'schizophrenia'. One particular application of the radical form of Lemert's theory of social deviance has therefore survived a certain amount of testing without being disproved.

There is, however, a lot more to be said. At the moment, an element of passionate advocacy tends to limit the vision of the proponents of the theory, so that they see it only as a weapon with which to batter those they regard as enemies. It could be more useful than that, but only at the cost of giving up claims to total explanation of the phenomena of social deviance, including all those legitimately denoted by the term 'psychiatric disorder'. In the case of any particular application of the theory, a set of qualifying conditions needs to be put forward from which specific predictions can be made and tested. This is not how the theory has been used hitherto.

Moreover, it is important to consider what alternatives are available. We know that people admitted to any type of public institution tend to be poor, single or divorced, old, relatively unskilled occupationally, not very good at making social relationships, and so on. The more severe these disadvantages, the longer they are likely to stay, irrespective of the ostensible reason for admission. The demographic analysis made by Morton Kramer,[86] of people admitted to British general hospitals with conditions as

diverse as hernia or duodenal ulcer, is a remarkable demonstration of the importance of social factors in helping to determine
what might appear to be purely medical decisions. But this influence may, of course, be entirely reasonable. What the radical
labelling theorists have to show is under what circumstances
admission to an institution (or other form of social disposal) is
harmful, because of the unnecessary creation of a special category
of deviance, rather than beneficial. We have seen that something
of the kind probably did happen in some hospitals in the United
States, where the label of 'schizophrenia' was incorrectly applied.
We do not, however, know what would have happened to the same
individuals if, instead of incorrectly being labelled 'schizophrenic'
and, because this label was incorrectly thought to indicate the
impossibility of living outside an institution, being interned for a
prolonged period in hospital, they had been dealt with in some
alternative way. There were many options to choose from, not all
of them necessarily less damaging.

Whether the radical form of labelling theory proves to be very
limited in its explanatory power, or whether it can usefully be
applied in a wide variety of social situations, demands more precise
specification, and then empirical investigation, of a kind that has
not so far been undertaken. It is clear that it cannot be used to explain *all* admissions to mental hospitals, as the evidence given in
chapter 4 demonstrates. Still less can it be used to explain all
attributions of mental illness, even when the individual concerned
is not admitted. For example, no evidence can be produced to
show that children who experience unusual fears or show head
banging or the other behaviour mentioned by Scheff, are more
likely, after referral to child guidance clinics, to become chronically impaired because of the application of some label such as
'conduct disorder' or 'neurosis'. Most children treated for neurotic
symptoms become non-neurotic adults, as do most neurotic children not so treated.[146, 147] There is little evidence that treatment,
or labelling, makes much difference either way. In many such
cases, the label carries far less social significance than the behaviour
that was responsible for the referral to an official labelling agent.
The objections to a general radical labelling theory of delinquency
(see p. 146), apply *a fortiori* in the case of an equivalent explanation, applied in a sweeping way to some unitary concept of 'mental
illness' or 'madness'.

The moderate form of the theory of deviance, however, fits very well with restricted theories of illness or handicap. This is the form in which Lemert recognized that blindness, for example, could be a primary deviation. Similarly, the symptoms and disabilities of schizophrenia can be regarded as a basis for primary deviation, and the theory of secondary deviation then applies. Institutionalism can occur in someone who has properly been diagnosed as schizophrenic according to the narrow concept; perhaps it is even more likely to develop in such a person than in someone merely given the label although the central syndromes are not present. I prefer the terminology of intrinsic, secondary, and extrinsic handicaps, described in chapter 2, to describe these relationships, rather than that of primary and secondary deviance. The former is more flexible and contains fewer semantic traps.

Two factors contribute to a possible explanation of why the idea that labelling theory might be a substitute for disease theory has been so vigorously espoused. Both are characteristically north American. (There are, of course, exceptions to both.) Maurice Lorr,[109] a talented clinical psychologist, pointed out that 'in much of American psychiatry, formal diagnosis is actually ignored as relatively unimportant and outmoded, or disparaged as non-dynamic and useless'. He was driven to develop his own system of classification, using checklists of proved reliability and statistical techniques that yielded empirical groupings. The trouble was that the resulting categories looked remarkably similar to the diagnostic system he had tried to leave behind. The sociologist, even more remote from guidance by scientifically minded psychiatrists than the clinical psychologist, must also try to put forward an alternative theory. With only lay ideas of 'madness' to go on, plus experiences such as Scheff gathered in Wisconsin, any sociologist worth his salt would have to make an attempt. The second factor is the organization of clinical practice in the United States. As David Mechanic has pointed out, those who could afford it went to private psychiatrists and were treated by some form of psychoanalysis, while those who could not, but who were severely enough disordered or disabled to need protective care, were forced to use the state mental hospitals, admittedly a second-class system. There have, of course, always been plenty of exceptions but, by and large, during the period when the theory under review was being formulated, it must have been difficult to practise the kind of psychiatry advocated in this book.

Psychoanalytical models

Another kind of model that does not use disease theories, although it is put forward by doctors and uses medical terminology, is psychoanalytical. Theodore Lidz[107, 108] is the leading exponent of a school of thought that regards the development of schizophrenia as an inevitable hazard of growing up in certain kinds of family. The marriages of schizophrenogenic parents, according to him, are characterized by schism or by skew. If by schism, the parents are in open conflict, each selfishly pursuing some private fantasy and ignoring the real needs of the rest of the family. If by skew, one partner passively but resentfully accepts the dominant abnormality of the other, and conflict is covert rather than open. In either case, the normal growth of self-awareness and individuality in the child is inhibited, because the parents are unable to allow, let alone encourage, the development of a separate identity. 'The mother does not establish boundaries between herself and her child and fails to differentiate her own feelings and needs from those of her offspring.' Such a failure on the part of the mother is thought to be particularly damaging to boys, while an equivalent abnormality in fathers has a specially harmful effect on girls. 'In all of these families, the patient's emergence as an individual is thwarted by his subservience to the completion of a parent's life or to salvaging his parents' marriage.'

In his collected papers, and in more summary fashion in *The Origin and Treatment of Schizophrenic Disorders*, Lidz and his colleagues present work that has been carried out at Yale over more than twenty years. A good deal of weight is given to the double-bind theory developed by Gregory Bateson and his colleagues at Palo Alto, California, which suggests that the child who becomes schizophrenic is constantly subjected to parental communications that are directly or indirectly incompatible with each other and yet demand a response acceptable to the parents. Dr. Lidz has developed a rather more complex version of this theory to explain how distorted communications lead to—indeed, are—schizophrenia.

Nowhere in his published work does Lidz claim to have tested his theory. He simply elaborates it. The edifice is erected largely on the basis of observations on seventeen families, nearly all of whom were wealthy enough to pay for the patient to have prolonged psychoanalysis in hospital. It seems possible that these highly unrepresentative families were selected in part because of the degree of disturbance in their relationships with each other. Without an epidemiological context it is difficult to know. Moreover, the nature of this disturbance is described only in general terms. No precise criteria are laid down whereby other workers could attempt to repeat and test the observations. Egocentricity is common; schizophrenia is rare. We need more than the private intuitions of an expert therapist before theories of this generality can be established on a secure footing, particularly when other experts have suggested that different parental traits are the schizophrenogenic ones.

The double-bind theory is more useful because it is testable. It would seem relatively easy for two observers, independently listening to tape-recorded interviews, to arrive at similar judgements as to when and how often double-binds occurred. It would then be possible to demonstrate with some confidence whether they were found only or predominantly in families with a schizophrenic member. The following simple example of how to spring the trap is taken from Dan Greenburg's *How to be a Jewish Mother*:

Give your son Marvin two sportshirts as a present. The first time he wears one of them, look at him sadly and say in your Basic Tone of Voice: 'The other one you didn't like?'

If there is an intense relationship between mother and son, and if the son feels unable to comment on the ambiguity (or does not recognize it), there is no way of responding without giving the impression that he has rejected a loving parent.

Steven Hirsch and Julian Leff[70] have reviewed the various studies that have been made in order to determine whether it is possible for experts to agree when a double-bind is present, and if so, whether double-binds are commoner in the relationship between parent and schizophrenic offspring. The results are disappointingly negative. The experts themselves are unable to agree as to what constitutes a double-bind, and much of the work on frequency is methodologically inadequate. 'What tentative results there are suggest that double-bind messages are not specific to the parents of schizophrenics.'

L. Wynne and M. Singer[211, 212] carried out a series of experimental studies to test the wider theory that schizophrenia is transmitted from parent to child via 'communication deviances', of which the double-bind is only one example. They used the Rorschach test in order to demonstrate the deviances and found that it could be scored objectively and reliably by independent raters. They were able to distinguish very clearly between the parents of schizophrenic patients and those of neurotic patients or normals; in fact there was only one discrepant result out of 89 cases. The parents of 25 patients with 'borderline' schizophrenic conditions were split evenly as to high and low deviance scores. Hirsch and Leff criticized this work on methodological grounds and pointed out that the 'schizophrenic' patients included were highly selected (perhaps selected because there were abnormalities in family relationships) and probably included many who would not be regarded as schizophrenic according to a stricter definition. Their own attempt at replication, using a rigorous experimental design, unselected patients and specific diagnostic criteria, failed to reproduce the clear distinctions found by Singer and Wynne.

Hirsch and Leff concluded, from a survey of the literature and from their own work, that there is evidence that more parents of 'schizophrenic' patients are psychiatrically disturbed than parents of normals, that they show more conflict and disharmony, and that they are more often concerned and protective, but that these factors can equally well be explained by a genetic theory or as a reaction to abnormalities in the child. Taken together with the work described in chapter 4, showing the influence of current environmental factors on the course of schizophrenia, it is clear that we cannot confidently assert that the early environment model of aetiology is valid.

Lidz's claims, however, are made confidently and the reason may be that he defines schizophrenia tautologically in terms of an internalization of the processes, themselves undefined, that are supposed to cause it. Schizophrenia, for Lidz, is an egocentric over-inclusiveness. 'The patient typically believes that what others do or say centers on him . . . that he is the focal point of events that, in actuality, are fortuitous or coincidental to his life.' This definition is so broad that only the expert—in the last resort, only

Lidz himself—can tell us who is schizophrenic and who is not. By way of example, Lidz has diagnosed Isaac Newton in this way and, by implication, Tennessee Williams and Eugene O'Neill as well. The advantages to the theorist of such flexibility in definition are obvious, but we should consider the danger to others. This is where the labelling theorists can reasonably be critical.

Lidz's final judgement is that 'the families of schizophrenic patients fail in global ways to carry out the tasks requisite for the adequate personality development of their children.' He emphasizes they cannot help themselves: 'their noxious influences upon the patient are not malevolent but rather the products of their own personal tragedies and egocentric orientations'. The effect that such statements have upon relatives, many of whom are well aware of what is said about them, can be imagined.

The ideas of Theodore Lidz and other American writers have been built upon by Ronald Laing,[91] who says that '*without exception* the experience and behaviour that gets labelled schizophrenic is *a special strategy that a person invents in order to live in an unliveable situation*' (italics in original). Laing does also say, of the disease concept of schizophrenia, that 'to regard it as an hypothesis is legitimate', but he does not discuss the extensive literature concerned with testing this hypothesis. The only evidence he himself has brought forward is a series of case-histories published in 1964 in *Sanity, Madness and the Family*.[92] The material consists of a series of extracts from interviews with various combinations of family members, summaries and descriptions of other parts of the interviews, and a linking commentary. There were 14–50 hours of interview for each of eleven patients.

The study falls into that large group of uncontrolled investigations in which an enormous mass of information is collected in an unstandardized and unsystematic manner about a very small number of people. From this material a personal selection is made in order to illustrate a highly complex theoretical interpretation. The extracts from the interviews are included as demonstrations of a theory whose truth is regarded as revealed. There is no question of testing it. For example, Laing and his colleagues suggest that the parents of schizophrenics are unduly rigid in applying discipline, in toilet training, in limiting their children's social or sexual activities and in restricting or preventing their ability to become individuals in their own right. All these factors are susceptible of a degree of definition and quantification, so that their frequency in different types of family could be measured. In fact, no one has shown that they are commoner among the parents of people with schizophrenia than among other parents. The same is true of the process Laing calls 'mystification'; which consists of the parent saying one thing while doing another, and expecting the child to react to what is said rather than to what is done (i.e. it is a version of the 'double bind'). He does not feel it necessary to give any evidence that the process actually is commoner among families with a schizophrenic member.

Laing has made some bitter accusations against his own colleagues and the temptation to reply in kind must be very strong. Theodore Lidz[106] observes:

Laing's philosophy in *The Politics of Experience* is really a philosophy of despair rather than one of hope . . . Laing says that it is impossible to love—that is a personal problem of his, I think. In fact, one of the terrible things about *The Politics of Experience* is that Laing generalizes so much from his personal experiences.

And further:

A therapist who generalizes from his own devastating experiences with an intrusive and impervious mother to those of all mankind is as egocentrically oriented as the parents of schizophrenic patients.

This sophisticated psychoanalytical in-fighting casts no light on Laing's theories. Their truth does not depend on his personal characteristics, and their error cannot be demonstrated by descrying psychological idiosyncrasies which the critic does not like. What is needed is evidence, following adequate trial, that Laing's ideas are not false. So far no such evidence has been forthcoming, and we have been shown no reason why they should not be disregarded.

Two other well-known writers on mental illness are Thomas Szasz and Herbert Marcuse. Neither seriously attempts, any more than Ronald Laing does, to consider the evidence for limited disease theories summarized in chapters 3 and 4. The way that Szasz argues can be seen very clearly in a recent paper on schizophrenia.[177] He quotes the very general criteria deliberately used in the International Pilot Study of Schizophrenia to ensure that a wide range of conditions would be included in the series (including a substantial group that would not turn out to be schizophrenic), as though they were the criteria used by the investigators to define schizophrenia. In fact, the report comes to the very opposite conclusion; that certain very specific and restricted criteria are sufficient to identify, among this very broad spectrum, most of the conditions called schizophrenic by psychiatrists in nine different parts of the world (see chapter 4). Szasz's exposition of what the report said is completely false. The most charitable, and also the most credible, explanation, is that Szasz does not read anything that might tell him he is wrong. Sir Martin Roth,[150] in a devastating reply to the article, pointed out that Szasz himself, during a period of 30 years, had made numerous pronouncements about the care and treatment of patients. 'But in no case has he submitted his views to formal tests that could have disposed of them or substantiated them.'

The curious thing is that, every now and again, almost as it were by accident, Szasz does come very close to hitting a target that thoroughly deserves attack. We have seen that some people, psychiatrists among them, use the terminology of disease in spite of the fact that they regard the whole apparatus of disease classification, and the process of making a diagnosis, as a sterile waste of time. Such psychiatrists need a good deal of education in order to ensure that they do not use illness labels when no disease theory is usefully applicable. But this is to propose an increase in the skilled use of diagnosis, not its abolition. And the suggestion applies most forcefully to psychoanalysts such as Szasz himself. One of Laing's disciples,[9] for example, confused hysteria with schizophrenia in much the same way as Szasz did, when he published a famous account of the cure of a case of supposed schizophrenia by Laingian methods.

Herbert Marcuse,[113] more than any other critic, has combined the political with the pseudo-scientific approaches. In his book, *Negations*, he discusses the physiological and the psychological concepts of normality, assuming that the physician invariably tries to promote a positive concept of health, rather than concentrating on the mere treatment and prevention of disability. This formulation allows him to demonstrate that any definition of 'normality' is social in nature and that the psychiatrist can therefore act as an advocate or as a saboteur of the social system in which he lives. But suppose the society itself is 'sick'?

... we can say that a society is sick when its basic institutions and relations, its structure, are such that they do not permit the use of the available material and intellectual resources for the optimal development and satisfaction of individual needs.

This is a classical example of a non-definition. Everything depends on the way the word 'optimal' is used (a value-laden term if ever I saw one) and Marcuse will not enlighten us. He simply assumes that bourgeois society is 'sick' and develops a theory of 'surplus-repression' which he thinks explains how vested interests keep control of the minds of the population.

This situation cannot be solved within the framework of individual psychology and therapy, nor within the framework of any psychology— a solution can be envisaged only on the political level: in the struggle against society. To be sure, therapy could demonstrate this situation and prepare the mental ground for such a struggle—but then psychiatry would be a subversive undertaking.

This chain of spacious arguments brings Marcuse to the point at which he can accuse psychiatrists of failing because they have not adopted his political philosophy. The idea that a doctor should restrict himself to reducing disabilities and leave the definition of health to his patient, who might be a member of an opposing political party or of none, is regarded at best as quietist acquiescence in bourgeois capitalism and at worst as a criminal conspiracy. Like the psychoanalyst, the Marxist can regard any opposing view as itself evidence for his theory, as a pathetic attempt at defence against revealed truth. As expounded by certain practitioners (by no means all), the two philosophies are not as far apart as they might seem. Neither has a criterion of validation. The attitude of both can therefore be: 'Take it or leave it. Whose side are you on?'

These views, however ambiguous and illogical, have become fashionable, so that it is the done thing to quote them on any occasion when it is important to make an impression of being intellectually and socially up-to-the-minute. Karl Popper[133] long ago described this tendency and also the remedy:

It appears that irrationalism, in the sense of a doctrine or creed that does not propound connected and debatable arguments but rather propounds aphorisms and dogmatic statements which must be 'understood' or else left alone, will generally tend to become the property of an esoteric circle of the initiated . . . We must take the trouble to analyse the systems in some detail; we must show that we understand what the author means, but that what he means is not worth the effort to understand it.

Medical and sociological expansionism

David Mechanic[117] has analysed the two main uses of the term 'illness' in very much the same way as that used in this book (see pp. 19 and 140).

On the one hand, it refers to a limited scientific concept . . . on the other, to any condition which causes, or might usefully cause, an individual to concern himself with his symptoms and to seek help. The term 'illness behavior' refers to any behavior relevant to the second, more general, interpretation. If we are to understand the process of illness, it becomes necessary to consider what goes on even before a person sees a doctor or some other health worker.

Illness behaviour may be positive or negative. In the positive case, someone thinks he is ill and acts accordingly. In the negative case, someone avoids behaviour suggestive of illness. In either case, the behaviour may be congruent or discordant with that thought to be appropriate by a competent doctor. If discordant, the doctor will regard the people concerned as 'over-concerned' or 'under-concerned' about some aspect of disease. If congruent, he will approve of their behaviour, since they will seek and accept advice when there is evidence of disease, and will not continue to worry if there is no such evidence. The 'competent doctor' himself has prejudices with which an 'intelligent layman' may very reasonably disagree. The permutations available for a thorough sociological analysis are therefore very numerous.

One way to analyse them is to study the circumstances under which people actually do or do not consult their doctors and, having made a consultation, under what circumstances they accept advice, assuming that any advice has been given. A very considerable body of knowledge has been built up in this way (see, for example, the book by David Mechanic,[117] and the more recent book edited by David Tuckett[180]).

Medical sociology and social medicine deal with the same central subject matter. Their theories differ but complement each other. Medical sociology uses theories of social normality, departure from which is called deviance. Social medicine is based, in the last resort, on theories of normal biological functioning, departures from which may lead to disease. There is always some degree of interaction between social and biological factors, not only in the causation of deviance or disease, but in treatment, in prevention, and in long-term management. However, because of the many striking cases in which disease is clearly best dealt with in purely biological terms (at least so far as causes and treatments are concerned, though even here the purely social effects on the patient's self-attitudes and on the attitudes of his social group must be considered), some doctors have not resisted the temptation to regard medical sociology as of little relevance to their practice. Similarly, the many instances in which deviant behaviour appears to have purely social causes, and to need purely social interventions, have led many sociologists to suppose that disease theories are rarely relevant to social deviance.

In practice, as well as in theory, it is important that doctors should be aware of the motivations that bring patients to them, irrespective of whether medical treatment is indicated or not. It is just as important that social workers, who are also 'primary care' agents, should be able to decide, with a fair degree of competence, when the social problems with which they are presented are secondary to disease or to intrinsic handicap. In each case, the major problem for decision is how best to help the patient or client to overcome illness, handicap or disadvantage. Usually both medical and social elements will be involved. From the medical point of view, a terminology of intrinsic, secondary, and extrinsic impairments is appropriate. From the social point of view, the element due to illness may often be secondary or extrinsic. The concept of social treatment, management, and rehabilitation, unites the two points of view, because of the necessity constantly to assess and re-assess the goals of all the parties concerned—the individual with the problem, his close social group, and his professional helpers.

One reason why medical practices have come under criticism in recent years is that some psychiatrists use a term like 'schizophrenia' in a non-technical, virtually a lay, sense, and make and act on a diagnosis when there is no reason to suppose that a disease theory can usefully be applied. The broader their concept of 'schizophrenia' the more liable they are to make such mistakes. It is particularly in those parts of the world where historicist theories have been most influential that the scientific process of diagnosis has been least valued and, paradoxically, where the terminology of disease has been most readily applied to purely social deviations. This has led to a psychiatric expansionism which must indeed be criticized. Some sociologists observing such tendencies, especially in countries where the public psychiatric services are not very well developed, have jumped to the conclusion that no disease theory can ever be held to apply, but this is a clear case of throwing out the baby with the bath water. What they should be condemning is the misapplication of disease labels. They should be pressing for better diagnosis, not no diagnosis. Otherwise, sociologists are likely to be trapped into an expansionism of their own, just as irrational and damaging to the prospects of reducing disability and suffering as the one they are criticizing.

Disease theories of mental disorders, like other scientific theories, should be specific, restricted, and not amenable to generalization outside technically specifiable referents. They are not theories about mental illness in general, still less about mental or social health. There is nothing in such a diagnosis to suggest that the individual needs to be separated from his relatives or friends, regarded as socially irresponsible, segregated for years in an institution, made subject to legal restrictions, or dealt with as a pauper or a criminal or an incompetent. Before discussing these important matters in detail and considering the benefit that a scientific partnership between psychiatry and sociology might produce, it will be useful to consider one example in rather more detail. Chapter 6 will be devoted to criticisms made of Soviet psychiatry. We shall then be in a position, in chapter 7, to consider how far a limited but scientifically based psychiatry can contribute towards the solution of serious social problems.

6. Psychiatry and political dissent

> *What sort of times are these, when*
> *A conversation about trees is almost a crime,*
> *Because it implies a silence about so many outrages.*
> *He who quietly crosses the street over there:*
> *May he not already be out of reach of his friends,*
> *Who are in need?*
>
> Bertolt Brecht

Through western eyes

During the past few years many reports have been published in Western Europe and the United States concerning the internment in mental hospitals of political dissenters in the U.S.S.R. Although it is said that similar practices have occurred in other countries, there has been nothing to equal the publicity given to the alleged abuse of psychiatry in the Soviet Union. Much of the evidence has been drawn from reports in the underground *samizdat* ('self-published') literature. The main burden of criticism of Soviet psychiatrists has been that they have consciously aided political repression by making diagnoses of mental illness in cases where they knew no illness existed. Public opinion in the West has also reacted to the accounts of political repression by Alexander Solzhenitsyn, Evgenia Ginsburg, Anatoli Marchenko, and others. Because of an interest in the effects of institutions of all kinds on their inmates, I have long had an acquaintance with this literature.

In cases such as these it is clearly difficult to separate the specifically medical issues from the broader political context. Against such a background, it is easy to assume that any official activity connected with political dissent is intended to be repressive. Even a readiness to suspend judgement on the medical aspects of the problem sufficiently to make further inquiries carries the risk that the motivation for doing so will be misunderstood. Thus when in 1973 the opportunity came for me to attend a meeting organized by the World Psychiatric Association (WPA) in the Soviet Union, the subject of which was to be schizophrenia, the temptation to refuse and to make a comfortable protest from London was very strong. The trouble was, however, that it would not have been fair. In the public debate on the question that ensued, virtually no one in the West suggested that it might be right to go in order to discover the Soviet side of the case. However, two outstanding Russians, Andrei Sakharov and Zhores Medvedev, did make this point, and suggested a number of questions that needed to be answered. I decided, therefore, to go and to take the opportunity to raise these issues in my paper. (This may be why the proceedings were never published.) In the event, I was the only speaker to do so.

During the visit several scientists, including myself, were invited to the Serbsky Institute to attend 'a full and free professional discussion of the alleged abuse of psychiatry in the Soviet Union'. Several 'cases' of prominent dissenters were discussed and a consideration of these is given below. But before coming to the 'cases' themselves it is important to consider two underlying medico–legal problems. These are (1) the definition of crimes against the state, and (2) the definition of mental illness, particularly schizophrenia. These two definitions determine the point at which someone found to have committed a serious crime can be said to be non-responsible because he is mentally ill. Public attention has been focused mainly on the problem of responsibility and it is clear that Soviet is very different from Western practice.

Crimes against the State

In the Soviet Union, the public expression of views that are regarded as political slander is dealt with severely as a crime against the State.[141] The concept appears to be analogous to earlier concepts of treason or even of heresy. On 25 August 1968, seven brave people raised banners in Red Square, Moscow, protesting against the Soviet invasion of Czechoslovakia.[55] This restrained and orderly demonstration took place in a part of the Square that was closed to traffic and lasted only a few minutes. The demonstrators were doing no more than any Hyde Park orator in London may freely do, at any time and for as long as he chooses. They claimed that they were not breaking any Soviet law but they were charged with deliberately fabricating slanders discrediting the Soviet political system. The five who were convicted were sentenced to between three and five years imprisonment or to exile. Vadim Delone, Konstantin Babitsky, and Larissa Daniel received fixed sentences and were eventually released. Vladimir Dremlyuga has only recently been released after his three-year sentence in a Siberian labour camp had been doubled for allegedly spreading slander among the inmates. Pavel Litvinov was banished from the Soviet Union after his release. Two others, Natalia Gorbanevskaya and Victor Fainberg, were regarded as non-responsible because of 'schizophrenia' and served a similar period of time in special psychiatric hospitals before being allowed to emigrate. Their fate, and that of many others like them, has led to accusations that the psychiatrists concerned were influenced by political considerations in making their diagnoses and thus were consciously aiding repression. The prosecution did not claim that any of the seven demonstrators had used or plotted violence. Their offence was their public declaration of political dissent; by definition, a socially dangerous act.

Many western countries have gradually and painfully acquired a toleration of political dissent and an appreciation of its value. The opportunity to denounce established views, freely, vigorously, and in public, is regarded as the very foundation of political democracy in Great Britain and the U.S.A. We no longer regard unusual ideas, even when expressed without restraint, with horror or distress, as we should have done in the seventeenth century. There is no need, therefore, for us to apply concepts such as treason, heresy, or illness in such cases. The last people to be executed for treason in Great Britain were William Joyce and John Amery[188] who had broadcast for the Nazis during the war. No psychiatric evidence was heard. The law on treason is old-fashioned and difficult to apply, not least because of the automatic penalty of death, and it is hardly ever used in peacetime. There have been charges under the Official Secrets Act, usually for handing classified information to foreign governments in a manner prejudicial to the safety of the interests of the State. We try to make a distinction between offences of this kind and political activity, though sometimes the distinction is difficult to draw and the Government is criticized in consequence. But even if political activity involves the advocacy of an independent Welsh or Scottish state, it is not

regarded as a matter for legal restrictions. It is open to anyone to
establish a party, to hold peaceful meetings and demonstrations,
and to publish bitter attacks on the Government's philosophy and
practice, if he wishes to do so.

The first problem encountered, therefore, by a westerner who
tries to understand Soviet medico–legal practice is that the actions
for which dissenters are incarcerated are not, by our standards,
crimes at all, and seem to pose no serious threat to the State. This
inevitably introduces a political element into the assessment; more
than that, a historical perspective becomes obligatory. To appreciate the problems of free-thinkers who criticize the basic dogmas of
Marxism and do battle with the gigantic Soviet bureaucracy, it may
be useful to make a comparison, not with recent relationships
between governments and dissenters in western countries but with
the threat posed by Galileo to religious orthodoxy in the sixteenth
century.

Giorgio de Santillana[154] said of the Catholic Church at that time:
'The working of great administrations is mainly the result of a vast
mass of routine, petty malice, self-interest, carelessness, and sheer
mistake. Only a residual fraction is thought.' Some people learn to
work the system, some speak out in protest, some work quietly to
change it, most simply conform. An element in heretics of sublime
self-confidence, and a nonconformity in behaviour as well as in
thought, are particularly provocative to orthodox believers and
administrators. Many progressive churchmen and scientists were
charged with heresy, or avoided that charge, according to the
skill with which they expressed their innovatory ideas. Galileo
challenged the Church on its own ground and his criticisms, expressed with consummate skill, cut very close to the bone. But
he laid himself open to his conservative enemies. 'The truth
of the Galileo affair,' says Santillana, 'is that a few individuals
manipulated events in order to bring about the solution they
desired. The Church, including the Commissary-General of
the Inquisition himself, must be absolved from the charge of bad
faith.'

It should be unnecessary to remark that Santillana was looking through the eyes of seventeenth-century orthodoxy when he
made this judgement. He was not condoning the practices of the
Inquisition. But the historical or anthropological approach
does not permit a moral examination of the system that could be

manipulated in this way. It is as though we were considering a particularly interesting example of decapitation in a society of head-hunters.

Dr. Pavel Litvinov,[55] one of the Red Square demonstrators, singled out the central weaknesses of all such totalitarian systems. He argued at his trial that the prosecution had incorrectly quoted Article 125 of the Soviet Constitution, which states:

... that in the interests of the workers and with the object of strengthening the socialist system, citizens of the U.S.S.R. are guaranteed freedom of speech, freedom of the press, freedom of assembly, meetings and demonstrations'. But in the Prosecutor's version these freedoms are guaranteed only *inasmuch as* they serve to strengthen the socialist system ... If one were to accept such an interpretation, who is to decide what is and what is not in the interests of the socialist system? The citizen Prosecutor, perhaps?

The Prosecutor calls what we did a disorderly assembly, we call it a peaceful demonstration. The Prosecutor speaks with approval, almost of tenderness, of the actions of those who detained, insulted and struck us ... It is obviously these very people who decide what is socialism and what is counter-revolution.

That is what frightens me. This is what I have fought and will continue to fight with all the lawful means known to me.

In the rest of this chapter, I shall try to avoid political comment and to concentrate on the psychiatric issues raised by the fact that some of the dissenters, perhaps one-fifth of those whose names are known in the West,[141] have been diagnosed as mentally ill.

The concept of schizophrenia

The International Pilot Study of Schizophrenia[209] (see chapter 4) demonstrated that there was little difference between psychiatrists working in various parts of the world so far as a relatively narrow diagnostic concept was concerned. This was as true of Moscow as of the other centres. But while, in seven of them, psychiatrists restricted themselves mainly to this relatively narrow concept of schizophrenia, in two—Moscow and Washington—they used the term to cover other conditions as well; in particular, to changes in personality and nonconformities in behaviour.

Consider by way of example the following case-summary:

A 27 year-old unemployed woman, separated from her husband, living in Moscow. No family history of mental disorder. Parents divorced. Childhood: motor development poor, fears of the dark, aged 3–7. Play monotonous and repetitive, e.g. rocking for hours. Reserved, few friends. Normal progress in school until about 11 years old, when she lost interest and often truanted without parents' knowledge. Stubborn and rude to parents; often out late with boys, smoking and drinking. Mother over-protective; once cut daughter's hair which provoked rudeness, obscenity and violence. On complaint of truanting from headmistress, put into mental hospital aged 14½. Refused treatment with phenothiazine drugs. Discharged two months later (diagnosis: abnormal personality). After discharge she slept during the day and went out with boys in the evenings. Began sexual intercourse at 16. Then a period of relative improvement occurred; she finished school and began work as a seamstress but subsequently returned to her former ways. Became pregnant and refused an abortion but then would not care for the baby, who was looked after by a grandmother. Had a second child at the age of 25 but immediately gave it to a children's home where it died. She then became interested in hippies 'in foolish clothes and strange beards', shortly afterwards being admitted to hospital because of aggression towards her mother. Again had gonorrhoea.

The diagnosis in this case was 'continuous form of schizophrenia, heboidophrenia'. An American psychiatrist, who was familiar with the complete case-history, diagnosed 'pseudo-neurotic or borderline schizophrenia'. Such a diagnosis would be much less likely (though not impossible) in Britain. The early history suggests that she was able to get by at school until the age of 11, because only rote learning was required, but that after that age cognitive impairments prevented adjustment to ordinary social and family expectations. She might have done better in a special day-school, particularly if her mother could have been helped to understand her difficulties. These diagnostic problems do not involve any question of political dissent, which was not a factor in the case.

Here is a clinical description of the 'mild progressive form of attack-like schizophrenia', paraphrased from a document on the system of sub-classification used at Professor A. V. Snezhnevsky's Institute of Psychiatry in Moscow:

The onset often occurs during puberty with emotional instability, problems of self-definition, odd interests and preoccupation with the meaning of life. Neurotic and obsessional symptoms, over-valued ideas, and paranoial phenomena occur, at first on occasions, subsequently more durably. The paranoial and over-valued ideas include sensitive ideas of reference, 'metaphysical intoxication' and unrealistic pre-occupation with special philosophical concepts without showing much talent. True delusion formation is rare during the early years. Attacks of depression and hypomania may subsequently occur, the latter with delusional ideas of an expansive character (invention, reformation, grandeur). After 15 years or so emotional blunting becomes more obvious but the patients are able to work and study.

Anyone who knows anything about the history of psychiatry will recognize this kind of classificatory exercise, which can be matched in the literature of every country with a psychiatric school. Compare it, for example, with the following description of 'simple schizophrenia' taken from a British textbook:[165]

The picture progresses over years leading slowly to destruction of the personality. In early phases, only an unexpected lack of consideration for the closest relatives and friends, or a reckless neglect of social obligations, may be conspicuous. The patient may even preserve a colourless amiability among strangers, but all deeper feeling seems lost . . . Many ineffectual, talentless and sterile dilettanti are simple schizophrenics, as also are the hangers-on of harmless sects and philosophies . . .

To scientifically minded psychiatrists, detailed systems of sub-classification have an old-fashioned air. The clinical descriptions are full of vague terms, very difficult to define operationally and therefore difficult to recognize reliably. Tests of validity are virtually impossible over a 15-year period. However, we are still on familiar clinical territory. The clash between the modern clinical scientist and the traditional physician supported by years of experience and authority is going on all over the world, and one often sees both tendencies represented in the same individual. Although certain countries may be in the forefront of particular movements, representatives of all sides of the controversy can be found everywhere.

Such arguments might be regarded as academic were it not for the fact that a diagnosis of 'schizophrenia' can carry the implications discussed in chapter 5: admission to hospital, perhaps compulsorily, the use of powerful drugs, and exposure to a possibly authoritarian hospital regime which imposes its own values on the inmate and, through the attribution of a sick role, may lead to a self-image of impairment and dependence. Such considerations are not of course so serious when the diagnosis is made on the basis of an acute attack, characterized by symptoms of the central condition which is recognized by psychiatrists all over the world. In such cases failure to treat is likely to lead to far more damage than treatment. On the other hand, a broader definition, which leads to the diagnosis being given to people like the woman described in the case-summary on page 172, inevitably takes into consideration behaviour and attitudes that are much more difficult to differentiate from normal. Once the diagnosis is made, decisions concerning responsibility and treatment may follow as though the individual concerned were suffering from a much more severe and lasting impairment. Precisely this point is made in films such as *Family Life* and *One flew over the cuckoo's nest*, which have given rise to a public fear that all 'schizophrenia' (and, indeed, all mental illness) is diagnosed in this way. That imputation is quite unjustified; but the fact remains that, while psychiatrists agree on a large central group of schizophrenias, they differ among themselves as to how much more than this should be called 'schizophrenic'. Moreover, the broader definition is commoner in some parts of the world than in others. It is therefore important to distinguish between the 'central' group universally regarded as schizophrenic and the more peripheral groups.

According to the most recent work, it is possible to set aside the central group of schizophrenias with a fair degree of accuracy and reliability. Some varieties of paranoid psychosis can also be recognized reliably if standard techniques are used. 'Paranoid personality' is a much more difficult concept. Nevertheless, even here, there are conditions that most psychiatrists recognize. Paranoia querulans is an example. A touchy and sensitive individual, egocentric and rather rigid, may suffer a fancied injustice (or sometimes a real one). He begins to devote his whole energy to trying to put the matter right. His life then has no meaning except in terms of the struggle. Eventually he may waste all his assets on litigation. He may have cranky ideas on many issues, some of them political. The fact that no one else agrees with him does not affect his view. Is he 'abnormal' or not? Is he 'psychotic' or not? If he commits an offence in connection with his unusual ideas (whether political or not), can he be regarded as responsible? Psychiatrists have often been called upon to try to answer such questions and, in the case of the last one, have come to different conclusions. There are also famous cases in fiction, such as Kleist's Michael Kohlhaas and Trollope's Robert Kennedy.

In a letter published in *The Guardian* on 29 September 1973, 21 leading Soviet psychiatrists blankly denied all the charges against them but made one considered argument:

There is a small number of mental cases whose disease, as a result of a mental derangement, paranoia, and other psycho-pathological symptoms, can lead them to anti-social actions which fall in the category of those that are prohibited by law, such as disturbance of public order, dissemination of slander, manifestation of aggressive intentions, etc. It is noteworthy that they can do this after preliminary preparations, with 'a cunningly calculated plan of action' . . . To the people around them such mental cases do not create the impression of being obviously 'insane'. Most often, these are people suffering from schizophrenia or a paranoid pathological development of the personality. Such cases are known well both by Soviet and foreign psychiatrists. The seeming normality of such sick persons when they commit socially dangerous actions is used by anti-Soviet propaganda for slanderous contentions that these persons are not suffering from a mental disorder.

The Soviet claim was that *some* ideological dissenters (Natalia Gorbanevskaya but not Pavel Litvinov, Zhores but not Roy Medvedev, Leonid Plyushch but not, on the last occasion, Vladimir Bukovsky) were suffering from disorders of this kind, and that their 'anti-social' opinions and activities were due to mental illness rather than to a process of intellectual political analysis and rationally based disagreement.[122] If this claim were valid, the principles involved would not be essentially different from those determining western medico-legal practice. It is difficult to test it against comparable western examples because the concept of 'crimes against the state' has been applied virtually only in wartime. It is nevertheless instructive to consider, first of all, two people who were accused of treason, one by an American and one by a Norwegian court, and whose culpability was regarded as diminished because of evidence submitted about their psychiatric state. Following this, three of the famous Russian 'cases' will be considered in the same way.

Ezra Pound

Ezra Pound was a poet of genius, a creative translator, and an extraordinarily successful promoter of other writers' talents.[172]

His views on usury, which he thought caused all the problems that beset mankind, came to him in a blinding flash of revelation in 1916. He began to express strongly anti-semitic views about the way the world's finances were controlled. He went to live in Rapallo and became strongly attracted to fascist and Nazi ideas. 'There is too much future and only me and Muss to attend to it.' During the Second World War he lived in Italy and made more than a hundred broadcasts for Mussolini's government. Many of these quite clearly advocated a fascist programme of action. In a broadcast to Britain he said, 'You let in the Jew and the Jew rotted your Empire.' He was indicted for treason in July 1943. When the Allies advanced into northern Italy in 1945, Pound gave himself up and was returned to the United States to face trial. Interviewed by an American reporter on 8 May 1945, Pound defended his views: 'If a man valued his beliefs, he valued them enough to die for them, and if they were worth having at all, they were worth expressing.'[67]

When it came to the trial, however, Pound's lawyer discussed with him the possibility of pleading insanity, and Pound made no objection. Four doctors were appointed to examine him, three chosen by the Government and one by the defence. The examination took a week and the report was unanimous that Pound was insane and unfit for trial.

At the present time he exhibits extremely poor judgement as to his situation, its seriousness, and the manner in which the charges are to be met. He insists that his broadcasts were not treasonable, but that all of his radio activities have stemmed from his self-appointed mission to 'save the constitution'. He is abnormally grandiose, is expansive and exuberant in manner, exhibiting pressure of speech, discursiveness and distractibility. In our opinion, with advancing years his personality, for many years abnormal, has undergone further distortion to the extent that he is now suffering from a paranoid state which renders him mentally unfit to advise properly with counsel or to participate intelligently and reasonably in his own defence. He is, in other words, insane and mentally unfit for trial, and is in need of care in a mental hospital.

Pound was sent to St. Elizabeth's Hospital and kept in close proximity with mentally ill people. He referred to his ward as a 'hell-hole'. The court hearing took place on 13 February 1946 (Pound's lawyer[30] has written an account of it). Government lawyers cross-examined the four doctors but did not shake their opinion. The psychiatrist selected by the defence, Dr. Wendell Muncie, had no doubt that Pound had a set of systematized delusions about the world and about his own powers. The defence lawyer said later that several doctors at St. Elizabeth's had regarded Pound as merely eccentric and thought that he was able to stand trial; however, they were not called.

The poet was found to be of unsound mind and spent the next twelve years in St. Elizabeth's. The indictment was then dismissed and Pound was released, at the age of 72. He died in Venice in November 1972. If he had been found guilty of treason he would have risked execution 26 years earlier.

The evidence that Pound was so seriously mentally ill that he could not have instructed counsel and stood his trial is not conclusive. His views on politics and economics were unusual and idiosyncratic, and even the Italian fascists he admired had thought him odd, but this does not constitute evidence for insanity. It is impossible to say how much the medical report on Pound was influenced by knowledge of his genius and by the severity of the penalty for treason. A great deal of responsibility rested on the clinical judgement of the four doctors. Further discussion will be withheld until the other 'cases' have been considered.

Knut Hamsun

Knut Hamsun, the Norwegian novelist, was accused of treason in 1945; specifically of having become a member of the Quisling Party and of carrying on intensive propaganda for the Party and for the German invaders against the legal Norwegian government. He was arrested in June 1945 and, because of his age (86), placed in a local hospital and later in a geriatric home. After four months he was transferred to the University Psychiatric Clinic in Oslo. The preliminary examination* indicated that there were mild mental changes of a kind common in the senium, leading to some doubt as to his legal responsibility. It is in any case very unlikely that the court would have sent him to prison at his age (the sentence would probably otherwise have been 2–4 years). Thus, the final psychiatric opinion, to the effect that Hamsun was not insane, though there were senile changes which accounted for his poor

---

* I am indebted to Professor Ønulv Ødegård for an account of these proceedings.

judgement in taking part in political activities during the occupation, probably had little relevance to the outcome. He was found
guilty of treason and fined.

The principles at issue in this case are nevertheless of interest.
Hamsun was not regarded as insane and he was therefore convicted.
If his offence had been punishable by death, would the judgement
of the psychiatrists have been different or, for that matter, would
the court have found some way of mitigating the penalty for an old
man of 86? It is difficult to predict, when the offence is political,
the penalty severe, and the evidence for mental disorder marginal,
how any of the parties will react. Their personal beliefs must surely
play some part. Hamsun's political activities were considered to be
related to his mental condition.

We may now consider the three famous Russian 'cases'. The
people concerned have all written about their experiences, so that
no problem of confidentiality arises. All three were discussed at a
meeting of Western and Soviet psychiatrists at the Serbsky
Institute of Forensic Psychiatry in Moscow on 15 October 1973.

Zhores Medvedev

The case of Zhores Medvedev[119] is perhaps the most famous of
those publicized in the West. Briefly, this well-known biologist
had, in widely circulated books, criticized the 'geneticist' Lysenko
and had also stated his forthright disagreement with restrictions on
communication with scientists abroad. He said that his dismissal
from his position as head of a laboratory at the Institute of Medical
Radiology had been illegal. Subsequently he was compulsorily
admitted to a mental hospital on a civil order although he had no
mental illness at all and was charged with no crime. He was
released as a result of the intervention of influential friends. The
diagnosis in the case-notes was 'incipient schizophrenia'. The
psychiatric commission made a diagnosis of psychopathic personality with paranoid tendencies. Subsequently, Medvedev was
expected to attend a psychiatric follow-up clinic. He did not do so
and eventually was allowed to accept an invitation to work in
England. While there he was deprived of his Soviet citizenship.

The account given at the Serbsky Institute was similar in its
main outlines but the interpretation was different. For example,
the reason given for calling Medvedev for examination was that an

investigation had to be held as to why he had been unemployed so long (it is illegal to be unemployed in the Soviet Union) in order to determine whether he should receive an invalidity pension. When he refused, an error was made by the local doctors, who should not have hospitalized him compulsorily but should have proceeded more cautiously. It was emphasized that no violence was used during the admission; the police were there only because they had been called by Medvedev's wife. The psychiatric commission recommended his discharge, and he left hospital after three weeks.

Zhores Medvedev[118] himself stands by his original account. The two brothers explained the reasons why psychiatrists became involved in this and other cases as follows: first to discredit political dissenters; second, to avoid the publicity of a trial on a charge that was manifestly absurd; third, to make use of the fact that offenders could be kept in hospital indefinitely. Perhaps because of the publicity given to the case of Zhores Medvedev, few other examples in which the civil, rather than the criminal, law has been invoked, have been reported.

Natalia Gorbanevskaya

A report on the forensic psychiatric examination of Natalia Gorbanevskaya on 6 April 1970 was published in English as an appendix to a volume of her poems.[56] The account given on the occasion of the visit by western psychiatrists to the Serbsky Institute did not differ in any substantial way from this, except that the conclusion of a psychiatric commission on 19 November 1969, to the effect that there were no grounds for a diagnosis of schizophrenia, was not mentioned. The diagnosis then made was 'psychopathic personality with symptoms of hysteria'.

In essence, the picture presented to us was of a girl given to disagreement with her relatives and to erratic and impulsive behaviour (for which she was expelled from University), who complained of socially limiting anxiety symptoms (in particular, a phobia of heights and, later, a burning sensation in the fingers) and of depression with occasional suicidal thoughts. At the age of 21 she was said to have 'heard voices' for two weeks. She had two illegitimate children but made no lasting relationships with men. A diagnosis of 'schizophrenia' was first made in October 1959, many years before her first act of political dissent, and she was then admitted to hospital voluntarily for two weeks. After 1960 she improved, and there was no further psychiatric contact. In February 1968 she was admitted to a maternity hospital because of a threatened miscarriage and was briefly transferred to Kashchenko mental hospital because of what the psychiatrist who examined her regarded as a risk of suicide. She was depressed and had not wanted to eat. She was discharged a week later. The baby was born in May 1968.

In October 1968 the famous demonstration in Red Square took place. She was required to attend the Serbsky Institute as an out-patient while being examined by the expert commission. She was found non-accountable but was not thought to need admission to hospital. However, following further political activity, including the writing of *Red Square at Noon*[55] and the report of an expert commission in April 1970 which recommended compulsory hospitalization 'in connection with repetitive socially dangerous behaviour', she was sent to a special psychiatric hospital where she remained for almost two years. The diagnosis was sluggish schizophrenia. She was discharged in February 1972 in a 'stable therapeutic remission' and lived at home in Moscow working as a translator. In 1974 she applied to emigrate but was refused permission. In 1975 she applied again and this time permission was granted.

Her medical reports did not mention that she is a poet who has received favourable notices for her writing. In an 'open letter to Soviet psychiatrists', also published as an appendix to the *Selected Poems*, two friends stated: 'What has happened to Natasha unfortunately convinces us, not that our psychiatrists are insufficiently qualified doctors, but that they can make a wrong diagnosis *on purpose*.'

Leonid Plyushch

The case of Leonid Plyushch[84] will be considered in rather more detail because in many ways it is crucial to an understanding of Soviet psychiatrists' reactions to political dissent.

Plyushch was born in 1939 at Naryn, in the Kirghiz Republic of Central Asia. His father, a civil servant, disappeared in 1941. His mother worked as a cleaner. In 1962, Plyushch graduated from Kiev University and began work as an engineer-mathematician in the Cybernetics Institute of the Ukrainian S.S.R. Academy of Sciences. He constructed a mathematical model of the biological system regulating blood sugar and published an article on the organization of neuron-structures. After being a Stalinist in his teens, he was encouraged by Khrushchev's reforms to consider more liberal views of Marxism. In 1964, after the fall of Khrushchev, he wrote a letter to the Central Committee of the Communist Party in which he put forward ideas about the democratization of the Soviet Union. The letter fell into the hands of the KGB who asked him to refrain from writing such documents for a period of two years. He retained his job and even continued as a political teacher. In 1966 he began to write *samizdat* articles about the nature of the Soviet state and its ideology and about the problems of nationalities in the U.S.S.R. He considered that a gradual democratization of the country was required, through reforms from above and the propagation of democratic ideas among the people.

He was regarded as a creative and conscientious worker by the head of his department, who gave him a testimonial to that effect early in 1968. There is no evidence that anyone at that time regarded him as in any way abnormal. In March 1968, Plyushch wrote an open letter to the editors of *Komsomolskaya Pravda*, in which he denounced the new wave of political trials. It is clear from the letter that he was thoroughly familiar with *samizdat* literature, and had read *Cancer Ward, The First Circle,* and *Candle in the Wind.* In July 1968, he was dismissed from his post at the Cybernetics Institute and was unable to find other work.

Together with other political dissenters, Plyushch signed letters to Brezhnev (9 October 1968) and the U.N. Commission on Human Rights (20 May 1969). He also signed an open declaration concerning such matters as the invasion of Czechoslovakia, the suppression of peaceful demonstrations, and political trials (20 August 1969). He became a founder-member of the Moscow-based Initiative Group for the Defence of Human Rights in the U.S.S.R., the first group of its kind to be set up in the Soviet Union for over 40 years. This resulted in his dismissal from a temporary job he had taken as a bookbinder. He was interrogated several times in connection with the trial of other dissenters and was finally himself arrested in Kiev on 15 January 1972, at the age of 33. The charge was 'anti-Soviet agitation and propaganda'.

Soon after his arrest, he was allowed to write one letter from prison, dated 20 January 1972, to his wife The letter has been published in full[84] and shows no evidence of thought disorder or other impairment. Not only does it demonstrate his intellectual clarity but it is full of feeling for his family and is totally free from self-pity.

In May 1972, Plyushch was sent from his Kiev prison to the Lefortovo prison in Moscow, where he was held for six months. He appeared before two psychiatric commissions, the first chaired by Dr. Lunts, the second by Professor Snezhnevsky. The diagnosis of both commissions was sluggish schizophrenia from an early age. The case was heard in a Kiev court in January 1973. Plyushch himself was not present, nor were his wife or sister, except for the reading of the decision. The investigation had lasted for a year and necessitated a special decision of the Supreme Soviet of the U.S.S.R. since, legally, provision is only made for extending the normal two-month period to six months. During that time, Plyushch had one meeting with his defence lawyer and none with his wife. He was not allowed to see the materials of his case as other detainees would be. His wife addressed an open letter, dated 14 February 1973, to Professor A. V. Snezhnevsky, chairman of the committee from the Serbsky Institute which had reported on the case. She asked whether it would not have been possible to arrest Jesus Christ or Leo Tolstoy on the basis of the same offences which her husband was supposed to have committed. After 14 years of married life, she could say that her husband was absolutely normal mentally and that she was proud of his independence of spirit. In April 1973, following an appeal, the Ukrainian Supreme Court revised the decision of the lower court and ordered Plyushch to be sent to an ordinary psychiatric hospital. However, this judgement was in turn contested because 'of the extreme social danger of his anti-Soviet acts'. From July 1973 to January 1976 he was interned in the Dniepropetrovsk 'special' mental hospital, an old Czarist prison, complete with barbed wire, soldiers, searchlights, and dogs. His account of this period is harrowing and suggests that the standards of medical and nursing care were low. He was given haloperidol and other drugs commonly used in the treatment of schizophrenia, but he regarded this as a punishment rather than as a therapy. He reported that he 'deteriorated intellectually, morally and emotionally from day to day. My interest in political problems quickly disappeared, then my interest in scientific problems, and then my interest in my wife and children. My speech became jerky and abrupt. My memory also deteriorated.' The orderlies in the hospital were criminals serving out their sentences, who required rewards from the patients (e.g. groceries from their parcels from home) in return for small 'favours' such as an extra visit to the lavatory. The parallels with Goffman's account of the underlife of a large, and very poor, institution are striking.

Throughout this ordeal, Plyushch's wife, Tatyana Zhitnikova, was able to continue at work, although constantly harassed by the authorities. She received help from friends and from abroad. For a brief period, one of her children was excluded from school because of alleged 'Tolstoyan propaganda' but, after the affair became known overseas, he was reinstated, although neither boy joined the official youth organizations. After that, 'the attitude of everyone, including the teachers, was very correct. . . . I think it was the fact that the Plyushch affair was so famous that served to protect the children, for I know plenty of people in whom no one is interested and whose children suffer the effects of the harassment of their parents.'

At the meeting which I attended at the Serbsky Institute in October 1973, the official account of Plyushch's condition (derived from my notes of the simultaneous translation) was as follows:

From the age of 15, Plyushch was interested in politics and philosophy and decided to fight against the remains of imperialism in this country. He trained himself by 'training his will, fighting with his softness and ambition'. Aged 23, he graduated as a mathematician.

He decided, while studying, to reconstruct the Communist Party and reorganize the Komsomol. He thought he had outstanding ability. He had lots of new ideas about clothes and music, and was also preoccupied with thoughts about hypnosis. He believed that people could perceive thoughts through breathing. He wrote many manuscripts. He overestimated himself and thought he had solved problems of great importance for humanity. He sought to have followers, to be called 'Plyushchists'. He complained: 'The head is pushed from its axis—I am becoming mental.'

After graduation, he became an engineer. His interests were in philosophy, psychology, telepathy, biology, and later he also became interested in the arts, literature, and the treatment of stammering. He was fussy and suspicious, and passive and indifferent at work. He lost his office pass and was reprimanded. He complained that he was deprived of his human rights and said the government wanted to kill people. His aim was to restore Soviet power. His wife thought him normal but his mother thought him strange; he did not look after his children, his appearance or his clothes.

After his arrest, he was examined by a psychiatric commission on 14 July 1972. He was not anxious over the arrest, thought that there would be radical changes in the country which would prove his views on the world and his policies correct. He said he wished to accelerate the coming of democracy in this country by protesting, for the sake of communism.

On 7 September 1972 he had a further psychiatric examination. He did not try to establish his rightness. He did not regret that he was arrested and was more interested in the problem of integral psychology. His attitude to the future was indifferent. He showed no concern about his family. The conclusion of the commission was that he was suffering from schizophrenia, that he was not responsible for his actions and that he needed treatment in a general psychiatric hospital.

Presumably this account contains all the positive evidence of schizophrenia that could be culled from the lifetime of this bright young mathematician. It does not amount to very much when it is recalled that his wife and friends regarded him as completely normal, letters written at the time of examination show him to have been coherent and highly intelligent, and those who have known him since his departure from the Soviet Union have not remarked any abnormality. The assumption that his ideas about reforming society were delusional in nature is completely unacceptable in the absence of any technical evidence. No justification is therefore apparent for the decision that Plyushch was unable to instruct a lawyer, see his wife regularly, or defend himself at his trial. Protests from all over the world mounted, and the participation of the French Communist Party may have been decisive in obtaining Plyushch's release. He arrived in Paris in January 1976. On 26 March 1976, he met a group of psychiatrists at the New York Academy of Sciences. He thought that the reason he was treated as insane, rather than as criminally responsible, was that he refused to answer questions or cooperate in the investigation. 'So they had no way of knowing how I would behave in court.' Another reason was that as a Marxist himself, 'I could dispute points using the same terminology they used. For example, I had criticized the high salaries of Soviet government officials by citing Lenin; they should have the same pay as average workers . . . they are very uneasy facing court proceedings in which a Marxist would demonstrate that they are at fault . . . That's why they didn't try Medvedev and Grigorenko, who were also Marxists.'

In reply to a question about how far public opinion accepted the psychiatric diagnoses, Plyushch remarked that he had heard many Communist Party members say, of Sakharov and Grigorenko, that 'they must be crazy to give up high status and privileges. Many psychiatrists in the special hospitals think along the same lines. Among these doctors, one of the main criteria of mental illness is maladaption. They tell you: you couldn't adapt to a situation, you risked your own and your family's life, so you must be abnormal. I contested that by citing the example of the Bolsheviks. The response of the doctors was: so you consider yourself the equal of Lenin, that is the grandiose feature of your condition.'

Dr. Alfred Freedman, who had been present at the Serbsky Institute meeting in October 1973, asked a number of pertinent questions concerning the case-history given there. Plyushch said that his mother had denied calling him eccentric. In his teens, he had been a Stalinist, and very vain, but later regretted these ideas. He had kept a diary that included a reference to a friend who had been enthusiastic about his views, whom he called, ironically, a 'Plyushchist'. Much of the material about his supposed abnormality had come from this diary. He gave an example of a conversation with a doctor at the Dniepropetrovsk hospital, during which he spoke of using mathematical ideas in psychology; this was regarded as proof of his 'philosophical intoxication', whereas all it actually proved was the doctor's ignorance. (Medvedev gives many examples of this sort.)

Leonid Plyushch also privately met three senior Fellows of the Royal College of Psychiatrists who 'saw no indication of schizophrenia or other mental illness'.

Procedural issues

The processes of diagnosis and medico–legal examination in the U.S.S.R., in cases of political dissent, do not 'fail safe'. Judge Bazelon[10] pointed out that the lack of judicial review of the commitment process leaves a dangerous gap:

Judicial review in [the United States] is not premised on the belief that psychiatrists will act in bad faith. It is predicated on the belief that even the most conscientious and well-meaning psychiatrist will sometimes depart from legal and medical standards . . . The absence of judicial review in the Soviet Union may reflect a belief that there is no need for the public at large to oversee government officials and ensure that they respect all substantive and procedural rights. Americans would have some difficulty with such a notion. We do not share this faith with respect to our government officials, whether they are experts in mental health or aeronautics or communications.

Bazelon was discussing civil commitment procedures, but the argument applies even more forcefully to the criminal law. An absence of independent judicial safeguards and of opportunities for conflicting psychiatric judgements to be heard in public could tend towards the adoption of diagnoses and verdicts acceptable to those in power. As we shall see in later chapters, a good deal depends on whether we can trust our doctors, but that, in turn, must also depend to some extent on how far we can trust the political system.

Some Soviet psychiatrists say, privately, that it is entirely humane to recommend that a dissenter whose mental health they question (albeit on very minimal grounds) should not be regarded as responsible, even though the individual concerned would rather stand trial. 'The court has no competence in matters concerning the nature and extent of personality changes brought about by any form of mental illness. The psychiatrist, in the light of his specialist knowledge, must help the court to determine the juridical criterion of responsibility.'[122] There is no form of partial or limited responsibility.[169] Thus a person with personality disorder not amounting to psychosis will be dealt with by 'participation in corrective labour, the rebuilding of his personality with the aid of new social stimuli. The Soviet corrective labour colony serves precisely these aims.'[221] The theoretical basis on which Soviet psychiatrists say they act is therefore clear. In April 1975, Plyushch's wife, accompanied by a member of the Armenian Academy of Sciences, is said to have visited Professor A. V. Snezhnevsky, who asked them: 'Would it really have been better for Plyushch to get seven years of strict-regime imprisonment?'

A comparison of the case of Ezra Pound with that of Leonid Plyushch may help to answer that question. The differences be-

tween their political views is, of course, irrelevant. The technical
evidence that they were 'schizophrenic' is rather poor in both
cases. Each of the two psychiatric reports contains curious echoes
of the other. The court procedures, however, were very different.
The defence entered the plea of insanity on behalf of Pound and
the psychiatrist chosen by the defence agreed with the conclusions
reached by the psychiatrists chosen by the prosecution. Leonid
Plyushch did not wish to plead insanity and his friends and
relatives denied that he was insane. His lawyer did not choose
any of the psychiatrists on the commissions that reported on his
mental condition. It would have been better to have declared that
Plyushch was not suffering from a 'psychosis', that his ideas were
not delusional, and that he was responsible for his actions.
If this meant that he would be condemned to the camps, that
would be a matter for politics, not for medicine. Plyushch knew
what the alternative to the mental hospital was and he preferred
it.

It is of greatest importance, if any medico–legal system is to
work and be accepted by society at large, that both the courts and
psychiatrists should be seen to be acting fairly and independently
of outside pressure. The defence should always be at liberty to
challenge the imputation of insanity and to ask that the accused
should be treated as a political offender. (This is not, in fact, possible in some European countries today. At most, the defence can
ask that the court appoint two new psychiatric experts.) And if the
philosophy of the prison is punitive, it should be clear that the aim
of the hospital system is not. This means that powerful drugs
should not be given against a person's will except in emergency,
that compulsorily detained individuals should not be incarcerated
with patients much more severely ill than themselves, that they
should not be held incommunicado, and that it should be recognized the hospital is their home and that therefore the amenities
should be appropriate.

In prison mental hospitals in the Soviet Union, common criminals quite often act as attendants, dissenters have no legal right to
appeal to a lawyer if they think that they are being dealt with
improperly (whereas in a prison camp such a demand will occasionally succeed), drugs are used as a form of punishment, and
political dissenters are sometimes deliberately kept with violent
patients. Even after discharge from hospital, there is a long period

during which the dissenter has to report regularly to the dispensary. It has several times been reported that there is a common practice to admit to mental hospitals all the prominent dissenters on the dispensary lists for a week or so before and after national holidays such as May Day, when there might be an opportunity for demonstrations.

Psychiatry and the bureaucracy

There is a strongly paternalistic element in the way Soviet psychiatrists are taught to think. This emphasis is not surprising. The pervasive morality in Soviet society is based upon social responsibility and group authority. As Marx said, 'It is not man's consciousness that determines his being, but on the contrary, it is his social being that determines his consciousness.' Psychiatric services and attitudes are thoroughly grounded on this premise. As we saw in chapter 1, it is only in imperfect Western societies that Marxists see dissent as a sign of the need for radical social change. In a Marxist society, dissent is regarded either as a socially dangerous act or it is a sign of madness.

The bureaucracy is organized on a gigantic scale. People must be selected for promotion in terms of orthodoxy and conformity. It is easy to suspect the motives of those who climb to the top of any political organization and it is tempting to say that exploitation occurs whenever the opportunity for it exists. The more monolithic the structure the greater the suspicion. At the least what might be called the Speer avoidance phenomenon must operate from time to time. Albert Speer, Hitler's architect, noticed a pool of blood on the office carpet the day after the Roehm purge. 'I looked away,' he wrote later, 'and from then on avoided the room. But the incident did not affect me more than that.'

An anonymous contribution to the *samizdat* literature,[4] published subsequently in English, analysed the state of psychiatry in the U.S.S.R. between 1968 and 1970. The author, who obviously knew the leading psychiatrists in Moscow well, was concerned to say that criticism should be aimed not at psychiatry as such but at 'its replacement by a handful of ever more over-simplified dogmas'. He described Eugen Bleuler (see p. 101) as the villain of the piece, and considered the Snezhnevsky school of diagnosis, in which (he said) virtually anybody could be regarded as schizophrenic, as no more than a logical extension of Bleuler's fabrications.

It is unlikely that this diagnostic system was constructed with the deliberate aim of catching political, or any other, dissenters in its net. There are similar systems elsewhere in the world, which can equally be criticized on clinical grounds. Given an appropriate administrative and political set-up, however, in which unconventional ideas and behaviour are regarded as anti-social, a theory that sets the threshold of mental illness at rather a low level and includes a wide variety of conditions under the most severe rubric of 'psychosis', can be utilized for the purposes of the State. The author of the *samizdat* document believed that there had been a deliberate selection of people who accepted this broad view of schizophrenia for high positions in psychiatry. Once its advocates achieved positions of prominence, it was inevitable that the doctrine itself would come to be widely adopted. There may even be active persecution of doctors (such as Semyon Gluzman) who fail to toe the line.

During the presentation at the Serbsky Institute referred to earlier, I asked for clarification of the term 'delusions of reconstruction or reformation'. The answer was given by a junior doctor but it is all the more illuminating for that:

They deal with social problems. The patient thinks it necessary to reform the system of government control in this country. He thinks that he himself is capable of undertaking leadership; that it is necessary to review theoretical problems of social science and that he himself is capable of explaining the theory and practice of Soviet industry and reconstruction. His ideas are so essential [he believes] that he should leave the Soviet Union and disseminate them in all the countries of the world.

If even a junior doctor can hold such views, the situation is certainly ripe for exploitation by manipulators. The fact that most dissenters charged with criminal offences are *not* referred for a psychiatric opinion still requires explanation. It seems probable that many factors are involved: the sophistication of the local KGB, the degree of local support for the dissenter, the nature and extent of protest abroad, the evidence that a law actually has been broken, the diagnostic habits of the psychiatrists chosen for the commission, and the presence or absence of mental disorder in the past. One can hope, therefore, that strengthening the opposition at several of these points may help to reduce the practice. But the power of manipulators behind the scenes should not be underestimated.

I have had personal experience of the fact that a visit to the Soviet Union can be used for political purposes. Following a tour of psychiatric services in Moscow and Leningrad in May 1972, which included a brief unscheduled visit to the Serbsky Institute, I had given an interview to a reporter from the Soviet weekly journal, *Medical Gazette*, in which I was asked to comment on accusations made about Soviet forensic psychiatrists. I said I knew some of the British psychiatrists who had made such statements and thought they were giving an honest opinion. I had not myself, at that time, reached a firm conclusion. In response to other questions I stated my admiration for certain aspects of the Soviet services, particularly those for the chronically handicapped (see chapter 7).

This interview was never published, but on 24 August 1972 a broadcast was made by Radio Moscow in Romanian, which included some of my more polite remarks, following a statement about the Serbsky Institute. The broadcast said that it was no secret that Western newspapers occasionally publish slanderous articles and news items regarding mental hospitals in the U.S.S.R. Georges Fully, General Inspector in the French Ministry of Justice and Secretary-General of the International Association of Criminology was quoted as saying, 'I have every reason to believe that everything that is written is mere anti-Soviet propaganda.' The broadcast then reverted to more general aspects of Soviet psychiatry and my own visit was mentioned, including the fact that I had visited the Serbsky Institute. I was quoted as saying, 'I admire the Soviet system because in the U.S.S.R. everything is done to restore the patient to normal life. I mean to say that here, in your country, the development takes the right path, as it does in our country. I cannot find anything to criticize. I find everything is beautiful.' On 18 January 1973, the British journal *Soviet Weekly* asked me if they might quote this passage from the broadcast in an article on Russian psychiatry. I made it clear that the transposition of my remarks to a different context gave them a meaning I had not intended. The article did not appear.

Since the meeting I described earlier between Western and Soviet psychiatrists in October 1973, a number of similar statements have been made in the Soviet press. For example, in the

Korsakov Journal of Neuropathology and Psychiatry (No. 3, 1974) there appeared the following summary:

After the close of the symposium's scientific programme its participants were, at the suggestion of the presidium of the All-Union Society of Neuropathologists and Psychiatrists, invited to Moscow to visit the U.S.S.R. Health Ministry's Institute of Forensic Psychiatry named after V. P. Serbsky. The aim was to give them wide ranging information on the system of forensic-psychiatric diagnosis in the U.S.S.R., on its professional level, and on the legislation which exists in this field in the U.S.S.R. In the course of a day, 13 foreign psychiatrists were informed in detail about the position of forensic psychiatry in the Soviet Union, they took part in the examination of a patient, and they familiarized themselves with the case-histories of those patients whose names are used in the foreign press for slanderous anti-Soviet propaganda. Two foreign psychiatrists, who expressed the desire to do so, visited one of these patients right in his hospital.

At the end of this session the foreign psychiatrists who had taken part in it made a favourable judgement about the professional level and the methods of psychiatric diagnosis of the Institute of Forensic Psychiatry named after V. P. Serbsky.

This is characteristic of the way the meeting has been reported in the Soviet Press, in spite of my own statements to the contrary, both to the Press and in an article in the *British Medical Journal*,[193] in which I said that Soviet psychiatric practice would be unacceptable to most British psychiatrists. The comments of other Western psychiatrists at the meeting, who made statements in their own countries, were similar to mine. Dr. Alfred Freedman, then chairman of the American Psychiatric Association, issued a press release on his return to the United States that was critical of Soviet medico–legal practice (*New York Times*, 3 November 1973). In spite of this, Professor Georgi Morosov,[123] Director of the Serbsky Institute, replying to my criticism in a letter to the *British Medical Journal* on 6 July 1974, again claimed that, 'those participating in the conference, like the Executive Committee of the World Psychiatric Association, verified that all five of the so-called dissidents, who had previously been acknowledged as irresponsible, were suffering from mental illnesses during the legal examination'. In my reply to this letter,[194] I said that it was not true that all the Western psychiatrists agreed on this point. 'I have no doubt that many of my colleagues were not satisfied, as I myself was not, that all five political dissenters whose cases we heard were so seriously mentally ill during the time of their legal examination as to be unfit to plead, to conduct their own defence, or to instruct defence lawyers.'

Members of the Executive Committee of the World Psychiatric Association were in a position to say whether they agreed with my conclusion, since four of them had attended the meeting, but they made no statement one way or the other. After the lapse of more than a year, the Secretary-General[96] wrote to the *British Medical Journal*, simply saying that the Executive Committee made no statement at all after the Serbsky meeting. That was fair enough, because he and other members of the Executive Committee attended in a personal capacity. But, by the same token, they were free to make their own personal statements.

Now that the political implications of a diagnosis of 'schizophrenia', in cases like those of Zhores Medvedev, Natalia Gorbanevskaya, and Leonid Plyushch are clear, it becomes even more important than before to attempt to achieve international agreement on the technical aspects of diagnosis and on its medico-legal consequences. A good deal of international attention is being focused on these matters, especially through the World Health Organization, and we may hope that, in due course, this will have its effect in making psychiatrists, throughout the world, more cautious in their use of terms like 'simple' or 'sluggish' schizophrenia. The British Royal College of Psychiatrists and the American Psychiatric Association have been outspoken in their comment, but international opinion also needs to be brought to bear. The World Health Organization, which is sponsored by national governments, is the right body to undertake a general procedural review and to lay down general ethical principles, but it can move only with extreme caution where political matters are concerned. The World Psychiatric Association would appear to be the appropriate group to consider specific clinical issues such as those arising in the case of Plyushch, or at the least to consider the basic issues underlying such complaints. However, it is a loose grouping of 76 member associations, meeting only at five-yearly intervals and held together in the interim by a small Executive Committee. This Committee's record has not been impressive but its membership was changed at the most recent Congress in Hawaii, in September 1977. Two resolutions were passed there.

The first specifically deplored Soviet practice but was passed only by a small majority of votes, while a majority of member associations was actually against it. The second, with a more substantial majority, set up a panel to investigate any future allegations, wherever they might originate. It remains to be seen how this panel will work in practice but in theory it could provide a useful forum for debate and for influencing professional and public opinion.

Motes and beams

We have been concerned, in this chapter, with issues arising from criticisms of Soviet psychiatry, but it is important not to evade the problems of motes and beams. It would be ludicrous to suggest that the West has no medico–legal problems; no doctors who cause harm by uncritical assumption of authority or omniscient judgement, and no instance of people diagnosed as mentally ill although no disease theory can usefully be applied. In the next chapter, some ideas pioneered by Soviet psychiatrists, from which Western specialists can learn, will be described, and compared and contrasted with practices in the U.S.A. and U.K. Other practices in Soviet as well as other branches of psychiatry, will be criticized.

I mentioned to a colleague in Soviet Georgia that his country and mine shared the same patron saint, St. George, and asked him which country he thought produced the dragon. His reply was that dragons always come from another country.

7. Services for the mentally ill

*Morality, like economics, is actually part
of the nature of things.*

Sidney Webb

Health services and politics

Health services in all countries, whether developed or developing, have ostensibly similar aims. They are intended to promote health, to postpone mortality and to prevent disability as far as possible. These three aims, particularly the first, contain a large element of value. They are interpreted in the context of local ideas about economics and morality. Everyone agrees that those in need should receive help and that the rest should contribute according to their ability, but in one country there are wide differences in personal wealth so that a substantial minority do not have to work at all, while in another to be unemployed is actually an offence. Terms like 'need' and 'ability' will mean different things because the political philosophies are different. If we leave the political dimension out of account we may as well give up any hope of understanding how services have developed in the past and how they may rationally be influenced in future.

Michel Foucault pointed out that, in contrast to the attitude generally prevalent during the middle ages, which left madmen to sink or swim, thrown on the mercy of those from whom they begged, public opinion during the classical period took a more specifically intolerant view. Aubrey Lewis[103] described the change vividly:

As the seventeenth century proceeded, there was a regrouping of those whom society wished to expel and exorcise. It paid regard chiefly to the moral aspect of conduct. Along with the beggars it included the mentally ill, the profane, the free-thinkers, libertines, and dabblers in sorcery. Into the closed world which it thought suitable for their aberrations, not then differentiated as they later were, it banished all who dealt in magic practices, blasphemy or perverse sexuality—conduct which seemed to have much in common with frenzy and delusion. Venereal disease bridged the gap between disease and immorality: the logic of the time did not find the gap wide or essential. All the conditions which the seventeenth and eighteenth centuries shut away had, in contemporary eyes, some moral fault, to be punished and cleansed away from impure mind or peccant flesh.

During the early years of the eighteenth century in England, pauper lunatics were dealt with by parish overseers under the old Poor Law, others went to prison (since there was no diminution of responsibility because of insanity), others were confined under the vagrancy laws in the local bridewell or house of correction, others were sent to private madhouses where they had virtually no legal protection, a few were treated in Bethlem Hospital, and a substantial number were confined alone in 'single care', often chained in coal-cellars or other out-of-the-way corners. The general assumption was that the able-bodied unemployed or destitute deserved their fate. Very little attempt was made to distinguish between the 'impotent' or handicapped and 'sturdy rogues or vagabonds'. All tended to be herded into the same workhouses, where living conditions depended upon local charity and the quality of the overseers.

The Poor Law was revised in 1834,[23] the new formulation being intended to reduce even further the charge paupers made on the public purse. Punishment by degradation became official policy, receiving its classical formulation in the principle of less eligibility; the pauper's condition must be less attractive than that of the lowest paid labourer. The workhouse system was designed to recover what profit might be had from the inmates by extracting as much work from them as possible while providing only the minimum subsistence.

Under the 1834 Poor Law Amendment Act, everyone receiving public assistance had to be in a workhouse. Congregated among the destitute were the handicapped, the chronically sick, and the old. Infirmaries were set up and later became a system of second-class public hospitals. There had been an attempt to establish a voluntary hospital system supported by charity to care for the chronic sick. St. Thomas's hospital in London was founded for this purpose, but already in the seventeenth century had restricted its admissions to short-stay cases. Doctors 'wanted to show results in terms of cure, and they were naturally reluctant to surround themselves with cases which showed the limitations of their professional skill. Doctors who taught particularly wanted to demonstrate successes.' In fact, after St. Thomas's hospital had excluded incurable cases, 'one of its governors (Mr. Guy) founded, with money he had made in speculation, a sister hospital specifically for incurable and mental cases. But the early decision of the governors of St. Thomas's hospital to concentrate on curable cases proved to be an important precedent. It was not many years before Mr. Guy's hospital began to exclude the type of patient it was founded to treat.'[1] This problem of finding the best means of caring for both acute and chronic conditions has not been solved today and is particularly evident in psychiatry.

The first public mental hospitals in Britain, as in the United States, were set up in reaction against these intolerable conditions. In both countries charitable reformers, together with pioneering doctors, began to campaign for new laws and new provisions specifically for the mentally ill and retarded. It takes a thorough-going romantic like Foucault, whose eyes are fixed on ineffable spheres, to regard this reform movement as retrograde. Small county asylums began to be established in England, following the act of 1808. Even the earliest of them were markedly better than the 'community' alternatives, the workhouses and private madhouses, and some were outstandingly good. Most had many acres of grounds and incorporated farms, although they were within fairly easy reach of town. The legal provisions were poor, however, making no stipulations about treatment but imposing penalties if a patient escaped.

These penalties were high, being equivalent to at least one month's wages. The maximum penalty of £10 was a keeper's total wages for five months. As a result, the staffs of county asylums were unwilling to take the slightest risk in allowing a patient liberty of movement; mechanical restraint provided a way of preventing escapes without exercising unremitting supervision.[78]

One of the main aims of the new 'moral' treatment was to foster self-restraint and thus to do away with the need for leather muffs with wrist locks, boot hobbles, straitjackets, and other ingenious devices. The advocates of 'non-restraint' were physicians at county asylums; Charlesworth and Gardiner Hill at Lincoln, John Conolly at Hanwell. Lincoln Asylum was small and relatively easy to staff. There were 'only 72 patients in 1829 and 130 in 1837, when the total abolition of restraint was finally achieved'. Hanwell, however, was the largest asylum in the country, with 1,000 patients, and Conolly's adoption of the 'moral' treatment methods used at Lincoln was courageous to say the least. He also advocated specialized education in methods of asylum treatment for doctors and keepers though he was never able to implement these ideas.

The principles of moral treatment spread widely, at least to the extent that influential people began to pay them lip service. An educational approach was adopted, great emphasis was placed on well-mannered behaviour, bleeding and purging were discredited and an atmosphere of optimism about the curability of mental disorders prevailed. The discharge rates were as high as those reached today. Charles Dickens, who had been appalled by the conditions in London workhouses, was greatly impressed by a small hospital he visited in the United States, where the physician and staff sat down to dine with their patients.

Unfortunately, the era of reform did not last, partly because the pioneers had been too optimistic and ran out of steam. Some of the claims for cures were clearly impossible. Another important factor, emphasized by Kathleen Jones,[78] is that the public in both England and the United States became fearful that improper detention might occur. The Lunatics Acts of 1845 had been chiefly concerned with the welfare of the mentally sick individual in need of protection from exploitation and physical ill-treatment. Admission to hospital ensured this, together with a minimal standard of living. The magistrates were involved as managers and they were empowered to charge the patient's maintenance to his parish. The term 'asylum' was appropriate. However, the Lunacy Acts of 1890 and 1891, which codified and systematized the various legal restrictions on the freedom of the mentally disordered, required at least one certificate of unsoundness of mind or mental defect and an order by a justice at the time of admission. The laws were interpreted so strictly that only severe, chronic, and probably incurable cases could be accepted.

Another important factor was that the earlier campaigns had been too successful. Larger and larger numbers of people were admitted, not all of them necessarily able to benefit from moral treatment. In the United States, many were immigrants with no social skills or resources. The carefully fostered family atmosphere of the small asylums could not be maintained as the wards became overcrowded and understaffed. Bockoven[15] has graphically illustrated this process occurring in an American state mental hospital. A similar evolution took place all over Europe. Much of the impetus towards the development of a comprehensive psychiatry, based on the principles of humane social treatment, was lost. Before the end of the nineteenth century, the custodial era had arrived.

More recent history has shown a turning away from the institution as a means of solving social problems, but this development has taken characteristic forms in different countries. Some aspects are curiously like the reform era of one hundred years earlier but in reverse. It is instructive to compare and contrast what has happened in countries with political philosophies as varied as those of the U.S.S.R., the United States, and Great Britain. There are many points of similarity in spite of the obvious differences.

Services in the United Kingdom

The philosophy of the welfare state has been adopted through a gradual and continuous process of trial and error. The turning point was the minority report of the Poor Law Commission published in 1909, principally the work of Beatrice Webb. She had two main principles; that prevention was better than cure and that charitable activity had its proper place in supporting a public service. The recent development of the British health and social services can best be evaluated in the light of these two aims. To start with, the goals were to end the Poor Law, to institute universal social insurance, and to establish education for all. The new attitudes were extended to the mentally ill in the Mental Treatment Act of 1930, which broke the stranglehold of the Lunacy Acts passed 40 years earlier. People could at last be admitted to a public mental hospital without being on a compulsory order. The Act also allowed for the development of out-patient clinics at general hospitals. Towards the end of the Second World War further large steps forward were taken, including legislation on pensions, family allowances, education, provision for the disabled, a complex of personal social services, and, above all, a national health service. All these were positive ideas, put forward in order to create a welfare state that would be an alternative to the old Poor Law system and not simply a continuation of it.

The main principle of the National Health Service, introduced in

1948, was that everyone who needed medical care or treatment should be able to receive it, irrespective of ability to pay. The mental hospital services, which hitherto had developed separately, were incorporated, with the general hospitals for the acutely ill and the hospitals for the chronic sick, into one system. An important but relatively small private sector survived, though in psychiatry it was a proud boast that the public service was actually better than the private. On the other hand, the three chief branches of medical service—'primary' care by general practitioners, hospital care by specialists, and public health care by local government agencies—remained in separate administrative hierarchies. Local authorities remained responsible for social and community services and this, too, represented a barrier to a comprehensive and continuous care system.

Nevertheless, the National Health Service was an important step forward. Mental illness lost a little more of its stigma. Admissions to mental hospitals again increased, as they had done after the Mental Treatment Act. Living conditions in the mental hospitals improved. First class doctors were attracted into psychiatry —indeed the proportionate increase in numbers was closely parallel to that in the United States, although psychoanalysis and 'office psychiatry' had much less influence. British psychiatrists prided themselves on an eclectic education, grounded firmly in the principles of diagnosis and treatment of the European schools, but with a strong and characteristic emphasis on the social aspects of the subject—social causes, social effects, social treatments. Two main currents of reform flowed strongly. One was the therapeutic community movement. It was assumed that groups of people with common problems could help each other, that an authoritarian approach was out of place when treatments could not be specified precisely, and that psychodynamic interpretations of events occurring in the group would provide useful insight. The movement provided fresh impetus and encouragement to psychiatry at a time when many older ideas about treatment were coming to be regarded as of little value, and the first two assumptions have proved of lasting value.

An even stronger progressive element was the introduction of methods of social and vocational rehabilitation and resettlement and the development of the view that many psychiatric patients were handicapped rather than ill. Paid work was provided for longstay

patients instead of diversionary arts and crafts or maintenance
work on the institution. Hospital farms were sold. Locked doors
were opened and transitional environments of various kinds were
provided in order to provide a ladder back to full community life.
At the same time there was an emphasis on early discharge in
order to avoid the disabilities of institutionalism. Many doctors
and nurses look back on this period during the early 1950s, when
a wind of change was blowing through the most progressive mental
hospitals, as the most useful time of their lives.

These developments led to a rapid reduction in the numbers of
patients, which occurred in hospitals like Mapperley at Notting-
ham long before the new phenothiazine drugs were introduced.
From 1954 onwards the number of beds occupied in mental hospitals in England and Wales began to decline (from 150,000 or
344 per 100,000 population, to 202 per 100,000 population in
1973). The numbers in Scotland and Ireland have always been
higher and the decline less rapid. The use of the new drugs added
to the effect of the social treatments and enabled them to be introduced universally.

The new optimistic mood was reflected in educated public
opinion. Practices that had been introduced piecemeal by the
pioneers were codified in the Mental Health Act of 1960 which
allowed for admission to psychiatric hospitals on the same informal
basis as to general hospitals and removed the judicial element
from compulsory admission except for the right of appeal to a legal
tribunal. Only a tiny proportion even of long-stay patients remained 'under certificate' and in 1971 only 16 per cent of all admissions were by compulsory order. In some areas, the proportion
is now down to 5 per cent.

Eileen Brooke pointed out that European countries with fewer
than 200 psychiatric beds per 100,000 population fell into two
groups; 'one comprising some less economically favoured countries and the other a group of Eastern countries with the dispensary system and socialized medicine'. The system put forward for
the future English service in the 1962 Hospital Plan was not consciously based on the Russian model but it did entail a similar
heavy dependence on forms of care other than the mental hospital.
It was calculated that, as the number of beds decreased, it would
reach a point at which all the 'old long-stay' patients accumulated
in former days would have been discharged or have died, while very

few 'new long-stay' patients would have accumulated to take their place. The latter could be accommodated in special units, the shorter-stay patients could be treated in residential or day wards in district general hospitals, and the 'old-fashioned' mental hospitals would no longer be needed, all their functions being covered in more acceptable ways.

At the end of 1973, there were 41 beds per 100,000 population occupied by people who had been resident for more than one, but less than five years—the 'new long-stay'. Whether the plan, which remains the basis of government policy, can be brought to fruition depends very much on whether these people can be catered for humanely. The problems are many: 'security' because of a danger to themselves or others—a small but important proportion; long-term treatment; likelihood of rapid relapse after discharge; need for much supervision or nursing care, e.g. in severe chronic schizophrenia or dementia; and a combination of mental illness with other types of handicap such as blindness, physical disability, or mental retardation.

Most of the alternative services required for people who remain handicapped after they leave hospital will have to be provided by the new social service departments of local government. Social workers now have their own administrative hierarchy and can regard themselves as a profession completely independent of medicine. There is a National Social Service as well as a National Health Service. Unfortunately, the better trained and experienced they are, the more likely are they to be in purely administrative positions without any 'case-load' of clients at all. Since the reorganization of medical services in 1974, in which the former tripartite medical structure has been unified into one system, the division between the social and medical hierarchies has become complete. There is no medical voice in local government and the social workers who sit on district health committees are often not senior enough to ensure local authority action. Eventually, the health and social services will have to be unified.

The minister responsible for the newly reorganized N.H.S. pointed to two major deficiencies which the changes were intended to remedy. Services for the disabled, mentally ill, and retarded 'have failed to attract the attention and indeed the resources which they need' and 'the domiciliary and community services are underdeveloped'. He thought that the reason was that responsibility

for providing adequately for each geographical area had never
been specifically invested in any one identifiable body. 'Real
needs must be identified' through the new and simplified management structure, 'and decisions must be taken and periodically
reviewed as to the order of priorities among them. Plans must
be worked out to meet these needs and management and drive
must be continually applied to put the plans into action, assess
their effectiveness and modify them as needs change or as ways are
found to make the plans more effective.'[80] Although it is very
doubtful whether the new administrative structure is simpler,
or more likely to meet these needs, the two large areas of deficiency identified by Sir Keith Joseph are certainly very marked in
the psychiatric services. One of them is an inadequate service at
'primary care' level. The two main professional agents at this
level are the general practitioner, working with nurses, and the
social worker. The former offers a service which covers 95 per
cent of the population, a large proportion of whom are in fact seen
during the course of a given year. The G.P. treats nearly all cases
of lesser psychiatric disorder and refers only a very small proportion to specialists. There have been complaints that the service
provided is often unsympathetic, uninformed and hasty, being
based mainly on symptomatic medication of anxiety, depression
and sleeplessness rather than on an understanding of social and
psychological causes and treatments. Local social workers tend to
see those with special problems—inadequate housing, difficult
children, welfare needs, and so on—who are also likely to be at
high risk of developing lesser psychiatric disorders. At the moment
there is little coordination between the two types of service and
little knowledge about the overlap between them. As we saw in
chapter 3, the interaction between social problems and emotional
reactions is beginning to be understood. Social action and counselling are more important than drugs, except where the emotional
reaction has 'gone out of control'. A promising idea is that of the
primary care team, in which medical, nursing, and social skills are
represented and regular communication ensures that the right
skills are deployed for the right needs, without too much duplication of effort. If the present trend towards group practice from
health centres continues and accelerates, there is even the prospect
that people with lesser psychiatric disorders, who so frequently
have physical illnesses and social problems as well, could receive

both medical and social help within the same building. Specialist psychological and psychiatric advice could also be available to the team, and to selected patients, within the centre.

The other large problem concerns the replacement of the functions of the mental hospital, in providing shelter, asylum, supervision, basic nursing, and security on a long-term basis, for a relatively small but particularly difficult group of people. The government has promised that no mental hospital will be closed until all its former functions have been adequately taken over.[35] This means the provision of well-staffed units for demented old people, at a time when the ordinary hospital facilities for geriatric medicine are seriously deficient. It means the provision of a wide range of protected environments, including hostels, group homes, and subsidized housing. It means the provision of 'secure' accommodation elsewhere than in mental hospitals. It means the provision of extra units with special facilities for physically handicapped people who are also mentally ill. Many of these extra services are supposed to be provided by local government social service departments rather than by hospital authorities, but the current financial climate is not favourable.

Meanwhile, however, changes are taking place in the hospital system that may make it impossible for them to continue to fulfil these social functions. Although the pressures affecting American state mental hospitals (see p. 212) are not felt with the same urgency, there is a tendency for staff to feel that a therapeutic atmosphere is impossible unless only people capable of 'informed consent' are admitted, thus excluding many mentally ill people who would benefit from treatment. Many hospitals no longer have the facilities or the staff to cope with seriously disturbed patients, whether under compulsion or not. This creates the necessity to set up special 'secure' prison-hospitals, with inevitably greater stigma, difficulties in staffing, and formalized decisions about the right time for discharge. The same is true of a large group of inadequate people, not necessarily manifestly ill, who used to use psychiatric hospitals as places of refuge. Judges have had some critical comments to make about this situation:

Her Majesty's courts are not dustbins into which the medical, welfare and social services can sweep difficult members of the public. And still less, Her Majesty's judges do not dispose of those who are socially awkward. If this was so, the road ahead would be terrible to contemplate. We stand on that road barring the way. And if anyone thinks they can dispose of people by having them sent to jail, they can think again.

The girl concerned was a social misfit who from her early teens had frequently been convicted of drug offences, soliciting, larceny and assaults on the police. She had had several illegitimate children. She had been in and out of special schools, hostels and hospitals where 'treatment' had failed to bring about any change. Psychiatrists have perhaps promised too much in the past by suggesting that their training equips them more specifically than that of social workers, say, to help such people. However, as psychiatrists (helped along by outside criticism) begin to divest themselves of some of their previously claimed powers, it begins to be evident that many social problems have been alleviated by the possibility of granting asylum and that no adequate substitute yet exists.

Thus British psychiatric and social services stand at the crossroads. Very few of the new psychiatric units in district general hospitals have been built and it is doubtful whether economic resources will allow the programme of building to go ahead as planned. It is also too soon to be sure that the new units can provide really comprehensive medical and nursing care of the new kind, that is, offering, in association with local authorities and voluntary organizations, a basis for long-term support to patients and relatives, who would be regarded as partners in the process of care. So much of the psychiatric work in a general hospital is of a new kind, additional to that previously undertaken but competing for the same personnel and resources. Meanwhile, the alternative services needed by social service departments are also competing for scarce funds. The running-down mental hospital system may thus receive a new lease of life. Fortunately it was, in its heyday, the best of its kind in the world and probably still retains the potential to adopt new roles.

Services in the Soviet Union

There has long been an emphasis on social and preventive factors in the provision of medical services in the Soviet Union and even in prerevolutionary times there was an early form of district service, with case registration and an emphasis on after-care. The social security programme introduced in Lenin's time provided pensions for the disabled and laid great stress on help to achieve full working capacity. During the 1920s and 1930s a system of extramural psychiatry was set up based on a network of dispensaries, day hospitals, and workshops and on services for social and industrial resettlement, such as rehabilitation units, training centres, vocational guidance units, and prophylactic workshops, in the factories themselves.

The system of dispensary care is better developed in Moscow and Leningrad than elsewhere and coverage is particularly thorough in the field of rehabilitation and community care. Thus Moscow No. 8 dispensary serves two districts with a total population of 500,000. There is one dispensary psychiatrist to 33,000 population, each working with a nurse. Such a doctor works a six-hour day, four hours of which are spent in the dispensary and two hours visiting patients' homes and places of work and engaging in health education and consultation. She will see 16–20 patients during the course of the day, mostly for long-term supervision, but a couple of them direct referrals from hospital or polyclinic. There are various schedules of visiting, ranging from patients recently discharged from hospital, who need to be seen twice weekly, to those who are seen only once a year. If a patient does not keep an appointment, the doctor or nurse visits him at home or at work.

Though the psychiatric hospital system is administratively distinct, patients from a given district are always admitted to the same hospital, and the dispensary and hospital doctors are in close contact. In Leningrad, for example, no patient has more than two doctors, one in the hospital and one in the dispensary. Detailed clinical summaries, containing specified information (for example, the maximum dose of drugs used, the recommended therapeutic and maintenance doses, etc.), are routinely supplied to the dispensary within a few days of discharge, and the patient is required to attend at the dispensary within five days of discharge. Again, there is a home visit or telephone call in the case of default.

There are many specialists at the dispensaries, notably for alcoholism, which accounts for 1 in 7 of all referrals. There is very little narcotic addiction. Other specialists deal with children, epilepsy, neurological disorders, mental retardation, etc. Special departments at the dispensary deal with various types of 'physiotherapy' (including electronarcosis, hydrotherapy, and many techniques that are uncommon in the U.K.: massage, ultraviolet light, electrical stimulation of muscles and skin, etc.), speech therapy, individual psychotherapy, and group and 'collective' psychotherapy. The last is concerned with patients in relatively large groups (what we would call a patient–staff meeting). A substantial department is responsible for patients with mental retardation; teachers with special training, known as 'defectologists', figure prominently, as do speech therapists on a most generous scale.

Each dispensary has a day hospital and one or more workshops. (The latter should be distinguished from the similar facilities provided by hospitals, which are used only for the rehabilitation of in-patients.) All patients must be able to travel by public transport (there is a home occupation programme for some of those who cannot). Patients stay in the day hospitals for up to six weeks, mainly during phases of 'decompensation' which do not require in-patient treatment.

The workshops attached to the dispensaries are large (often taking over 100 people) and provide the opportunity for realistic work as a means of rehabilitation. Patients get an invalidity pension, depending on the severity and chronicity of the condition, a wage for their work, and free food and excursions. They do not pay tax on this money. The average budget, counting everything, is said to be not very different from that of non-handicapped workers. Since the goods produced are sold at ordinary prices but no government tax is paid, the workshop makes a 'profit' which can be used for various purposes including, in at least one case, putting up new buildings.

People do not stay in such workshops for more than a year or so; usually for shorter periods of time. In some of the larger industrial concerns there are factory psychiatrists whose function is to care for the mental health of workers. A great deal of attention is given to the optimal placement of people who have been psychiatrically ill. Many factories have special workshops for handicapped people. For example, a sewing-machine factory in the neighbourhood of No. 8 dispensary in Moscow is said to have up to 100 people with psychiatric impairments in such a shop, as well as providing sheltered conditions for other handicapped people within the open workshops. The standard of work required is, of course, very much higher in the open factories than in the sheltered workshops. For example, such workers need to be members of a trade union and they need sickness certificates if they wish to stay away from work. In addition, there are special factories equivalent to those of the British Remploy organization, some of them with homes attached. Psychiatrists have a good deal of power to say who should work in sheltered conditions. There are no hostels or group homes, and handicapped patients without families are mainly in long-stay psychiatric hospitals. There are two mental hospitals for Leningrad patients in the country outside the city, for the longest-stay patients. Such hospitals have from 100 to 600 beds. It is now recognized that the open-door system should apply to these hospitals, too, and considerable improvements are being carried out. They usually have attached farms and workshops in the neighbourhood belonging to collective farms.

The staffing ratios for these dispensaries are most generous by the standards existing elsewhere. One dispensary in Leningrad (serving the Moscow district of 400,000 people), has a total staff of 160, including 27 doctors, 56 nurses and 50 occupational supervisors. Ten of these doctors are district psychiatrists, responsible for sub-areas of about 40,000 people each (and paid overtime, to the extent that they work longer hours to make up the norm of one to 33,000), dealing only with out-patient supervision, follow-up, and health education. Doctors tend to specialize rather narrowly. Those concerned with functional psychosis, for example, may know rather little about neurosis or about dementia. Doctors in charge of dispensaries tend to describe their activities 'by numbers', as though this is how they train their staff in a system that covers most routine situations. There does not seem to be much necessity to exercise independent judgement, hence the categories determining how often the patient should be seen. There is a routine for almost every occasion. It is unusual to depart from the routine of follow-up or treatment laid down. Major decisions (for example, moving from one category to another) are referred to a commission. This is not unlike the system being used in some developing countries.

Local authorities run an emergency service, staffed by psychiatrists and nurses 24 hours a day. There is no general practitioner system. All patients are seen first in polyclinics for diagnosis and treatment. There are neuropathologists among the many specialists represented but most of the severe and chronic psychiatric conditions are referred to a psychiatric service that is administratively and geographically separate from the general health system. There are very few psychiatric units in general hospitals. Most of the 25,000 psychiatrists work in the large mental hospitals or in the dispensaries.

There is no extensive social service and no separate development of the professions of social work, occupational therapy or clinical psychology. All the work is undertaken by doctors and nurses, though there is a good deal of subspecialization. The general level of medical and nursing education tends to be lower than in the United Kingdom. The administrative distinctions of the psychiatric service ensure that an unpopular section of health care (for stigma is as great as the U.S.S.R. as elsewhere) receives an adequate degree of attention. As with the services for the mentally retarded in Sweden, there are advantages and disadvantages in such a separation.

The very thoroughness of the Soviet service may carry a disadvantage. A certain insistent paternalism and over-protectiveness are characteristic throughout the whole society and are plainly evident in attitudes to the mentally ill and retarded. In many cases it brings good results; probably the more severe the handicap the more satisfactory the care. But there is, for example, no legal process of compulsory admission to hospital. Once the relatives or others have requested admission and the psychiatrist has agreed that it is necessary, the patient's own consent is taken for granted. All admissions are therefore 'voluntary'. Similarly there is no appeal procedure following admission.

It is very unlikely that the service available generally reaches the standards of the showpiece areas in Moscow and Leningrad. Nevertheless, one cannot imagine a voluntary organization being set up to represent the interests of some consumer group, like the National Association for Autistic Children or the National Schizophrenia Fellowship in Britain, simply because it is regarded as inconceivable that all needs are not already being met.

The dispensary psychiatrists also serve as public mental health officers for their local areas. During their work in factories and cafeterias and housing estates, and in cooperation with school physicians, they engage in health education. Health is a social concept and its definition depends on social traditions and values. Isidore Ziferstein,[213] an American psychoanalyst who spent more than a year working at the Bekhterev Institute in Leningrad, made some very interesting observations about the health education activities of psychiatrists. They deal not only with obvious problems like alcoholism and the work placement of individual patients but also with broad issues of mental hygiene; the best way of organizing work and recreation, attitudes to health, techniques of child-rearing. The way to prevent alienation is to impress on children and adults, through daily life experiences from the cradle to the grave, the two ideals that originated in the pre-Soviet agricultural commune; 'You are not alone in the world', and, 'Never be a bystander'. These principles are part of a pervasive morality in Soviet society, which is based on social responsibility and group authority. Psychiatric attitudes and services are thoroughly grounded on a premise of social consciousness. But a general acceptance of a definition of health based upon a strict interpretation of such principles can mean that dissenting opinions or behaviour may come to be regarded not just as 'non-health', but as 'illness', and more specifically as 'psychosis'. The results have been examined in chapter 6.

Services in the United States of America

During the nineteenth century, when the political philosophies of the two countries were approximately the same, the development of a mental hospital system followed similar lines in the United States and the United Kingdom. Nothing equivalent to the coherent British welfare system has yet emerged in the U.S., however, although there are signs that it may one day do so. There has been a tremendous expansion in psychiatric services nevertheless and, because the entrepreneurial system has allowed a wide variety of natural experiments, it is instructive to compare developments with those in the Soviet Union and the United Kingdom.

Before the Second World War there were about 3,000 psychiatrists in the United States. By 1971 there were more than 25,000. Two-thirds were in private practice, spending most of their time in office consultations with fee-paying clients. Four out of ten were engaged only in private work. Henry Davidson[33] characterized the early stages of this vast expansion as follows:

Psychoanalysis as a treatment method was available only to those patients who were well enough to stay out of hospitals, articulate enough to talk freely, prosperous enough to pay substantial fees, sophisticated enough to talk comfortably about matters previously dismissed as un-mentionable, and intelligent enough to co-operate in a complex pro-gram. Thus analysis became identified with the smart, the articulate, the mildly ill, the wealthy and the sophisticated. So it acquired the glamor which it has never lost.

Private psychiatrists need never leave their offices, or have to deal with the problems of the old, the poor, the severely ill or dis-abled, the dangerous, or the markedly deviant. They need not worry about emergencies or court appearances or the drudgery and hard work associated with hospital practice.

Before 1960, the public sector was relatively neglected since an inability to pay for services was seen as a reflection of the unwilling-ness of the individual to work hard, prosper and pay his own way. The state mental hospitals have been frequently and justly criti-cized for being large, poor, overcrowded, and staffed by untrained attendants and by doctors who were not good enough to gain entry into the commercial system. (Nearly half had been trained abroad.) A high proportion of patients were there compulsorily. Many of the private health insurance corporations refused to cover psychiatric disorders or imposed strict limitations which excluded severe and chronic illness. General hospitals, by and large, would not admit mentally ill patients. Only some of the university and voluntary hospitals and the Veterans' Administra-tion, set up to deal with ex-servicemen, provided a service which to some extent cut across this double standard of care. A number of psychiatrists, influenced by an excellent public health tradition, also took a markedly social line, based on epidemiological research and an awareness of developments in community psychiatry in Europe. However, all the psychiatric services were affected by the fact that most of the ambitious and able doctors wanted to become psychoanalysts in private practice. The postgraduate training courses with the highest prestige were devoted to providing this kind of experience. As Davidson put it: '90% of training time is spent in teaching its happy beneficiaries to handle only 5% of the patients. The remaining 10% of the trainees have to treat the re-maining 95% of the patients.'

Under the influence of the new ideas in social psychiatry de-veloped in Europe, there was an emphasis during the late 1950s and early 1960s on trying to provide more broadly based services that were linked to need rather than to ability to pay. Several state legislatures passed Community Mental Health Acts, and the National Institute of Mental Health offered consultant services, field demonstrations, and grants in aid. The report of the Joint Commission on Mental Illness and Health,[77] in 1961, emphasized the new ideas about community responsibility. The main recommendation was that mental health centres should be available in all districts, staffed by full-time personnel, and that they should provide in-patient, out-patient, partial-hospitalization, and consultation services. The Community Mental Health Centres Construction Act of 1963 authorized the appropriation of funds to be disbursed by the National Institute of Mental Health. Subsequent amendments carried the programme through to mid-1970.

The emotional drive behind the new programme had two sources. First, there was the humanitarian feeling that the state mental hospitals were snake-pits, that chronic mental illness had largely been created by them, and that closing them down would prevent much of this long-term disability. Second, there was an idealistic assumption that community mental health could be achieved by treatment, by psychotherapy and by health education. Each area of 200,000 was to have a 120-bed centre providing a 24-hour service. Thus acutely ill patients could be treated near their own homes and admission to the more remote institutions avoided. But, as Elaine and John Cumming[32] have pointed out, the ability of clinics of this kind to deal with the most severe and chronic problems of mental illness is questionable. Their aims are directed towards prevention and cure; concepts such as support, supervision or shelter find little place. Moreover, many of the staff would still be part-time psychiatrists whose main interest remained in private psychotherapy. Rather than acting as a bridge between the over-privileged and the under-privileged streams of American psychiatry, they might exacerbate the division. Finally, the necessary field social work and the apparatus of pensions, financial supplements, home welfare services, rehabilitation units, and sheltered day and residential environments, was not only lacking but entirely foreign to the American way of looking at things. It smacked of 'socialized medicine' and the Welfare State.

This kind of criticism of the mental health centre idea has been repeated at intervals and, although there are some notable exceptions, it is not yet clear that the programme is successful. A report to Congress by the General Accounts' Office at the time that Federal funding for centres was due for renewal pointed out that, compared with the original estimate by the National Institute of Mental Health that 2,300 centres would be needed nationwide (subsequently scaled down to about 1,500), only 392 were operational by the middle of 1974. Twelve of these were studied in detail and a number of critical points made about them. Their planning had often depended more upon the interests of staff than upon the needs of the area. Without continued Federal assistance some of the services (particularly those that produced little revenue) would have to be run down. Most of the patients served came from lower income groups and had only a limited ability to pay for services. In most instances, local communities had not provided significant financial support. There was poor coordination between the centres, state hospitals and other community organizations. This last problem, difficult enough within a public service such as that in Britain, is extremely difficult to solve in the United States.

Characteristically, all sorts of solutions have been tried.[214] One means of bringing pressure to bear on the state hospital system has been through the courts. Several judgements, in different states, have required the local mental hospital to improve the standard of care provided. A century of pauperism, neglect, isolation, and institutionalism cannot, however, be put right by court order.[45, 166] One action, brought by a committed patient who claimed he had been unable to obtain reasonable treatment, illustrates the problem. The Chief Judge of the Federal District Court, sitting in Montgomery, Alabama, ordered a complete restructuring of the state's mental health services, including a comprehensive code of patients' rights, minimum staff–patient ratios, and the establishment of an individual treatment plan for every patient. (These standards had earlier been suggested by the American Psychiatric Association.) Although the plaintiff won his case, the state could not comply with the ruling because of lack of funds. Such actions have, however, led to some improvement in standards.

Another approach, also through the courts, has been to restrict the grounds on which patients can be compulsorily admitted to hospital and to ensure that those who are so admitted have access to legal advice. There is much to be said for such an arrangement though provision is still needed for emergency admission. There are also proposals, however, that those who are admitted informally should be subjected to legal examination in order to make certain that they are able to give 'informed consent'. This requires full knowledge, competence to make the decision, and willingness to be admitted. It is difficult to know how these criteria would be interpreted; but, with a lawyer eager to demonstrate his skill at saving people from a fate he regards as invariably damaging, one can well imagine many people who would benefit from residential care either being turned away or being committed. Others, of course, would pass the test and be certified as fit subjects to be voluntarily admitted to a psychiatric hospital. This brings us back full circle to the situation under the English Lunacy Acts, when everyone admitted to hospital had to undergo legal investigation in order to ensure that no one was improperly admitted. The result was a greater horror of admission than had existed previously, and it is arguable that these Acts did much to inaugurate the custodial era. A narrow and conservative legalism can do more harm than good, even when the motives are of the best.

Both these preoccupations—the 'right to treatment' and the right not to be casually committed to hospital—thus represent avenues forward and avenues backward, depending on how they are implemented. It is argued that the large mental hospitals are costly, that they do not provide adequate 'treatment', and that it is therefore wrong to confine people in them, just as in the U.K. a movement has grown up suggesting that they should be abolished altogether. This would save money, some of which could better and more economically be spent on community services, and prevent a good deal of extra disability.

As we saw in chapter 5, there is a kernel of truth in these arguments, so far as state hospitals in the U.S. are concerned. But they can be over-generalized. What many people need is not so much treatment as shelter or 'asylum'. This is particularly true of schizophrenia which still leads to chronic disability in about one-quarter of cases (see chapter 4). Because the impairments are invisible, it is not obvious that a protective environment is necessary. It may not even be necessary to take preventive medication if the environment is appropriate. Secondary and extrinsic types of impairment and inadequacy are even less visible.

It is by no means clear that providing alternative services for such people outside the hospital is cheaper. That needs to be demonstrated, but it would depend very much on the standard of care provided. Even if states, attracted by the idea of saving money, did close their large psychiatric hospitals, it may be doubted whether the funds would then be put into providing suitable alternative facilities outside. All sorts of claims can be made for spending the money in other ways. Even the community mental health centres do not necessarily care for the chronically disabled.

Finally, the rights of individuals other than the patient, particularly those of relatives, are frequently overlooked. In due course, they too may combine, find themselves able lawyers, and start a movement of their own.

Meanwhile, mental hospitals have been running down faster in some states than in others. A very substantial factor has been negative, rather than positive. The admission of people with dementia and other brain diseases has been discouraged and a commercial system of 'nursing homes' has grown up to cater for them instead. The income for these homes was derived from social security payments. A very similar tendency occurred in England though on a lesser scale. In New York, there were complaints that patients were being exploited or even that they had been turned out on the streets to fend for themselves.

The *New York Times* investigated practices, 'in which patients released from state hospitals often wind up in cheap hotels or other poor accommodations, get little medical help and eventually return to hospitals; a lack of high-security facilities for those who are criminally insane; the reluctance of the state to accept severely disturbed children for treatment, and the existence of deplorable conditions in a number of state mental institutions'. The new Governor of New York State proposed, at the end of 1974, a sweeping overhaul of the whole system in order 'to end the indiscriminate release of mental patients who get little or no aftercare; to build close cooperation between the state and community agencies working with mental patients, and to greatly increase the emphasis on preventive mental health treatment'. The Commissioner of Mental Health who had been associated with the earlier policy was replaced.

These objectives were very comprehensive but they were to be pursued within the same budget as before. It remains to be seen whether the essence of the problem—the fact that there is a core of chronically handicapped individuals who remain dependent even when good services are provided—has really been understood. It is a straightforward question of priorities; whether sufficient funds are devoted to their adequate care and maintenance or whether there will simply be a partial restoration of the old system, warts and all.

The overall numbers of people in mental hospitals and residential treatment centres declined from 405 per 100,000 population in 1950, to 350 in 1960, and 215 in 1970. Much of this sharp decline is accounted for by a reduction in numbers of elderly people with dementia. Nevertheless, as Morton Kramer[87] has pointed out, if residence in an institution of any kind is taken into account, there has been no change in numbers over this period. The term 'institution' covers homes and hospitals for the aged, ill and chronically handicapped, as well as prisons, training schools for delinquents, etc. At the time of the censuses in 1950, 1960, and 1970, approximately one per cent of the U.S. population were in institutions. The decrease in mental hospital provision was made up by an increase in numbers in homes for the aged and in correctional institutions.

Throughout the United States there are examples of the highest quality of diagnosis, treatment and care. In many places, new types of service are being built up and evaluated that may yet be found to serve as a national model. There is always the great saving grace of an opportunity for personal initiative to succeed in filling local gaps. What is lacking is a stable administrative structure that will apply these high standards to a national or state-wide health and social service. The wealthy can buy more and, on the whole, better care than the poor and disadvantaged. The public services have not yet escaped from the image of the Poor Law. Politically, a high national standard is not a goal that can be achieved within the near future, and powerful interests argue that it would be thoroughly undesirable to attempt to do so.

A comparison of three systems

An ideal system might combine the manpower and resources put into the best Soviet dispensaries (and the power given to their physicians to implement decisions about sheltered or part-time work), with the overall comprehensiveness and standards of the British national health and social services, and the flexibility and opportunity for innovation that is possible in the United States.

Unfortunately, the advantages of the three systems derive from the underlying social and political structures and cannot be divorced from the corresponding disadvantages: authoritarian inflexibility, with consequent inadaptability; a bureaucratic assumption that increasing administration means increasing service; and transient overselling of doubtful remedies in anticipation of consumer demand, with consequent disillusion and inequitable distribution of resources.

The United States and the Soviet Union are both large countries, and this may be one reason why there has appeared to be a certain intolerance of nonconformity, though recent developments in the U.S. have tended to diminish its impact. The pre-revolutionary Russian communes prepared the soil for 'social consciousness'. Deviation has been dealt with by 're-education' in labour camps or, in special cases, since health and social conformity have not been regarded as separable concepts, has been treated as mental illness (in practice, as 'schizophrenia'). Health is defined within rather narrow limits, outside which, non-health is regarded as illness. The north American ideals of self-reliance, individualism, and the ability to pay one's own way are quite different, but there is a similar tendency to equate conformity and health, and a similar liability to regard deviation from the norm as illness. Psychoanalysis provides a theoretical justification for diagnosing a disregard of social reality as a form of psychosis (in practice, as 'schizophrenia').

It is very doubtful how far the comprehensive psychiatric services in some areas of Moscow and Leningrad are available nationally. There is no doubt that a general extension of such standards would be extremely expensive and could only be attained by diverting resources from elsewhere. Services in all three countries face this problem though it is illustrated most starkly in the Alabama court judgement mentioned on page 212. The United States spends a higher proportion of its gross national product on medical care than does Britain, and since it is a richer country the difference in terms of dollars per head of population is very large—something like three hundred dollars per person per year compared with one hundred.[115] But much of this money is spent on types of care that have a lower priority in Britain, since in the U.S. consumers control more of the spending. Mortality rates, for example, are lower in Britain than in the U.S. If psychiatric services are left to free market forces, the largest number and, on the whole, the wealthiest consumers will be those with 'lesser psychiatric disorders'. Practitioners eager to supply their needs will not be lacking. Potential demand can be stimulated by salesmen (see p. 35) and there will never be any lack of customers even for useless or harmful forms of treatment.

The supply of doctors in most countries is not related to the way income is distributed in the population, although income is related to the distribution of morbidity and mortality. If the average risk of dying within a working lifetime is 100, the risk for unskilled labourers is 143 compared with 76 for professional people. But the latter group gets more, and better, care.

Needs and priorities

The more effective the democracy, the greater the pressure on society, from every conceivable interest group, to spend more money and resources on its own particular problems.[189] The new insistence, in the western world, that every human being is entitled to insist upon a wide range of rights, has created a new situation for medicine, the law and the social services—one with which many professional people find themselves ill-equipped to cope. The possibilities for expanding medical and social care are infinite. Even useful and helpful forms of treatment can never be made available to the extent that would seem theoretically desirable. Postponing mortality ensures that there will be more disability, not less, much of it chronic, so that the numbers of people in need accumulate from year to year. As medical and social knowledge grow, our ability to replace damaged functions will improve still further. Already there are complaints every Christmas (the time when newspapers devote space to such matters) that some elderly person, alone in her apartment and beyond earshot of the neighbours, falls and breaks a leg and is found only days later. This leads to calls for regular patrols by social services departments or voluntary bodies or neighbours in order to ensure that all old people living alone are under some sort of surveillance. This one costly item could be multiplied a thousand times and there would still be others not yet contemplated.

In medical terms, one can say that the fact that an acceptable and effective form of treatment or care exists for a recognizable

form of illness or disability automatically creates a state of potential
need in anyone who could benefit from it. Services are set up in
order to provide effective and acceptable treatments or methods of
care as economically as possible. Whether identification of this
potential need occurs, and whether it is followed by demand or
utilization, will depend on many complex factors, including the
knowledge and attitudes of the patient, relatives, general public
and professional people. The final decision as to whether a service
is made available that will supply the appropriate treatment or care
is made by the people who control access to the service. 'Need' is
then judged within the clinical transaction between doctor or other
professional worker and patient. This is 'personal' need—for heart
transplants, renal dialysis, nursing care in severe dementia, a
sheltered environment in chronic schizophrenia, or simply for
advice. At this level, terms like 'consumer' are misleading and
likely to distort understanding of the doctor–patient relationship.

But there is also a 'social' need, seen from the viewpoint of those
who represent society as a whole, and their civil servants. Given
limited resources, how many hospital beds, operating theatres,
doctors or nurses, can be provided? The answer, in turn, limits the
professional choice of the doctor, who cannot prescribe what is not
available. As we have already seen, it is impossible to satisfy all
potential need. Of course, if we consider, not just the problems of
one particular group—say the elderly—but those of every variety
of severely handicapped person, and of their families, their
neighbours, their employers, and those who try to help them
professionally, then we are considering the problems of society as
a whole. But it does not work like this. I may be very sympathetic
towards the problems of people with multiple sclerosis, because I
have a relative with that disease, but that does not necessarily make
me any more tolerant towards the problems of people with schizophrenia. I may well come to regard the claims made on behalf of
the mentally ill as detracting from the chance my own handicapped
relative has of receiving a decent service.

Some economists argue that it is possible to deal with the element of value in all these personal points of view, not by leaving the
provision of services to the free struggle of market forces, but by
placing a valuation on them that can ultimately be translated into
cash terms. The amount that any particular individual is prepared
to pay towards a given service can be estimated. The same is true

of two, or ten, or thousands of individuals. Whether existing resources should be spread thin so that everyone gets an equal share, irrespective of 'merit', or whether some individuals (say, the severely physically handicapped) should get an extra share because of their inability to help themselves, can thus be determined. But this does not get us closer to real values. Whose opinions are to be sampled? How are the questions to be determined? Should the opinions of those who are best informed be given greater weight? Suppose opinions change from one week to another, how is it possible to continue monitoring them? In practice, politicians, administrators, and clinicians will take the important decisions. There will never be sufficient information to make the decisions fully rational or automatic. It is impossible, therefore, to get away from the underlying value judgement. That does not, however, mean that planning and administration cannot be made more rational, only that it can never become completely rational (not even in a totalitarian system or in the freest of market economies).

Brian Abel-Smith[2] points out that what matters ultimately is the ethos and commitment of those working in health services 'to serve not only individual patients but the health of the community as a whole. This is not true only of doctors, dentists or of administrators and managers, but of nurses, social workers, and paramedical workers as well. Value for money in health care will not be secured until health professionals see it as part of their responsibility to see that it is. This has major implications for the original education and continuing education of those working in health services.'

The introduction of a Chief Scientist's organization into some of the major English government departments, including the Department of Health and Social Security, is intended to ensure a more systematic canvassing of outside scientific opinion about problems currently subject to policy review, and the work that could be undertaken to explore new solutions to them. It is too soon to say whether it will be successful. Another approach, much spoken of by British governments, is to bring the processes of decision-making, both centrally and locally, more into the open, so that the reasons for decisions can be subjected to criticism from outside. The United States has been more successful in this respect than the United Kingdom, although it is arguable that the British system cannot survive unless more openness is achieved. The alternative is to become more authoritarian as in the Soviet system. An arbitrary element in decision-making must always remain, but it should only be tolerated when the fullest possible explanations have been given, so that, in the last resort, the electorate know what they are voting about.

This arbitrary element would still remain, even if many more potential needs were turned into 'rights', enforceable at law, like the minimum standards that are laid down for housing or for safety at work. In the long run, as in the Alabama decision (see page 212), unless sufficient funds and resources are made available, legally sanctioned standards cannot be met. At the moment, in England, the social service departments have to meet certain statutory requirements concerning problem families and children at risk of injury, and this has given these groups high priority. There is no equivalent requirement to set up homes or hostels for people with chronic psychiatric illness who otherwise must stay in hospital. Making the provision of such services mandatory would redress the balance, but if the total available budget is not increased, then either present resources must be spread more thinly, or one or other group of the needy must suffer.

How to increase the amount of money that can be spent on those in need in our society (essentially a matter of increasing national production) is beyond the scope of this book. There is, however, the option of making better use of what we have. We already spend enormous sums on the health and social services. Do we get the best value for money?

There are many points at which it is possible to investigate the extent to which treatments and methods of care are, in fact, acceptable and effective, and that the services providing them are as economical as possible. Many expensive social and medical practices may be found to be ineffective in decreasing and preventing morbidity, and others may carry their own iatrogenic risks.[24] Health and social services research of this kind is only just beginning, and it is particularly needed in the field of psychiatry, where pharmacological, psychological, and social methods of treatment often have no reasoned justification.

Self-help, for example, is an area where investigation could prove useful. As we saw in chapter 4 many patients with schizophrenia, and their relatives, would be better able to cope if they were given expert advice about the various ways of responding to the symptoms. Should delusions be humoured or denied? Should social withdrawal be allowed or combated? Is there any way in which patients can anticipate a stimulus which might set off a hallucinatory or delusional episode, and learn to control it? By trial and error, patients and relatives come to conclusions about these matters, sometimes beneficial, sometimes harmful, but they are rarely given useful advice, largely because professional people have neglected to learn from them. However, the amount of technical knowledge required to counsel all the handicapped groups is enormous and no one individual could master it. Quite different technologies are required for the blind, the spastic, the schizophrenic, and the retarded. Some specialist professionals are required but they need not all be highly trained and expensive doctors.

Experiments in developing countries have shown that it is possible to train relatively inexperienced people to give certain treatments, such as injections of fluphenazine to control acute schizophrenia. Other studies have shown that nurses can become skilled in applying behavioural treatments under supervision. Health visitors and district nurses can undertake quite a lot of a general practitioner's work so long as they know that help will always be forthcoming if they get out of their depth. They can take charge of the immunization of babies, prescriptions for birth control medication, the stitching or treatment of minor wounds, advice on management of chronic illness, and so on. Relatives and patients can often themselves acquire a detailed knowledge of how to minimize chronic disabilities. Relatives are highly motivated to help. In administrative jargon, they are 'primary care' agents. But, far from getting the help they need, they have often been vilified as the major causal agents. Voluntary organizations such as Neurotics Nomine and Alcoholics Anonymous have already proved their worth.

There is already a tendency towards the use of day, rather than residential, care and of primary rather than specialist services, using psychiatrists more frequently in a consulting role. It is necessary to make sure that an increased emphasis on primary care does not mean that only the lesser disorders are treated. It is simple enough to save money by letting the severely handicapped shift for themselves without any help.

The enormous expenditure on major and minor tranquillizers

and sedatives is another area deserving study. The results of controlled trials have suggested, on the whole, rather limited and specific uses for such drugs. On the other hand, there is evidence that some people who would benefit from them do not receive them or do not receive sufficiently high doses. Better training of general practitioners in psychiatry would lead to more effective and economical care being given.

One of the severest critics of scientific professional medicine (as of other professional disciplines) has been Ivan Illich,[72] but a careful study of his work in order to obtain suggestions for improving and pruning medical services is disappointing. Illich is an inverse historicist, always harking back to a mythical golden age when a scientific medicine had not developed and healing was a magical art. He also seems to put forward a free market view in which the customer controls the transaction by paying for the services of the doctor, completely ignoring the strong class bias of such an analysis. There are three links in his denunciation of iatrogenesis. The most direct is the undisputed fact that doctors can cause disability as well as ameliorate it; the cure is sometimes worse than the disease. The second link is 'social iatrogenesis', a dependence on medical help that prevents non-medical health-enhancing mechanisms from operating. For example, the sickness certificate legitimizes laziness, and the label of schizophrenia absolves an individual from responsibility. The third link is 'structural iatrogenesis', an inability to cope with one's own personal problems because the current ethic assumes that they can be overcome only with medical help. Pain, for example, can be dealt with by stoicism or by self-dosing with opium or alcohol. The doctor's presence at the deathbed is regarded as an intrusion on privacy whereas the priest's is not. Illich does not put forward reasoned alternatives. Nearly all his examples are taken from other authors, and in most cases where there is any substance in the criticism, there appears to be a fairly satisfactory practical solution. Illich, however, only accumulates the examples as a kind of launching platform for a grand idea, that of 'deprofessionalizing' medicine, giving responsibility for health back to society. 'Society' means whatever Illich chooses it to mean—often a grossly romanticized version of Lévi-Strauss's 'little, savage tribes'.

One of the problems that arise when popular prophets like Illich take over and promote, for their own purposes, the useful ideas produced by other people, is that the work of the original thinkers comes to be seen only through distorting lenses. It is clear enough that the first basis for planning health services in developing countries ought to be preventive: ensuring adequate nutrition, clean water, eradication of disease-bearing insects, health education, and other methods of primary prevention. The second basis is a cheap but universal service provided, at the primary level, not by doctors but by specially trained health workers who themselves remain part of the community they serve. Useful services of this kind have been developed in China, Cuba, and rural Tanzania. The values of individual curative medicine, with its more and more expensive technology, should not be allowed to determine the planning of services. Many developing countries have now learned these lessons. More developed countries have overcome the first set of problems. We already have clean water and adequate nutrition. Our primary prevention problems are concerned with matters such as pollution, cigarette smoking, traffic accidents, overeating, alcoholism and under-exercise. With the expenditure of a great deal of money we might (it is not certain), ensure that some middle-aged people stay alive for a few years longer. The prevention of accidents is one of the few factors that could affect younger people. Eventually, countries that at the moment are 'developing' will encounter the same problems. What we can learn from them is the adaptation of caring services to the level of expenditure available. This will need much public debate before politicians can include it in their programmes.

The way in which these two points can be applied to the planning of psychiatric services deserves further consideration. First of all, we will consider the concept of prevention.

Prevention is better than cure

Beatrice Webb's first principle is still valid; prevention is better than cure. There are three types of prevention: primary, or stopping disease occurring in the first place; secondary, or detecting disease at an early stage in order to limit the development of residual chronic disabilities; tertiary, or preventing the accumulation of extra handicaps if clinical disabilities are unavoidable.

Primary prevention of the severe functional psychoses is not yet feasible in any systematic sense, since we do not know enough about their biological or social causes to be able to spot, early enough to do something about it, which people are vulnerable. A twenty-year study of the children of schizophrenic parents now under way may give some relevant information. We do already know that many people with schizophrenia have behaved unusually in youth.[185] Even if a precise predictive test could be perfected, however, it is not clear that any remedial action could be taken to postpone or prevent onset. None of the family theories offers any specific suggestions, and empirical counselling and support might well make matters worse by focusing the family's attention on the possibility of later illness. Pasamanick put forward a theory concerning a 'continuum of reproductive casualty' which posited that certain preventable paranatal abnormalities (e.g. those due to malnutrition) could increase the risk of schizophrenia and other psychiatric conditions. There is some statistical evidence for such an argument, but the basis for intervention is usually more direct. We do not need additional reasons for trying to prevent malnutrition during pregnancy. It should, of course, be remembered that a decrease in foetal and infantile mortality has led to an increase in the prevalence of conditions like Down's syndrome.

It is important to recognize a trap in the idea of primary prevention, particularly so far as severe psychiatric disorders are concerned, since the most well-meaning people may fall into it. Because social factors are undoubtedly very important in causing mental illness, it is tempting to suppose that all that is *really* needed is social action. In one version of this argument, social action means changing society in some radical fashion. In another, it means changing family relationships, since mental illness is seen purely as a manifestation of interpersonal disturbances. Between the two lies a spectrum of other alternatives. Such theories must do harm if they are based on a denial of handicap rather than an attempt to reduce or limit or prevent it. It will, of course, very often be necessary to attend to problems in relationships when one family member is schizophrenic, but to ignore the schizophrenia as simply one of the ways in which these relationships are manifested, without any other meaning of its own, is to give up hope of helping the situation. Similarly, rehousing such a family may be an extremely useful measure and, sometimes, all that is needed. One sometimes hears the slogan; 'The best way to improve mental health is to spend all our spare money on housing,' but to think that schizophrenia will be prevented in a society where everyone is well-housed, is to indulge in fantasy. The welfare state in Britain was largely founded on Beatrice Webb's idea that if poverty could be prevented, much disease, handicap and misery would be prevented with it. The kind of poverty she was concerned with arose out of the very low wages paid to workers. Many of us who live in the temporarily rich societies of the 1970s cannot imagine ourselves as we might have been in Victorian times. Henry Mayhew's *London Labour and the London Poor* is a help. A street prostitute told him: 'You folks as has honour, and character, and feelings, and such, can't understand how all that's been beaten out of people like me. I don't feel. I'm used to it . . . I don't want to live. And yet I don't care enough about dying to make away with myself.'

Universal education, subsidized housing, health care based on national insurance, pensions, unemployment and sickness benefits, and welfare supplements, have done much to prevent pauperism and its ill-effects. Such poverty as still exists tends to be concentrated in certain groups of disadvantaged people; those with large families, the long-term unemployed, the aged, the ill and the handicapped. There are specially deprived areas in which poverty is particularly apparent, although it is recognized that most people in such areas are not in fact living below the poverty line, and that, from a national point of view, most poor people are not living in deprived areas.[151] The strategy of concentrating extra resources in economically declining inner-city areas (the community development projects) has not proved very successful. These problems need to be tackled on a regional or national basis. Alternative strategies of income-maintenance, or job-creation in areas of high unemployment, have therefore been proposed.

Some research carried out at the reception centre for homeless men in Camberwell, London, lends support to the idea that much of the destitution found in cities in modern times has complex social causes.[208] The earlier background of the men showed one predominant characteristic: a general lack of any advantage or privilege that would facilitate the acquisition and maintenance of a recognized position in society. The following description pertains to the group as a whole rather than to individuals but it gives a fair picture of their lives. They tend to come from large families housed in poor and overcrowded conditions, and their fathers were often unskilled manual workers. They achieved little at school, truanted a good deal, and acquired few vocational skills. They were at a disadvantage compared with their siblings. On leaving school they found themselves in an area where unemployment was high, particularly in unskilled occupations, and where it was difficult to find cheap accommodation away from home. Many moved to other cities in search of work. During their twenties, they did not, like most of their contemporaries, marry and have children. Instead they tended to move from job to job in single-sex trades, cut off from the rest of society. Kitchen portering was probably the single commonest job. Some were in the armed forces. They tended not to save money or to contribute to pension schemes, and were quickly out of pocket when they became unemployed, and so had to accept social security. A very high proportion had criminal records, particularly offences connected with alcoholism and vagrancy. Racial prejudice was not prominent at that time but has become important since. Even when working at their best, many of these men were living in a financially precarious situation and the accidents of life, together with drinking or gambling, could easily move them towards real destitution. Their first contact with the reception centre was made, on average, in their mid-thirties, and for some this was the first of many visits.

Recently the age at which men become destitute has been getting lower. A report on young Scotsmen in London, published in 1976, described the increase in numbers of young people from Glasgow, who come south to find work but find, not only that they remain unemployed, but that the price of decent accommodation is entirely beyond their means. The process described by Susanne Wood[208] then comes into operation, but at a much younger age than hitherto. There seems to be little doubt that, as unemployment rises in the most deprived areas, more and more young people are affected, and that it is not only the marginal youngsters described by Wood who are now at risk.

A case can certainly be made for primary prevention. Creating job opportunities for unskilled young men, and improving the supply of cheap accommodation where they could live after leaving home, would reduce the number who migrate in search of work and who, ten years later, become destitute. This, in turn, might prevent a good deal of alcoholism, depression, and other handicaps. Unfortunately, it has not been demonstrated, so far, that income maintenance schemes are successful. A recent OECD report shows little correlation, in Europe and the United States, between expenditure on income maintenance and indices of poverty. This may simply mean that the money often goes to the wrong people, rather than to the low-paid, the unemployed, those with large families, and the handicapped. Some of it may, of course be given to legitimate recipients, but spent unwisely. There is no reliable means of picking out individuals at highest risk. It is also necessary to consider the negative incentive effect so troublesome to those who framed the New Poor Law. A 'social' wage for an unemployed man with a large family may ensure that he does not try to obtain work, since the effort is simply not worth his while. This will particularly be true of those who have no vocational skill and no chance of obtaining work that is rewarding in itself, quite apart from the pay. The numbers in this marginal category are likely to be very small.

There is still another point to be considered. A very high proportion of chronically destitute men using the reception centre in Camberwell are mentally or physically ill or disabled.[179] The onset of illness or handicap often appears to be related to the process of becoming destitute, particularly when a general background of social disadvantage is present as well. Of course, the life of the deprived and destitute itself contains more risk of developing physical diseases (particularly respiratory) and psychiatric disorders (particularly alcoholism and depression).

There is now good evidence that people who accumulate in long-term residential accommodation, whether hospitals, prisons, nursing homes, hostels or reception centres, are often 'homeless single people', in the sense that they have no home to go to, and that they also have a long history of unemployment and inability to cope with everyday social problems.[66, 112] The protected environments in which they accumulate provide an alternative to destitution. What happens when the less capable are discharged or turned out is all too evident. They tend to wander the streets, to end up in lodging-houses or unsuitable rooms, or to be exploited by 'hotel' proprietors for their social security money.

Thus the problem of destitution must be tackled throughout the whole process, not only at its beginning. Destitution has multiple causes and it would be unwise to think that even massive housing and employment schemes would prevent it altogether. Physical and mental illness and disability are extra factors which, particularly when combined with social disadvantage, may make it impossible for men to avoid destitution. Methods of secondary and tertiary prevention therefore need to be taken just as seriously, and we shall take up this point again.

So far as the lesser psychiatric disorders are concerned, the work described in chapter 3 shows that there are rarely single causes and that it is difficult to predict which individual will find which environmental factor most distressing. As in the case of malnutrition, many of the factors that contribute towards mental ill-health are clearly worth preventing in their own right. We should not need the argument that poverty or unemployment or bad housing cause psychiatric disorders in order to initiate social action. At quite a different level, one can argue that many people need a quiet life. If they are clever enough they will be able to find a way of life that does not put them under pressure. But not everyone is clever and lucky. Many are under constraints of various kinds, whether owing to physical handicap, psychological vulnerability or social disadvantage, and they are at a higher risk of breakdown. It would be optimistic indeed to assume that all such unfair distinctions between human beings can be eliminated by social action.

Professional roles

People who enter the professions of medicine and social work are usually, at least initially, attracted by the idea of helping others with a wide variety of problems. It is only later during training that attention becomes restricted to certain kinds of problem, perhaps those that can be dealt with by the use of techniques that the newly qualified professional feels most competent to use. There is then a danger of over-using one particular brand of expertise, whether it is medication or case-work or psychotherapy or social action, in spite of the complexity of the problems that are presented.

Quite often, of course, the most important problems, the ones that most need intervention, will not be the ones presented. The doctor may not hear about the awful housing situation, the disastrous marriage or the retarded child who cries all night. He may hear only the complaints of sleeplessness, dyspepsia or tension headache. Quite often, too, the key problem will be psychological rather than social in nature; lying in the individual's attitude to him or herself. Skills analogous to those of the novelist may then be needed to work out a satisfactory solution. But often, the quickest way to reduce suffering and restore function is to diagnose an illness or a disability and to recommend an effective and acceptable treatment or method of coping. Here the meaning of the term 'mental illness' or 'mental disability' is quite specific. It has no necessary connection with 'madness' in the general sense although, of course, deviant behaviour may occur as a result of the illness or disability.

In the first two cases, once it is clear that the third type of solution is not relevant, there is no particular reason why the practitioner should be a doctor. In the third case a medical training is important but more general healing arts and an ability to prescribe social changes or welfare benefits will often be needed as well. This is to say no more than that there are biological, psychological and social components in every problem presented. The essence of diagnosis is to determine what combination of interventions will bring the most effective and economic relief of suffering and disability.

The practical problem is that no single individual can be expert in all three fields but yet people like to be able to take their problems to one professional person, such as a general practitioner, whom they can trust. Doctors develop a good deal of confidence, during their training, in their ability to make a medical diagnosis, and to a lesser extent in their capacity to advise about normal biological functioning and development. They are least likely to be confident about their social and psychological skills. If social workers and general practitioners worked from the same health centres they could do a great deal to teach each other how to cope with problems that arise in overlapping areas of practice and how to recognize types of problem that are most effectively dealt with by the other profession. This could eventually cut out a good deal of duplication of effort.

It might turn out that the area of overlap was very considerable. In fact, all professional workers tend to over-value the uniqueness of their own talents. How much of a doctor's job could be undertaken by nurses; how much of a nurse's by nursing assistants; what are the essential differences between a psychiatrist and a clinical psychologist; could a health visitor undertake most of a social worker's job so far as general practice is concerned? Each profession tends to feel that the essential skills of the others could be acquired within a few months. As we have seen, experiments in developing countries have demonstrated that brief, highly specific and concentrated training can indeed produce an effective practitioner, at least in limited technical fields. The new roles that psychiatric nurses are finding, in behaviour therapy and in the community management of chronic illness and disability, suggest ways in which services may usefully develop in future. The staff of day centres and hostels should also be regarded as an underutilized resource. But however 'deprofessionalized' a service becomes there will always be a tendency towards more and more learning and specialization, since knowledge accumulates, principles are formulated and other people want to learn them. When a seemingly inevitable tendency towards increasing bureaucracy is added, together with a developing rivalry towards the group of practitioners exercising the most closely similar functions, all the elements for the creation of a new profession are present.

The process of professional evolution takes different forms in different parts of the world and it does not seem of great general interest to attempt a prediction about the future of any one particular group, such as psychiatrists. Each separate function *could* be taken over by some other type of professional. If general practitioners and social workers were really well trained and motivated to cope with the psychiatric aspects of their work; if the neuropsychiatrist of former days could be reintroduced in order to deal with the smaller volume of acute in-patient work; if experienced nurses could take over the job of effective long-term counselling; if clinical psychologists took on more responsibility; if geriatricians looked after everyone with dementia; the psychiatrist could quietly fade away. At the moment, the psychiatrist is the only professional person able to combine the elements of these roles and to provide a link between all those concerned with the diagnosis, treatment and care of psychiatric illness and disability. It certainly makes a satisfying and rewarding as well as a necessary and socially useful job. But to be properly effective, psychiatrists and other professional people need to be able to prescribe the right combination, not only of treatments, but of services.

The future of psychiatric services

Predicting the future of psychiatry is as hazardous as predicting the weather. Virtually every condition of importance in psychiatry has multiple causes, many of them psychological or social in nature. Services for people with psychiatric disorders depend on the social climate of the time, and on the changing social priorities given to the milder and the more severe disorders. In recent years, we have seen the development of an anti-psychiatry movement that carried considerable conviction, in spite of the lack of evidence for its more extreme assertions and the strong body of evidence against them. That movement is now in disarray, perhaps because it tried both to destroy and to promise too much. The fantasies of revolutionaries have tended, in our time, to be expressed in psychiatric (or anti-psychiatric) terms, just as, in the seventeenth century, they found expression in the form of religious (or anti-religious) experiences. The realities of schizophrenia, mania, depression, mental retardation, dementia, and other severe disorders have not, however, been touched by these fantasies, although for a time many people were beguiled into believing that they would be. Although we cannot look very far into the future in order to discover what further social reactions will influence the development of psychiatric services, two, at least, of their key functions ought to be considered; the provision of sheltered environments, and the use of compulsory admission to hospital.

Both the official English and the official American plans for the future envision a time when the present psychiatric hospitals will have been replaced by a range of alternatives. (Russian psychiatrists remain profoundly sceptical). Let us suppose that adequate funds were available to develop the district general hospital units that would treat the acutely ill. We may assume that at least 50 'new' long-stay patients aged under 65, per 100,000 total population, are accumulating at the moment, either in hospital, or at home, or in unsuitable accommodation elsewhere. Of these, about one-third need hospital accommodation (17 per 100,000) because of functional psychiatric conditions.[112] If accommodation on a suitably domestic scale could be made available near a general hospital psychiatric unit, this might be the best solution. It is out of the question for this group to sleep in a busy acute ward but the day hospital facilities, suitably enlarged and equipped for rehabilitation, could be shared. A few would be high security cases and it might be that a regional unit would be more suitable, because of the very specialized accommodation required. The problem about this solution would be that such units would inevitably attract a wider group of people, including acutely ill patients who were too disturbed for modern general hospitals to want to cope with, and chronically disturbed prisoners who were not wanted in the prison system.

Even within the age-group under 65, there would be people with pre-senile organic conditions, many of whom do not need specialized psychiatric care. The solution of this most complex problem is tied up, on the one hand, with that of the younger 'chronic sick' and, on the other, with that of senile dementia.

Yet another group is composed of people who need considerable supervision, usually because of chronic disabilities associated with schizophrenia, though not necessarily in a hospital setting. These are people who need help because otherwise they neglect their toilet, their nutrition, or their appearance, and who tend to wander about without awareness of common dangers or social responsibilities. They do not need very specialized medical or nursing services, but they need help and supervision throughout the 24 hours. This could be provided in night hostels and day centres, with transport laid on between the two, thus eliminating the appearance of an institution while preserving the protective nature of the environments. The residential setting would need to be surrounded by a protected space (gardens or grounds) in which the patient could wander without being exposed to public scrutiny. A minimum of 15 places of this kind, per 100,000 population, would be required.

A similar number of places would be required in less supervised accommodation such as group homes, in which people otherwise accumulating as 'new' long-stay in psychiatric hospitals could look after themselves.

Yet a further set of places would be required for the people with special needs, who at present accumulate in psychiatric hospitals because, as well as being blind, or deaf, or epileptic, or mentally retarded, they have also acquired the diagnosis of 'psychosis'. This diagnosis might well have been justified at some time in the past, but following recovery from the psychiatric disorder, it has proved impossible (often because of prejudice) to find more suitable accommodation for them.

All these requirements are extra to what is available at the moment and the estimates are minimal. Double this provision might well be required. Moreover, since there has been no rationally designed scheme based upon the needs of a complete area, there has been no evaluation either. These estimates are quite hypothetical. Nevertheless, if the large psychiatric hospitals are to be closed, these functions have to be carried out in other ways.

The essential reasons for living in a protected environment are nearly always social, since most psychiatric investigation and treatment does not in itself necessitate a residential setting. The main functions to be undertaken, apart from the obviously medical ones, are supervision, active rehabilitation and shelter (including long-term management). These may sometimes best be carried out in a hospital setting. Once the acute condition has improved but has left either residual disabilities (such as slowness and withdrawal in schizophrenia) or a vulnerability to various environmental stressors (often very clearly predictable in schizophrenia, in frequently recurring affective psychoses, and in severely disabling neuroses), a decision about discharge has to be carefully balanced, taking the patient's wishes and the social circumstances into account. If the patient is discharged too quickly the risk of relapse may be high with a consequent loss of confidence and motivation and increase of 'stigma'. On the other hand, if the patient stays too long he may come to appreciate the protection of the hospital too highly and fear to leave. A period of rehabilitation while still in hospital, particularly if environmental modification can also be effected during this time, may then be more beneficial than discharge to the care of some other agency (even if available). The supervision of seriously disturbed behaviour is not likely to be challenged as a hospital function; at least, not by anyone who wants to take it over. This is traditionally a nursing function. There is also a medical component even in the provision of sheltered accommodation, since considerable skill and knowledge are required to prevent disabilities from getting worse. Psychiatric handicaps are highly reactive to the environment and, in this sphere as in most of the others discussed earlier, medical and social aspects of care are so closely linked as to be indistinguishable for practical purposes. Other mundane reasons for a patient staying in hospital for some time are to give a respite to relatives, to keep the goodwill and trust of patients and to fill gaps in other social or health services.

On the other hand, the discussion in the preceding paragraph could be turned upside down, in order to show that some non-hospital settings do manage to contain seriously disturbed patients, that psychiatrists can advise on treatment very effectively even when the handicapped individual is not living in hospital, and that the social components in rehabilitation and the provision of shelter are quite as important as the medical.

In practice, there is always a medical and a social component in treatment and in care, and fluctuations in any individual case are such that it is often difficult to say where medical responsibility ends and social responsibility begins. Nevertheless, this artificial split is what the administrative separation of medical and social hierarchies tends to emphasize and even require. No matter how one preaches 'integration', or sets up liaison committees and multidisciplinary teams, there is a fatal tendency to compartment-alize thinking and action in terms of one or other model. This has meant that social processes have sometimes been overlooked or even denied in hospital practice, while the client's handicaps and specific vulnerabilities have been overlooked or even denied in social practice. A transfer of responsibility merely perpetuates this barrier and substitutes one set of disadvantages for the other. Obviously an effective service ought to be accommodated to the needs of the handicapped individual rather than to the niceties of preserving separate administrations.

This principle applies across the whole range of accommodation needed, which includes 'hospital' provision (for those recovering slowly from psychiatric illnesses, those requiring 'transitional' rehabilitation before discharge, and those in need of supervision because of disturbed behaviour), 'hostel' provision (for those who need supervision but can be closer to the everyday life of the community), and less supervised but still partially protected accommodation in group homes, bed-sitters, supervised lodging or family care. An equally wide range of day and leisure-time provision is also required.

The overlap between the roles of hospital nurse and day-centre or hostel supervisor, between community nurse and social worker, between psychiatrist and general practitioner, between occupa-tional therapist and occupational supervisor, is very obvious to anyone who knows the entire range of services provided by these apparently different professions. The contribution of the psychologist in the management of disturbed behaviour and handicap is now becoming clearer but overlaps with that of all the other workers.

Some mitigation of the split might be achieved if the highest area and regional health authority committees overlap a substantial part of their membership with local authority social service committees and if senior officers of the two hierarchies also have voting rights on each other's executive committees. Staff of the social services department who have functions in connection with the mentally ill or disabled should, of course, have specialist training. Finally, hospitals should be encouraged to set up hostels and group homes for chronically handicapped individuals who need long-term medical or nursing attention but who nevertheless need a home of their own. When the hospital is in the centre of its catchment area, a house on the periphery of the site, with the front door opening to a public street and the back door opening to a private open space, would have considerable advantages.

Various models of sheltered care need to be investigated and experiment encouraged. For example, a range of units for handicapped people, occupational and residential, hospital and local authority, might be linked together functionally but scattered geographically over a convenient city area. Several adjacent houses with large gardens, perhaps situated in a residential square, might be linked to others within easy walking distance and yet others an easy bus-ride away. Such a cluster of units could serve a wide range of functions for a sizeable group of handicapped people, while retaining a domestic and human scale. The staff numbers would be sufficient to make communication, supervision and training feasible. Links between relatives and friends and with the sympathetic public would be simple. The use of family care, particularly on the Dutch model,[190] and even the construction of one or two experimental sheltered communities jointly between a hospital and a local authority, should also be considered. Local authority day-centres also need re-evaluation. At least one in each area might be upgraded closer to the status of a Remploy factory.

It would be a great pity if the opportunity for imaginative development were missed because rigid building specifications led to the construction of identical slab blocks all over the country.

Perhaps there are sufficient ideas here to suggest how innovations might be made in the present pattern of psychiatric service for chronically handicapped or relapsing patients without decreasing the amount of support available. If no such innovations are possible, the very least we should aim at is to make sure that our present services do not get worse.

The concept of responsibility

A second key function of psychiatric hospitals is to provide for people who are regarded as temporarily non-responsible by reason of mental illness. Before deciding that this function is unnecessary, we need to consider the concept of responsibility itself. We all try to influence each other's opinions and behaviour. In the ordinary give and take of social interaction it is assumed that most people can look after themselves but even so it has been found necessary to pass various restrictive laws, for example protecting consumers against unscrupulous salesmen. A toddler in a busy street, or a young man with profound mental retardation, or an old lady with severe dementia, would come into this category. Even if we were total strangers, we should quickly assume from their behaviour that they were not fully responsible and that they needed a good deal of guidance and supervision in order to protect them from getting into situations in which they might come to harm. We should usually adopt some sort of theory of immaturity, illness or disability, although this might not be made explicit.

Much the same reasoning is involved if someone like this appears about to make an injudicious will or to dispose of assets unwisely or to act in a way that will harm other people. A major problem occurs, however, in cases where there is a fluctuation in the same individual between periods of full responsibility and partial or absent responsibility. This can occur during the course of many psychiatric illnesses, notably mania, severe depression, schizophrenia, and delirium.

In English practice, no court need be involved in deciding whether a person regarded as mentally ill should be compulsorily admitted to hospital. The Mental Health Act of 1959 was hailed at the time as a piece of progressive legislation because it removed the previous requirement for a magistrate to be involved in all but emergency admissions. Instead, a Mental Health Review Tribunal could be invoked as an appeal procedure. It has become clear that the Tribunal system has varied in practice between regions and that applications are much more likely to be successful when the patient is assisted by an advocate.[58] There have also been notorious cases when medical advice was ignored, and the patient discharged, with disastrous consequences. The system could be improved, by ensuring that all compulsorily detained patients should regularly be considered by Tribunals, by ensuring that patients were represented, and by laying down clear criteria for continuing compulsion.

The problem of emergency admission under compulsion is more difficult. The onus of deciding whether the patient is likely to harm himself or others, as well as deciding the degree of rationality and the severity of any causal mental illness, falls upon the doctors involved. It has been suggested that the procedure is sometimes applied too casually. The wording of the relevant sections of the English Mental Health Act leaves no doubt that the doctor must decide how far any particular aspect of a patient's behaviour is a manifestation of illness and only if he is satisfied that a patient is 'mentally ill' may he apply compulsion. But with schizophrenic patients whose illness runs a fluctuating course and whose antisocial behaviour is not accompanied by florid symptoms such as delusions or hallucinations (at least, these are not described by the patient and may be controlled whenever he is under observation by someone in authority), it is the behaviour that provides the main evidence of the mental condition. The psychiatrist can apply strict or flexible criteria to make his decision, depending of course also on information from the other people involved. This decision may look quite different to the patient and to the relatives. Some 17 per cent of admissions to English psychiatric hospitals are under compulsion. In one area the proportion is as low as 5 per cent, so that further progress may be expected. Many admissions last only a few days. It would not seem that a fundamental change in the English law is necessary but a useful innovation would be to increase the provision of legal advice. A new breed of lawyers is needed to supply this service that, as yet, hardly exists in England.

Criticism of psychiatrists has already resulted in fewer patients being admitted under compulsion, and the situation in the U.S.A. and U.K. described earlier suggests that sometimes this has resulted, not in a defence of the patient's civil rights, but in a substantial decrease. This will particularly be the case if those opposing a compulsory order do so for irrelevant ideological reasons, having been persuaded that 'mental illness does not exist' and that relatives who ask for admission must inevitably be prejudiced. Presumably this will be unlikely to happen as advocates become familiar with the problems and find out for themselves what happens after people are, or are not, admitted to hospital. However, psychiatrists themselves are much affected by the current climate of opinion. There are common stories from relatives that they cannot obtain help for people who are clearly unable to help themselves.

Six weeks after his release, I knew my son was becoming ill again. I contacted the social worker, who was fully in the picture, and begged him to go and see my son. He flatly refused, telling me that the person who was ill had to make the appeal himself and nothing could be done by a relative or friend ... my son was eventually arrested and committed to a mental hospital by the court but he has absconded from the hospital three times and is still at large.[128]

Another man was brought to the emergency clinic of a psychiatric hospital because his wife said he was over-active, elated, and sleepless and was beginning to speak of spending their joint savings on some grandiose and impossible scheme. She thought his judgement completely irrational. She also feared violence if she crossed him although this was not her principal worry. On two previous occasions similar symptoms had developed into full-blown mania but, because he convincingly denied abnormality when seen by doctors, he was not compulsorily admitted before he had ruined their small business and behaved in a grossly abnormal way in public. Admission to hospital had been a humiliating experience because it had taken place in full view of the neighbours. He had responded quickly to treatment on both occasions and had then been extremely sorry for the trouble he had caused. The marriage was otherwise a contented one. Now his wife pleaded that he be admitted in time to prevent the same thing happening a third time. The man was in control of himself during the interview, denied all symptoms, and refused voluntary admission. The psychiatrist did not agree that emergency admission under order was indicated and he was not in fact admitted for another week, during which time he again spent all their savings.

A recent inquiry into the death of a nurse who had been stabbed while trying to persuade an informal patient (who had earlier shown signs of violence) to move to a locked ward concluded:

that by letting mentally ill people retain their ordinary freedom, society gives them the freedom also to remain ill, the freedom to refuse treatment and indeed the freedom to deteriorate mentally.

If 'society' insists that all other considerations, including the human rights of others in contact with them, must be subordinated to the overriding freedom of severely mentally ill people, then even sensible everyday decisions will become impossible in the absence of a lawyer. In the United States it is now quite possible to come across a psychiatrist who will refuse to advise a relative what to do about schizophrenic behaviour. (Suppose, for example, someone refuses to use her bedroom because she says the neighbours are pumping gas under the bed.) The reason given will be that, if the individual herself does not ask for help, there is no problem. In the last resort, if the relative cannot tolerate the situation, one or other party has to leave, preferably the one who is complaining, i.e. the relative. In fact, it is possible to give useful advice that might avoid the necessity for subsequent compulsory admission. The psychiatrist taking the *laissez-faire* view will be convinced that he is behaving in a liberal, enlightened, and humane way. He is pushing the idea of civil rights as far as it can be taken, in the interest of a theoretical average client, even though evident disability has to be denied in order to maintain the fiction that everyone is fully responsible. To those who feel compassion for the ill and handicapped, and for the relatives who try to help them, this turning of the back is similar to Cain's: 'I am not my brother's keeper.' The idea that compulsion may only be used if the patient is clearly dangerous can be incompatible with a proper respect for patients' interests and rights, let alone those of others.

At the other extreme, the absolutist assumption that all socially unusual or undesirable behaviour can be regarded in a deterministic way as part of a 'psychosis', thus excluding individual responsibility altogether, is equally likely to lead to harmful consequences. In the *Ann Arbor News* of 3 August 1975 it was reported that a man had been arrested because he was begging for dimes. He was carrying a suitcase containing $24,087 in small bills. A few days later a judge committed him to a psychiatric hospital because he 'lacked good judgement'. Most of his money then had to be used to pay for the drug treatment and hospital care ordered by the court. He even had to pay the fees of the prosecuting lawyer. He was an eccentric, solitary person who worked hard and lived frugally; his only oddity being that he was obsessed with saving money. There was no suggestion that he had ever harmed anyone. No mention was made of the diagnosis but presumably it hardly mattered. He was 'psychotic' because he 'lacked judgement'. In practice, this would mean that he would be treated as 'schizophrenic'.

This case may be used to introduce a discussion of the issues that arise in criminal as opposed to civil cases. Assuming that the individual did commit the offence with which he was charged,* and that this was not due to pure accident or circumstances beyond his control, two central issues arise. The first is whether he can be regarded as capable of rationally choosing between various courses of action, in the light of a full appraisal of the foreseeable consequences, including those that may be harmful to himself or others. The second concerns the degree of probability that any incapacity of judgement is caused by mental illness or defect.

In severe cases of impaired judgement it will usually be found impossible to separate the two central issues. Someone who is grossly 'psychotic' (see pp. 44–48) because of acute delirium or mania or schizophrenia will show impaired judgement as one of the symptoms of the illness. However, this is not true at lesser degrees of severity. If judgement is impaired by alcohol, by foolishness, by jealousy, or by a combination of such factors, the defence of mental illness will not commonly arise at all. Even if the individual has acted in a 'blind rage', it will usually be assumed that he could have been in control of his actions.

This is the point at which controversy can arise. If, for example, it is a person's political judgement that is being questioned (suppose that he had committed an offence for political motives), the term 'psychosis' may be used to cover both the supposed aberration in judgement and the mental illness that is hypothesized to have caused it. This involves the begging of both questions. In other words, someone with a questionable lack of judgement may be committed because it is thought to be evidence of 'psychosis' and, vice versa, someone with a mild 'psychosis' may be regarded

---

* There is an anomaly if someone found 'unfit to plead' subsequently improves. Should he then come to trial? The alternative may be over-long detention.

as necessarily suffering from lack of judgement. Either way, the interpretation of the term 'psychosis' may, if the courts are willing, become the prerogative of psychiatric experts who might be influenced by extraneous factors such as the political or economic or social climate of the time.

Richard Arens[5] suggested that a judgement made in Washington in 1954, which came to be known as the Durham rule, was too permissive in its effect:

The legal and moral traditions of the western world require that those who of their own free will and with evil intent . . . commit acts which violate the law, shall be criminally responsible for those acts. Our traditions also require that where such acts stem from and are the product of mental disease or defect . . . moral blame shall not attach, and hence there will not be criminal responsibility.

This judgement was an innovation in American law but it might have had certain harmful consequences, in that psychoanalytic doctrine was becoming popular with the educated (particularly the literary) public and various minor conditions were interpreted by lawyers and defence psychiatrists as mental illnesses absolving from responsibility. Mental hospitals, hitherto resistant, were called upon to 'treat' committed 'neurotic' offenders. 'Hence they acquiesced in policies that progressively transformed hospitals into prisons.'

Arens argued that people accused of serious crimes were committed to mental hospitals although very little in the way of mental illness could really be demonstrated, and that sometimes, as in the case of Lincoln Rockwell, the American Nazi leader, a political motivation was involved. The term 'mental illness' could be used so elastically that it would cover one case in which extraneous circumstances seemed to make hospital more desirable than prison, while another case, otherwise very similar, would not be covered. Neither private nor public psychiatry resisted these pressures.

Bruce Ennis,[41] another critic of American procedures, has documented cases in which the law decided that previous decisions on responsibility, based on psychiatric evidence, were wrong. David Mechanic[117] observed:

Just as the label 'mental illness' may be useful under some circumstances, there are other situations where such a designation may do harm to a person's reputation and standing. In the minds of many people, 'mental illness' implies the inability to act rationally and responsibly and thus such labels are frequently discrediting. There are occasions when a prominent person holding unpopular views may be labelled mentally ill because the community has no other adequate way of coping with him. This phenomenon is extremely difficult to document since such persons often hold views or behave in a manner which is sufficiently deviant to substantiate in the minds of many the claim that they are mentally ill. However, there is a considerable danger in equating deviant views with mental disorder, and there are occasions when the mental illness label is used for political or social purposes unrelated to illness. For example, a Negro civil rights leader was sent involuntarily to one of New York's psychiatric observation wards after he attempted a citizen's arrest on the mayor for failing to enforce the law regarding discrimination. This was clearly a political gesture meant to embarrass the mayor and the use of psychiatry in this situation was also politically motivated.

Several other examples were considered in detail in chapter 6. There seem to be no famous British cases, though one could perhaps point to a negative case, that of William Joyce, executed for treason. No question as to his sanity was raised but some sort of a case could no doubt have been made out.

Judge D. L. Bazelon,[11] the author of the Durham rule, himself subsequently came to regard it as unsatisfactory:

... I favored the abandonment of the Durham rule because in practice it had failed to take the issue of criminal responsibility away from the experts. Psychiatrists continued to testify to the naked conclusion instead of providing information about the accused so that the jury could render the ultimate moral judgement about blameworthiness.

What the psychiatrist must do is to provide evidence of mental illness so severe that it is likely to interfere with the ability of the accused person to reach a fully informed judgement. That evidence must be of a precise and technical nature. It should not be sufficient to diagnose a 'psychotic' condition; in fact a severe anxiety state or hysterical condition or obsessional neurosis might theoretically be accepted as sufficient. The judgement as to 'blameworthiness' can then be taken by the court. It is not a matter for psychiatrists.

There remain a number of difficulties concerning the determination of causality. For example, it is now Russian practice to assume that, even if a mental illness were in remission at the time an offence was committed, responsibility will not be imputed (see p. 122). The more usual case would be one in which the illness had improved since the time of the offence. These issues have to be decided by the jury. A recent government committee reporting on the English law[143] recommended that severe mental illness present at the time of the offence, or occurring thereafter, should be regarded as sufficient reason for the special verdict, 'not guilty on evidence of mental disorder'. Following French practice, the issue of causation would not be considered. 'It is true that it is theoretically possible for a person to be suffering from a severe mental disorder which has in a causal sense nothing to do with the act or omission for which he is being tried but in practice it is very difficult to imagine a case in which one could be sure of the absence of any such connection.'

Once the issue of responsibility has been settled it should be left to the court to take evidence on the question of any further action needed such as absolute discharge, discharge on probation, compulsory admission to an ordinary or a special psychiatric hospital, with or without a restriction on discharge.

These provisions would not necessarily prevent the kind of action taken in the case of Leonid Plyushch. The report of the Committee on Mentally Abnormal Offenders, referred to earlier, contains a definition of 'severe mental disorder'. There are several clauses to the definition but each contains a term that would allow experts to testify that Plyushch was deluded (no definition of delusions is given) if the court were willing to accept their testimony. However, the fact that, in British and American courts, it is ordinarily the defence that enters a plea of mental illness, makes it unlikely that this particular problem would arise.

The discussion of 'aggressive psychopathy' on page 65 suggests the conclusion that, at present, there are insufficient grounds for including it under the heading of 'mental illness' for purposes of evidence to the courts.

A separate word needs to be said on the allied subject of depressive disorders, in which an individual is more likely to harm himself than others, although rarely there is a tragedy in which an individual kills his family rather than let them suffer the fate he thinks he has brought upon them. Some critics have suggested that compulsion should not be used even in these cases, on the ground that mental illness does not 'exist'. If someone wants to kill himself, why not let him get on with it? Most people, whether medically qualified or not, would find this attitude repellant. In any case, all that the doctor can do is to help the individual through his current phase of depression and thus give him another opportunity for choice. There is no way of stopping people from killing themselves if they really wish to do so.

Medico–legal practice tends to fluctuate backwards and forwards under the influence of public opinion. In England and America, at the moment, psychiatrists are under a good deal of public pressure not to admit patients under compulsion and not to treat people who do not wish to be treated. The pressure is applied by those who doubt the validity of psychiatric judgements about illness or disability. We have seen that their doubts have sometimes been justified but the problem of providing a better framework for action remains. The criticisms that will be made in future may tend to go the other way. Everyone in society has civil rights. We feel on humanitarian grounds that the balance has been tipped against the disadvantaged in society but if it is weighted too much in the opposite direction there will undoubtedly be a public reaction. Public attitudes are also likely to be influenced by accounts of mentally ill individuals who, after discharge from hospital, have repeated bizarre and apparently motiveless crimes. In such cases, most people would have been only too thankful if those responsible for allowing the discharge had adopted more generally restrictive criteria.

In summary, there are opportunities, in the situations dealt with by psychiatrists, for an overuse and an underuse of compulsion based on diagnosis of seriously impaired judgement due to mental illness. A great deal depends on how broadly or narrowly medical concepts are used. Changes in public opinion can shift psychiatric practice one way or the other. In the last resort, it is a matter of whether we can trust our doctors, our lawyers and our courts, and that depends on whether we trust our social system in general. If we can, a narrow legalism will tend overall, to restrict liberty, not enhance it. If we cannot, there are plenty of current examples to show that the existence of laws guaranteeing human rights is not, in itself, effective. There are several ways in which the English law could usefully be modified but basically it is sound.

8. The Traditions of Medicine

> *I shall be pardoned for calling it by so harsh a name as madness when it is considered that opposition to reason deserves that name and is really madness; and there is scarce a man so free from it but that if he should always on all occasions argue or do as in some cases he constantly does, would not be thought fitter for Bedlam than civil conversation. I do not here mean when he is under the power of an unruly passion but in the calm steady course of his life.*
>
> John Locke

John Locke carefully distinguished between 'madness' in the sense of unreasonableness, which is common, and 'madness' in the sense of being overpowered by 'an unruly passion', which is rare. This is a surprisingly modern distinction but Michel Foucault[46] would have none of it. To him, madness is always a form of opposition to *established* reason and the way people react to it is a function of the historical epoch in which they live. He thinks that in modern times, psychiatrists are simply agents of reaction whose covert function is to suppress the creative forces of opposition.

As for a common language, there is no such thing; or rather, there is no such thing any longer; the constitution of madness as a mental illness at the end of the eighteenth century, affords the evidence of a broken dialogue, points the separation as already effected, and thrusts into oblivion all those stammered imperfect words without fixed syntax in which the exchange between madness and reason was made. The language of psychiatry, which is a monologue of reason *about* madness, has been established only on the basis of such a silence.

In fact, one of the strongest tendencies in modern psychiatry is towards accepting Locke's differentiation between 'madness' (folly, unreasonableness, deviation) and 'unruly passions' (illness). Psychiatrists of this school put forward disease theories concerning certain restricted psychological syndromes and apply them in individual cases when they think they can thereby reduce suffering

and disability. They do their best to test these theories and are
ready to give them up if they do not prove useful. They do not
think that a disease theory explains the total personality and behaviour of the patient but only very specific and restricted aspects.
They will use many other types of 'model' as well as that of disease.

On the other hand, Foucault is right in assuming that many
psychiatrists throughout the world do not make Locke's distinction.
They regard any form of folly, unreasonableness or deviation as
falling on a continuum between relative normality and 'psychosis'
and they may be much more ready to apply labels such as 'schizophrenia' because some aspect of attitude or behaviour is socially
unintelligible or out of touch with 'reality'. In general, these schools
are likely to use highly complex and relatively unvalidated theories,
in a non-scientific way, i.e. they are not meant to be tested. The
theories may be social, psychological or somatic in nature.

It should be noted that metapsychological theories can be used
without attaching disease labels, simply to facilitate the process of
finding a satisfying explanation for the individual's current condition that can be used as a basis for further constructive action.
W. H. Auden described this process in his poem in memory of
Sigmund Freud: 'so many long-forgotten objects revealed by his
undiscouraged shining are returned to us and made precious again;
games we had thought we must drop as we grew up, little noises
we dared not laugh at, faces we made when no one was looking . . .
but he would have us remember most of all to be enthusiastic over
the night, not only for the sense of wonder it alone has to offer, but
also because it needs our love'. This process is essentially aesthetic
or moral rather than scientific in nature. It is applied privately
between therapist and client and does not carry the same social
dangers as when it is connected with a pseudoscientific disease
model.

In the light of these distinctions we can see that the scientific
approach to illness does not lead to deep insights concerning
historical forces. When Christopher Hill invites us to learn from
the 'lunatic fringe' of the seventeenth century, and also of our own
time, we should not look to Oliver Cromwell's depression or Isaac
Newton's obsessions but to 'deviance' that can clearly be defined in
social terms. Some psychiatrists are eager to play the game of
historical interpretation but if they do so by indiscriminately
attaching disease labels to historical or contemporary 'deviants'

they are fudging the distinction made by Locke and they fully deserve the strictures of Foucault.

Two great traditions have set up a creative tension within medicine. One is the gradual development over centuries, greatly accelerated during the past hundred years, of a tradition of clinical science. The other is the development and handing down of a tradition of healing based on experience, intuition and the use of the doctor's personal resources in interaction with those of the patient. The case of Gilbert Pinfold (see p. 107) can be used to illustrate both approaches. The superb clinical description forms the basis for comparison with experiences reported by others and for the recognition of syndromes; in this case, the central and paranoid syndromes are dominant but disorientation and memory disturbances are also present. The presence of these syndromes raises important further questions concerning possible causal factors. Two obvious possibilities are alcohol and the bromide prescription. The course of the condition, which continued for some time after both factors had been discontinued, suggests that 'bromism' is the most appropriate diagnosis, since bromide accumulates in the body and continues to have a toxic effect for a time even after no more is being taken. Similar clinical conditions, which eventually cleared up completely, had earlier been described following bromide intoxication. This process of diagnosis, using clinical description and comparison with the accumulated experience of other doctors, is essentially scientific. The descriptions of early 'childhood autism' by Itard (see p. 22) and 'aggressive psychopathy' by Haslam (see p. 65) are so vivid that to read them is to have the feeling of witnessing a creative act.

The other approach is different but complementary. An overdependence on alcohol can be seen as dissatisfaction with a way of life and an attempt to put it right using artificial means. Dependence is an acknowledgement that something is wrong. Perhaps in Pinfold's case the extreme reaction could, in retrospect, be regarded as part of a healing process. Waugh's own therapy was writing the book. He would not have thought he needed the help of psychoanalytic or other 'professional' theories but no doubt his religion was a great resource. Whether he was 'better' or not, in the end, for having been through the experience and having achieved his own aesthetic synthesis of it, is impossible to judge. It is a matter of value. But helping the healing process in this way is part of the tradition of medicine and it can never be eradicated.

The traditions of medicine have developed over centuries in response to the needs and the healing talents of human beings. They have deviated on occasion in one direction or another but always within limits, and always, controlled by the same human forces, they have returned to a central path. To separate people into physicians and patients is, of course, at the deepest level, no more possible than to divide them into good and evil. This assertion was the basic theme of Albert Camus' novel, *The Plague*. Dr. Rieux, the narrator, kept a journal of the plague year in which he has spoken for all of us, whatever our nationality:

Yet he knew that his chronicle could not be one of definitive victory. It could be no more than a witness to what had had to be done and to what, without doubt, would have to be done again, in order to combat the never-wearying arm of terror, by all who, not being able to be saints but refusing to yield to the plague, try, in spite of their personal conflicts, to be doctors.

References

1. ABEL-SMITH, B., 1964. *The Hospitals, 1800–1948: A Study in Social Administration in England and Wales.* London (Heinemann).
2. —— 1976 *Value for Money in Health Services.* London (Heinemann).
3. ABEY-WICKRAMA, I., A'BROOK, M. F., GATTONI, F., and HERRIDGE, C. F., 1969. 'Mental hospital admissions and aircraft noise.' *Lancet 2,* 1275–7.
4. ANON., 1973. '*Samizdat:* Ignorance in the service of arbitrariness.' *Survey 19,* 45–65.
5. ARENS, R., 1969. *Make Mad the Guilty.* Springfield (Thomas).
6. ARGYLE, M., 1974. 'Explorations in the treatment of personality disorders and neuroses by social skills training.' *Brit. J. Med. Psychol. 47,* 63–72.
7. BAHN, A. K., GARDNER, E. A., ALLTOP, L., KNATTERUD, G. L., and SOLOMON, M., 1966. 'Comparative studies of rates of admission and prevalence for psychiatric facilities in four register areas.' *Amer. J. pub. Hlth. 56,* 2033.
8. BAKER, J. R., 1974. *Race.* London (Oxford University Press).
9. BARNES, M., and BERKE, J., 1971. *Mary Barnes.* London (Mac-Gibbon and Kee).
10. BAZELON, D. L., 1969. In: *Special Report of First U.S. Mission on Mental Health to the U.S.S.R.* Public Health Service Publication No. 1893. Washington (U.S. Department of Health, Education, and Welfare).
11. —— 1974. 'Psychiatrists and the adversary process.' *Scientific American,* 230.
12. BERNAL, J. D., 1969. *Science in History: Vol. 4, The Social Sciences.* Harmondsworth (Penguin).
13. BETTELHEIM, B., 1967. *The Empty Fortress.* London (Collier-Macmillan).
14. BLOCH, S., and REDDAWAY, P., 1977. *Russia's political hospitals: the abuse of psychiatry in the Soviet Union.* London (Gollancz).
15. BOCKOVEN, J. S., 1956. 'Moral treatment in American psychiatry'. *J. nerv. men. Dis. 124,* 167–94 and 292–321.
16. BÖÖK, J. A., 1953. 'A genetic and neuropsychiatric investigation of a North-Swedish population.' *Acta Genetica et Statistica Medica 4,* 1–10.
17. BOYER, P., and NISSENBAUM, S., 1974. *Salem Possessed: The Social Origins of Witchcraft.* Boston (Harvard University Press).
18. BROWN, G. W., BHROLCHAIN, M., and HARRIS, T. O., 1975. 'Social

class and psychiatric disturbance among women in an urban population.' *Sociology 9*, 225–54.

19. —— and BIRLEY, J. L. T., 1970. 'Social precipitants of severe psychiatric disorders.' In: *Psychiatric Epidemiology*. Eds: Hare, E. H., and Wing, J. K. London (Oxford University Press).

20. —— BIRLEY, J. L. T., and WING, J. K., 1972. 'Influence of family life on the course of schizophrenic disorders: a replication.' *Brit. J. Psychiat. 121*, 241–58.

21. —— BONE, M., DALISON, B., and WING, J. K., 1966. *Schizophrenia and Social Care*. London (Oxford University Press).

22. CARSTAIRS, G. M., 1965. 'Cultural elements in the response to treatment.' In: *Transcultural Psychiatry*. Eds: Reuck, A. V. S., and Porter, R. London (Churchill).

23. CHECKLAND, S. G., and CHECKLAND, E. O. A. (Eds), 1974. *The Poor Law Report of 1834*. Harmondsworth (Penguin).

24. COCHRANE, A., 1971. *Effectiveness and Efficiency*. London (Oxford University Press).

25. COHN, N., 1975. *Europe's Inner Demons*. London (Chatto, Heinemann).

26. COLES, R., 1972. In: *Laing and Anti-Psychiatry*. Eds: Boyers, R., and Orrill, R. Harmondsworth (Penguin).

27. COOPER, B., and MORGAN, H. G. 1973. *Epidemiological Psychiatry*. Springfield (Thomas).

28. COOPER, J. E., KENDELL, R. E., GURLAND, B. J., SHARPE, L., COPELAND, J. R. M., and SIMON, R., 1972. *Psychiatric Diagnosis in New York and London*. Maudsley Monograph No. 20. London (Oxford University Press).

29. COPELAND, J., KELLEHER, M. J., GOURLAY, A. J., and SMITH, A. M. R., 1975. 'Influence of psychiatric training, medical qualification, and paramedical training on the rating of abnormal behaviour.' *Psychol. Med. 5*, 89–95.

30. CORNELL, J., 1966. *The Trial of Ezra Pound*. New York (Day).

31. CREER, C., and WING, J. K., 1974. *Schizophrenia at Home*. London (National Schizophrenia Fellowship, 29 Victoria Road, Surbiton, Surrey KT6 4JT).

32. CUMMING, E., 1968. 'Community psychiatry in a divided labor.' In: *Social Psychiatry*. Eds: Zubin, J., and Freyhan, F. New York (Grune and Stratton).

33. DAVIDSON, H. A., 1967. 'The double life of American psychiatry.' In: *New Aspects of the Mental Health Services*. Eds: Freeman, H., and Farndale, J. London (Pergamon).

34. DAVISON, K., and BAGLEY, C. R., 1969. 'Schizophrenia-like psychoses associated with organic disorders of the central nervous

system.' In: *Current Problems in Neuropsychiatry.* Ed: R. N. Herrington. London (R.M.P.A.).

35. Department of Health and Social Security, 1975. *Better Services for the Mentally Ill.* Cmnd. 6233. London (H.M.S.O.).

36. DUBOS, R., 1965. *Man Adapting.* New Haven (Yale University Press).

37. DUNHAM, H. W., 1965. *Community and Schizophrenia : An Epidemiological Analysis.* Detroit (Wayne State University Press).

38. DURKHEIM, E., 1952. *Suicide : A Study in Sociology.* Trans. Spaulding, J. A., and Simpson, G. London (Routledge).

39. EATON, J. W., and WEIL, R. J., 1955. *Culture and Mental Disorders.* Glencoe, Illinois (Free Press).

40. ELLENBERGER, H., 1970. *The Discovery of the Unconscious.* London (Allen Lane).

41. ENNIS, B., 1972. *Prisoners of Psychiatry : Mental Patients, Psychiatrists and the Law.* New York (Harcourt Brace Jovanovich).

42. EYSENCK, H. J., and EYSENCK, S. G. B., 1969. *Personality Structure and Measurement.* London (Routledge).

43. FARIS, R. E. L., and DUNHAM, H. W., 1939. *Mental Disorders in Urban Areas.* Chicago (Hafner).

44. FESTINGER, L., and KELLY, H. H., 1951. *Changing Attitudes through Social Contacts* (Research Center for Group Dynamics, Institute for Social Research, University of Michigan).

45. FLASCHNER, F. N., 1975. 'Constitutional requirements in commitment of the mentally ill: rights to liberty and therapy.' In: *The Future Role of the State Mental Hospital.* Eds: Zusman, J., and Bertsch, E. F. Lexington, Mass. (D.C. Heath & Co.).

46. FOUCAULT, M., 1967. *Madness and Civilization: A History of Insanity in the Age of Reason.* Trans. R. Howard. London (Tavistock).

47. FOULDS, G. A., and BEDFORD, A., 1975. 'Hierarchy of classes of personal illness.' *Psychol. Med. 5,* 181–92.

48. FRIED, M., 1964. 'Effects of change on mental health.' *Amer. J. Orthopsychiat. 34,* 3.

49. FULLER, P., 1975. 'A chat of analysts.' *New Society 33,* 237–8.

50. GATTONI, F. and TARNOPOLSKY, A., 1973. 'Aircraft noise and psychiatric morbidity.' *Psychol. Med. 3,* 516–20.

51. GOFFMAN, E., 1961. *Asylums: Essays on the Social Situation of Mental Patients and other Inmates.* Harmondsworth (Penguin).

52. GOLDBERG, D., 1972. *The Detection of Psychiatric Illness by Questionnaire.* London (Oxford University Press).

53. GOLDBERG, E. M., and MORRISON, S. L., 1963. 'Schizophrenia and social class.' *Brit. J. Psychiat. 109,* 785–802.

54. GOLDHAMER, H., and MARSHALL, A. W., 1955. *Psychosis and Civilisation*. Glencoe, Illinois (Free Press).
55. GORBANEVSKAYA, N., 1970. *Red Square at Noon*. Harmondsworth (Penguin).
56. —— 1972. *Poems, The Trial, Prison*. Ed. D. Weisshart. London (Carcanet).
57. GOTTESMAN, I. I., and SHIELDS, J., 1972. *Schizophrenia and Genetics: A Twin Study Vantage Point*. New York (Academic Press).
58. GREENLAND, C., 1970. *Mental Illness and Civil Liberty*. Occas. Papers on Soc. Admin. No. 38. London (Bell).
59. GRINKER, R., WERBLE, B., and DRYE, R. C., 1966. *The Borderline Syndrome*. New York (Basic Books).
60. GRUENBERG, E. M., 1957. 'Socially shared psychopathology.' In: *Explorations in Social Psychiatry*. Eds: Leighton, A. H., Clausen, J. A., and Wilson, R. N. New York (Basic Books).
61. HAGNELL, O., 1966. *A Prospective Study of the Incidence of Mental Disorder*. Lund (Berlingska).
62. HARE, E. H., and SHAW, G. K., 1965. *Mental Health on a New Housing Estate*. London (Oxford University Press).
63. HASLAM, J., 1809. *Observations on Madness and Melancholy*. London (Hayden).
64. HEMPEL, C. G., 1959. 'Introduction to problems of taxonomy.' In: *Field Studies in the Mental Disorders*. Ed. Zubin, J. New York (Grune and Stratton).
65. HESTON, L. L. 1966. 'Psychiatric disorders in foster home reared children of schizophrenic mothers.' *Brit. J. Psychiat. 112*, 819–25.
66. HEWETT, S., RYAN, P., and WING, J. K., 1975. 'Living without the mental hospitals.' *J. soc. Policy 4*, 391–404.
67. HEYMANN, C. D., 1976. *Ezra Pound: The Last Rower*. New York (Viking).
68. HILL, C., 1972. *The World Turned Upside Down: Radical Ideas During the English Revolution*. London (Temple Smith).
68. HIRSCH, S. R., GAIND, R., ROHDE, P. D., STEVENS, B. C., and WING, J. K., 1973. 'Outpatient maintenance of chronic schizophrenic patients with long-acting fluphenazine: double-blind placebo trial.' *Brit. Med. J. 1*, 633–7.
70. HIRSCH, S. R., and LEFF, J. P., 1975. *Abnormality in Parents of Schizophrenics: A Review of the Literature and an Investigation of Communication Defects and Deviances*. London (Oxford University Press).
71. HOLLINGSHEAD, A. B., and REDLICH, F. C., 1958. *Social Class and Mental Illness*. New York (Wiley).
72. ILLICH, I., 1975. *Medical Nemesis*. London (Calder and Boyars).

73. ITARD, J. M. G., 1801, 1807. *The Wild Boy of Aveyron*. Eng. trans. by G. and M. Humphrey, 1932. New York (Appleton-Century-Crofts), 1962.

74. IVERSEN, L. L., and ROSE, S. P. R. (eds), 1973. *Biochemistry and Mental Illness*. London (The Biochemical Society).

75. JAHODA, M., 1958. *Current Concepts of Positive Mental Health*. New York (Basic Books).

76. JASPERS, K., 1963. *General Psychopathology*. Trans. J. Hoenig and M. W. Hamilton. Manchester (Manchester University Press).

77. JOINT COMMISSION ON MENTAL ILLNESS AND HEALTH, 1961. *Action for Mental Health*. Final report of the Joint Commission. New York (Basic Books).

78. JONES, K., 1972. *A History of the Mental Health Services*. London (Routledge).

79. JONES, M., 1962. *Social Psychiatry in the Community, in Hospitals and in Prisons*. Springfield (Thomas).

80. JOSEPH, K., 1972. *Foreword to : National Health Service Reorganisation : England*. Cmnd. 5055. London (H.M.S.O.).

81. KANNER, L., 1943. 'Autistic disturbances of affective contact.' *Nerv. Child 2*, 217.

82. KESSEL, N., 1960. 'Psychiatric morbidity in a London general practice.' *Brit. J. prev. soc. Med. 14*, 16–22.

83. KETY, S. S., 1974. 'From rationalization to reason.' *Amer. J. Psychiat. 131*, 957–63.

84. KHODOROVICH, T., 1976. *The Case of Leonid Plyushch*. London (Hurst).

85. KING, R. D., RAYNES, N. V., and TIZARD, J., 1971. *Patterns of Residential Care*. London (Routledge).

86. KRAMER, M., 1969. *Applications of Mental Health Statistics*. Geneva (World Health Organization).

87. —— 1975. *Psychiatric Services and the Changing Institutional Scene*. Presented at the President's Biomedical Research Panel. Unpublished.

88. KREITMAN, N., 1973. 'Prevention of suicidal behaviour.' In: *Roots of Evaluation : The Epidemiological Basis for Planning Psychiatric Services*. Eds: Wing, J. K., and Häfner, H. London (Oxford University Press).

89. KUSHLICK, A., 1973. 'Evaluation of residential services for mentally retarded children.' In: *Roots of Evaluation : The Epidemiological Basis for Planning Psychiatric Services*. Eds: Wing, J. K., and Häfner, H. London (Oxford University Press).

90. LABETZ, L., 1970. *Solzhenitsyn : A Documentary Record*. London (Allen Lane).

91. LAING, R. D., 1967. *The Politics of Experience*. Harmondsworth (Penguin).

92. —— and ESTERSON, A., 1964. *Sanity, Madness and the Family*. London (Tavistock).

93. LAKATOS, I., 1970. 'Falsification and the methodology of scientific research programmes. In: *Criticism and the Growth of Knowledge*. Eds: Lakatos, I., and Musgrave A. London (Cambridge University Press).

94. LEACH, E., 1974. *Lévi-Strauss*. Revised edition. London (Fontana, Collins).

95. LEFF, J. P., and WING, J. K., 1971. 'Trial of maintenance therapy in schizophrenia.' *Brit. med. J. 3*, 599–604.

96. LEIGH, D., 1975. 'World Psychiatric Association and Soviet psychiatry.' *Brit. med. J. 3*, 539–40.

97. LEIGHTON, A. H., LAMBO, T. A., HUGHES, C. C., LEIGHTON, D. C., MURPHY, J. M., and MACKLIN, D. B., 1963. *Psychiatric Disorder Among the Yoruba*. New York (Cornell University Press).

98. LEIGHTON, D. C., HARDING, J. S., MACKLIN, D. B., MACMILLAN, A. M., and LEIGHTON, A. H., 1963. *The Character of Danger: Psychiatric Symptoms in Selected Communities*. New York (Basic Books).

99. LEMERT, E. M., 1951. *Social Pathology*. New York (McGraw-Hill).

100. LÉVI-STRAUSS, C., 1967. The Scope of Anthropology. Inaugural lecture, chair of anthropology, 1960. London (Cape).

101. LEWIS, SIR AUBREY, 1953. 'Health as a social concept.' *Brit. J. Sociol. 4*, 109–24.

102. —— 1958. 'Social Psychiatry.' In: *Lectures on the Scientific Basis of Medicine*. London (Athlone Press). 6, 116–42.

103. —— 1967. 'Review of *Madness and Civilisation*.' In: *The State of Psychiatry. Essays and Addresses*. London (Routledge).

104. —— 1973. 'Manfred Bleuler's *The Schizophrenic Mental Disorders*: an exposition and a review.' *Psychol. Med. 3*, 385–92.

105. LIBERMAN, R. P., KING, L. W., DE RISI, W. J., and McCANN, M., 1975. *Personal Effectiveness*. Champaign, Illinois (Research Press).

106. LIDZ, T., 1972. 'Schizophrenia, R. D. Laing and the contemporary treatment of psychosis.' In: *Laing and Anti-psychiatry*. Eds: Boyers, R., and Orrill, R. Harmondsworth (Penguin).

107. —— 1975. *The Origin and Treatment of Schizophrenic Disorders*. London (Hutchinson).

108. —— FLECK, S., and CORNELISON, A. R., 1965. *Schizophrenia and the Family*. New York (International Universities Press).

109. LORR, M. (ed.), 1966. *Explorations in Typing Psychotics*. London and New York (Pergamon).

110. LUKES, S., 1973. *Emile Durkheim: His Life and Work*. London (Allen Lane).
111. MAIN, T. F., 1946. 'The hospital as a therapeutic institution.' *Bull. Menninger Clinic 10*, 66–70.
112. MANN, S., and CREE, W., 1976. 'New long-stay psychiatric patients: A national sample of 15 mental hospitals in England and Wales, 1972/3. *Psychol. Med. 6*, 603–16.
113. MARCUSE, H., 1968. *Negations: Essays in Critical Theory*. Harmondsworth (Penguin).
114. MARKS, I. M., 1969. *Fears and Phobias*. London (Heinemann).
115. MAXWELL, R., 1975. *Health Care: The Growing Dilemma*. Second edition. New York (McKinsey).
116. McKEOWN, T., 1976. *The Role of Medicine*. London (Nuffield Provincial Hospitals Trust).
117. MECHANIC, D., 1968. *Medical Sociology: A Selective View*. New York (Free Press).
118. MEDVEDEV, Z., 1974. 'Three years later.' Appendix to *A Question of Madness*, Penguin edition. Harmondsworth. (Penguin).
119. —— and MEDVEDEV, R., 1971. *A Question of Madness*. London (Macmillan).
120. MEEHL, P., 1962. Schizotaxia, schizotypy, schizophrenia.' *Amer. Psychol. 17*, 827–38.
121. MEZEY, A., 1960. 'Personal background, emigration and mental disorder in Hungarian refugees.' *J. ment. Sci. 106*, 618–27.
122. MINISTRY OF HEALTH OF THE U.S.S.R., 1964. 'Some problems of psychiatric service organization and forensic psychiatric examination in the USSR.' Moscow.
123. MOROSOV, G., 1974. 'Letter in reply to Wing.' *Brit. med. J. 3*, 40.
124. MORRIS, J. N., 1964. *The Uses of Epidemiology*. London (Livingstone).
125. MUMFORD, L., 1966. *The City in History*. Harmondsworth (Penguin).
126. MURPHY, H. B. M., 1968. 'Cultural factors in the genesis of schizophrenia.' In: *The Transmission of Schizophrenia*. Eds: Rosenthal, D., and Kety, S. London and New York (Pergamon).
127. —— and RAMAN, A. C., 1971. 'The chronicity of schizophrenia in indigenous tropical peoples: results of a 12-year follow-up survey.' *Brit. J. Psychiat. 118*, 489–97.
128. NATIONAL SCHIZOPHRENIA FELLOWSHIP, 1974. *Living with Schizophrenia: by the Relatives*. London (National Schizophrenia Fellowship, 29 Victoria Road, Surbiton, Surrey KT6 4JT).
129. NEWMAN, O., 1974. *Defensible Space*. London (Architectural Press).

130. NGUI, P. W., 1969. 'The Koro epidemic in Singapore.' *Australia and New Zealand J. Psychiat. 3*, 263–6.
131. ØDEGÅRD, Ø., 1932. 'Emigration and insanity: a study of mental disease among Norwegian born population in Minnesota.' *Acta psychiat. neurol. scand.* Suppl. 4.
132. PLEDGE, H. T., 1939. *Science Since 1500.* London (H.M.S.O.).
133. POPPER, K. R., 1945. *The Open Society and its Enemies.* London (Routledge).
134. —— 1960. *The Poverty of Historicism.* Second edition. London (Routledge).
135. —— 1972. *Conjectures and Refutations: The Growth of Scientific Knowledge.* Fourth edition revised. London (Routledge).
136. POWER, M. J., BENN, R. T., and MORRIS, J. N., 1972. 'Neighbourhood, school and juveniles before the courts.' *Brit. J. Criminol. 12*, 111–32.
137. PRIMSOSE, E. J. R., 1962. *Psychological Illness: A Community Study.* London (Tavistock).
138. PRITCHARD, D. G., 1963. *Education of the Handicapped 1760–1960.* London (Routledge).
139. RADZINOWICZ, L., and KING, J., 1977. *The Growth of Crime.* London (Hamish Hamilton).
140. RAPOPORT, R. N., 1960. *Community as Doctor.* London (Tavistock).
141. REDDAWAY, P., 1972. *Uncensored Russia: The Human Rights Movement in the Soviet Union.* London (Cape).
142. REPORT OF THE COMMITTEE OF INQUIRY INTO WHITTINGHAM HOSPITAL, 1972. Cmnd. 4861. London (H.M.S.O.).
143. REPORT OF THE COMMITTEE ON MENTALLY ABNORMAL OFFENDERS, 1975. Cmnd. 6244. London (H.M.S.O.).
144. REPORT OF THE COMMITTEE OF INQUIRY INTO ST. AUGUSTINE'S HOSPITAL, 1976. London (S.E. Thames Regional Health Authority).
145. RIESMAN, D., GLAZER, N., and DENNEY, R. 1950. *The Lonely Crowd.* New Haven (Yale University Press).
146. ROBINS, L. N. 1970. 'Follow-up studies investigating childhood disorders.' In: *Psychiatric Epidemiology.* Eds: Hare, E. H., and Wing, J. K. London (Oxford University Press).
147. ROBINS, L. N., 1973. 'Evaluation of psychiatric services for children in the United States.' In: *Roots of Evaluation: The Epidemiological Basis for Planning Psychiatric Services.* Eds: Wing, J. K., and Häfner, H. London (Oxford University Press).
148. ROSENHAN, D. L., 1973. 'On being sane in insane places.' *Science 179*, 250–8.
149. ROSENTHAL, D., and KETY, S. S., 1968. *The Transmission of Schizophrenia.* London (Pergamon).

150. ROTH, M., 1976. 'Schizophrenia and the theories of Thomas Szasz.' *Brit. J. Psychiat. 129*, 317–26.
151. RUTTER, M., and MADGE, N., 1975. *Cycles of Disadvantage.* London (Heinemann).
152. —— and QUINTON, D., 1977. 'Psychiatric disorder: ecological factors and concepts of causation.' In: *Ecological Factors in Human Development.* Ed: McGurk, H. Amsterdam (North Holland).
153. SAINSBURY, P., 1955. *Suicide in London: an Ecological Study.* London (Chapman and Hall).
154. SANTILLANA, G. DE, 1958. *The Crime of Galileo.* London (Heinemann).
155. SARTORIUS, N., JABLENSKY, A., and STRÖMGREN, A., 1978. 'Validity of diagnostic concepts across cultures.' In: *The Nature of Schizophrenia.* Eds: Wynne, L. C., Cromwell, R. L., and Matthyse, S. New York (Wiley).
156. SCHARFETTER, C., MOERBT, H., and WING, J. K. 1976. 'Diagnosis of functional psychoses: comparison of clinical and computerized classifications.' *Arch. Psychiat. Nervenkr. 222*, 61–7.
157. SCHEFF, T. J., 1963. 'The role of the mentally ill and the dynamics of mental disorder: a research framework.' *Sociometry 26*, 436–53.
158. —— 1966. *Being Mentally Ill.* Chicago (Aldine).
159. SCHNEIDER, K., 1959. *Clinical Psychopathology.* Fifth edition. Trans. Hamilton, M. W. New York (Grune and Stratton).
160. SCHULSINGER, H., 1976. 'A ten-year follow-up of children of schizophrenic mothers.' *Acta. psychiat. scand. 53*, 371–86.
161. SHEPHERD, M., COOPER, B., BROWN, A. C., and KALTON, G. W., 1966. *Psychiatric Illness in General Practice.* London (Oxford University Press).
162. SHIELDS, J., 1975. 'Some recent developments in psychiatric genetics.' *Arch. Psychiat. Neurol. Sci. 220*, 347–60.
163. SIMPSON, G. M., and ANGUS, J. W. S., 1970. 'Drug-induced extrapyramidal disorders.' *Acta. psychiat. scand.* (Sup.) *212*, 17–19.
164. SLATER, E., 1961. *Hysteria 311. J. ment. Sci. 107*, 359.
165. —— and ROTH, M., 1969. *Clinical Psychiatry.* Third edition. London (Cassell).
166. SLOVENKO, R., 1973. *Psychiatry and Law.* Boston (Little, Brown).
167. SNOW, J., 1965. *On Cholera.* A reprint of two papers. New York and London (Hafner).
168. SNYDER, S., 1974. *Drugs, Madness and the Brain.* London (Hart-Davis, MacGibbon).
169. SPECIAL REPORT, 1969. *The First U.S. Mission on Mental Health to the USSR.* Public Health Service Publication No. 1893. Washington (U.S. Department of Health, Education and Welfare).
170. SROLE, L., LANGNER, T. S., MICHAEL, S. T., OPLER, M. K., and

RENNIE, T. A. C., 1962. *Mental Health in the Metropolis: The Midtown Manhattan Study.* New York (McGraw-Hill).

171. STARKEY, M. L., 1949. *The Devil in Massachusetts.* New York (Knopf).

172. STOCK, N., 1970. *The Life of Ezra Pound.* London (Routledge).

173. STREIB, G. F., 1975. 'Changing perspectives on retirement: role crises or role continuities.' In: *Life History Research in Psychopathology.* Eds: Wirt, R. D., Winokur, G., and Roff, M. Minneapolis (University of Minnesota Press).

174. SZASZ, T., 1961. *The Myth of Mental Illness.* New York (Hoeber-Harper).

175. —— 1971. *The Manufacture of Madness.* London (Routledge).

176. —— 1972. Introduction to Ennis, B., *Prisoners of Psychiatry.* New York (Harcourt Brace Jovanovich).

177. —— 1976. 'Schizophrenia: the sacred symbol of psychiatry.' *Brit. J. Psychiat. 129,* 308–16.

178. TAYLOR, S. and CHAVE, S., 1964. *Mental Health and Environment.* London (Longmans).

179. TIDMARSH, D., and WOOD, S., 1972. 'Psychiatric aspects of destitution.' In: *Evaluating a Community Psychiatric Service.* Eds: Wing, J. K., and Hailey, A. M. London (Oxford University Press).

180. TUCKETT, D. (ed.), 1976. *An Introduction to Medical Sociology.* London (Tavistock).

181. VAUGHN, C. E., and LEFF, J. P., 1976. 'The influence of family and social factors on the course of psychiatric illness.' *Brit. J. Psychiat. 129,* 125–37.

182. VENABLES, P. H., and WING, J. K., 1962. 'Level of arousal and the subclassification of schizophrenia.' *Arch. gen. Psychiat.* 7, 114–19.

183. WALLWORK, E., 1972. *Durkheim: Morality and Milieu.* Cambridge, Mass. (Harvard University Press).

184. WALSH, D., 1971. 'Patients in Irish psychiatric hospitals in 1963: A comparison with England and Wales.' *Brit. J. Psychiat. 118,* 617–20.

185. WATT, N. F., and LUBENSKY, A. W., 1976. 'Childhood roots of schizophrenia.' *J. cons. clin. Psychol. 44,* 363–75.

186. WEISSMAN, M. M., and PAYKEL, E. S., 1974. *The Depressed Woman.* Chicago (University of Chicago Press).

187. WEST, D. J., 1973. *Who Becomes Delinquent?* London (Heinemann).

188 WEST, R., 1965. *The Meaning of Treason.* Harmondsworth (Penguin).

189. WILLIAMS, A., and ANDERSON, R., 1975. *Efficiency in the Social Services.* London (Blackwell and Robertson).

190. WING, J. K., 1957. 'Family care systems in Norway and Holland.' *Lancet 2,* 884.

191. —— 1966. 'Social and psychological changes in a rehabilitation unit.' *Soc. Psychiat. 1*, 21–8.

192. —— 1974. 'Housing environments and mental health.' In: *Population and its Problems*. Ed: Parry, H. B. London (Oxford University Press).

193. —— 1974. 'Psychiatry in the Soviet Union.' *Brit. med. J. 1*, 433–6.

194. —— 1974. 'Letter in reply to Morosov.' *Brit. med. J. 3*, 408.

195. —— (ed.), 1975. *Schizophrenia from Within*. London (National Schizophrenia Fellowship, 29 Victoria Road, Surbiton, Surrey KT6 4JT).

196. —— 1975. 'Impairments in schizophrenia: A rational basis for social treatment.' In: *Life History Research in Psychopathology Volume 4*. Eds: Wirt, R. D., Winokur, G., and Roff, M. Minneapolis (University of Minnesota Press).

197. —— 1976. 'A technique for comparing psychiatric morbidity in in-patient and out-patient series with that found in general population samples.' *Psychol. Med. 6*, 665–71.

198. ——(ed.), 1976. *Classification of Psychiatric Disorders. Psychiatric Annals*, Vols. 6 and 7.

199. —— 1978. '*Schizophrenia: Towards a New Synthesis*. London and New York (Academic Press).

200. —— BENNETT, D. H., and DENHAM, J., 1964. *The Industrial Rehabilitation of Long-stay Schizophrenic Patients*. Medical Research Council memo. No. 42. London (H.M.S.O.).

201. —— and BROWN, G. W., 1970. *Institutionalism and Schizophrenia*. London (Cambridge University Press).

202. —— COOPER, J. E., and SARTORIUS, N., 1974. *The Description and Classification of Psychiatric Symptoms: An Instruction Manual for the PSE and Catego System*. London (Cambridge University Press).

203. —— and FREUDENBERG, R. K., 1961. 'The response of severely ill chronic schizophrenic patients to social stimulation.' *Amer. J. Psychiat. 118*, 311.

204. —— and HAILEY, A. M. (eds), 1972. *Evaluating a Community Psychiatric Service: The Camberwell Register, 1964–1971*. London (Oxford University Press).

205. WING, L. (ed.), 1976. *Early Childhood Autism*. Second edition. London and New York (Pergamon).

206. —— 1971. *Autistic Children: A Guide for Parents*. London (Constable), New York (Brunner Maizel).

207. —— WING, J. K., HAILEY, A. M., BAHN, A. K., SMITH, H. E., and BALDWIN, J. A., 1967. 'The use of psychiatric services in three urban areas: an international case register study.' *Soc. Psychiat. 2*, 158–67.

208. WOOD, S. M., 1976. 'Camberwell Reception Centre: a consideration of the need for health and social services of homeless single
men.' *J. soc. Pol.* 5, 389–99.
209. World Health Organization, 1973. *The International Pilot Study of
Schizophrenia.* Geneva (W.H.O.).
210. —— 1974. *Glossary of Mental Disorders and Guide to their Classification.* Geneva (W.H.O.).
210. WYNNE, L. C., 1968. 'Methodologic and conceptual issues in the
study of schizophrenics and their families.' In: *The Transmission of
Schizophrenia.* Eds: Rosenthal, D, and Kety, S. S. London and
New York (Pergamon).
212. —— 1971. 'Family research on the pathogenesis of schizophrenia.'
In: *Problems of Psychosis.* Eds: Doncet, P., and Laurin, C.
Excerpta Medica International Congress Series, No. 194.
213. ZIFERSTEIN, I., 1968. 'Speaking prose without knowing it.' *Int. J.
Psychiat.* 6, 366–70.
214. ZUSMAN, J., and BERTSCH, E. F., 1975. *The Future Role of the State
Hospital.* Farnborough (Lexington Books).

Index